STUDIES IN HISTORY, ECONOMICS AND PUBLIC LAW

EDITED BY THE FACULTY OF POLITICAL SCIENCE
OF COLUMBIA UNIVERSITY

Number 297

THE SPEAKER OF THE HOUSE OF REPRESENTATIVES
SINCE 1896

THE SPEAKER OF THE HOUSE OF REPRESENTATIVES SINCE 1896

BY

CHANG-WEI CHIU, Ph.D.

NEW YORK

COLUMBIA UNIVERSITY PRESS

LONDON: P. S. KING & SON, LTD.

1928

To

My Grandfather

SHI-CHANG CHIU

WHO EXHAUSTED HIS LITTLE MEANS FOR MY EDUCATION

THEODORA RHOADES

WHO NEVER FAILED TO GIVE ME ENCOURAGEMENT AND COUNSEL

AND

A. G. McKENNA

WHO MORE THAN ONCE GENEROUSLY RENDERED ME FINANCIAL HELP

THIS WORK IS AFFECTIONATELY AND

GRATEFULLY DEDICATED

PREFACE

THE office of the Speaker of the House of Representatives has occupied an important place in the political history of American Government. It was first objectively studied upon by Miss M. P. Follett who in 1896 published her remarkable book *The Speaker of the House of Representatives*. In this book she traced the genesis and character of the office of the Speaker, discussed his power, influence and duty in relation to legislation in the House, and finally appraised his place as a political leader in the American system of government. The usefulness of this book was evidenced by the fact that it subsequently went through three reprintings.

Since 1896 many changes have been brought about in both the organization and the rules of procedure of the House. The purpose of the author in the following pages is to show in what ways and to what extent these changes have affected the power as well as the influence of the Speaker over legislation, in his threefold position, as (1) presiding officer of the House, as (2) the titular leader of his party in the House, and as (3) a private member of the House. In method of general approach the author, with a view to making the present volume a parallel study to Miss Follett's work, has adhered to the method of the latter, to whom he owes a word of deep gratitude. But viewing the office of the Speaker in its relation to the House as a whole, the author is minded to quote one of the sayings of the Chinese sage Mencius: " There are cases of praise which could not be expected, and of reproach when the parties have been seeking to perfect."

As to facts prior to 1896, the author almost entirely relied on Miss Follett's book and Mr. Hind's monumental work on *Precedents of the House of Representatives,* and only in a few cases for this period did the present writer consult the original sources. For facts since 1896 he has made a diligent search into the voluminous *Congressional Record.* General works, such as books and articles in periodicals, have been made use of. In cases where material in daily papers was drawn upon for want of direct sources of information, pains were taken to have them verified by competent authorities. Biographies and autobiographies of members of the House, by far too few in number, have been of aid, as they throw inside light upon the working of the House. Indeed the author feels that there is a real need for more Congressmen to write of the actual working of the House, not merely on the negative side, to answer adverse criticism of Congress, but also on the positive side to advance public education in the methods of Federal legislation.

The author has received valuable suggestions and criticism from specialists familiar with the working of the House. He wishes to thank Honorable Robert Luce who has not only read through the entire manuscript but also has generously given him suggestions and information of the most helpful sort; Mr. Lynn Haines, editor of the *Searchlight,* who kindly consented to read the whole of the manuscript; Mr. Middleton Beaman, of the House Legislative Counsel, who has read Chapter I of the manuscript; Mr. Frederic P. Lee, of the Senate Legislative Counsel, who has read Chapters II and VI of the manuscript; Honorable John Q. Tilson, the majority floor leader, Mr. William Tyler Page, Clerk of the House, and Mr. Lehr Fess, Parliamentarian of the House —all of whom have given the author information of great value. In the Department of Public Law, Columbia University, Professor Howard Lee McBain and Professor Lindsay Rogers were helpful.

But to Professor Joseph P. Chamberlain the author is under heaviest obligation. His inspiration as a teacher and his patience as a scholar have sustained the zeal of the author during his two full years of labor on this subject. Professor Chamberlain has read the manuscript, making invaluable suggestions and corrections as to facts and style. Without his direction this book can hardly have attained its present form. To Miss Margery Grant thanks are due for her help in proofreading. Needless to say, for whatever omissions and errors occur in this little volume, the author alone is responsible.

CHANG-WEI CHIU.

NEW YORK CITY,
NOVEMBER, 1927.

TABLE OF CONTENTS

CHAPTER I

THE SPEAKER AND HIS OFFICE

CHAPTER II

The Speaker and the Committee System

CHAPTER III

The Committee on Rules

CHAPTER IV

Power Through Recognition

CHAPTER V

Power Through Suspension of Rules

CHAPTER VI

CALENDAR WEDNESDAY

CHAPTER VII

The Discharge Calendar

CHAPTER VIII

The House Under Six Speakers

CHAPTER IX

LEADERSHIP IN THE HOUSE

CHAPTER I

THE SPEAKER AND HIS OFFICE

THE character of the Speakership of the House of Representatives is twofold—political and judicial.[1] Both in its essence and form this office may be said to have been a direct heir of the colonial assemblies, for the colonial Speaker was almost uniformly a political leader, an active politician, one who had " the push and the energy necessary to accomplish certain definite purposes." [2] It also inherited, as an immediate influence upon its course of development, traditions which flourished in the Continental Convention and in the Congress of the Confederation (1774-1788) and in the Philadelphia Convention over which George Washington presided.[3] This dualistic character of the office has little re-

[1] In offering the resolution of thanks to Speaker Henderson, Mr. Richardson, of Tennessee, said: "...The position of the Speaker of the House is both judicial and political. It is judicial in this, that the occupant of the chair is at all times bound by and obedient to a code of rules prescribed for the government and control of the House, and in the execution of which he is but its organ and servant. It is at the same time political. In the very nature of the things, he is expected in his position to look carefully to the interest of his party, and while he is to administer the affairs of his great office in a manner to best promote the public weal, it is not expected that he will fail to use all legitimate and proper methods to build up his party and fortify it against attack..." *Cong. Record*, 56th Cong., 2nd Sess., p. 3604.

[2] Follett, *The Speaker of the House of Representatives* (New York, 1909 ed.), p. 15. The genesis of the Speakership was adequately treated in *ibid.*, chapter i. Asher C. Hinds held that the Constitution did not create the Speaker, but adopted an existing officer. Hinds, " The Speaker of the House of Representatives," *American Political Science Review*, vol. iii, p. 156.

[3] George Washington, while presiding over the Convention, did not hesitate to make his influence felt over the adoption of the amendment,

semblance to the Speakership of the House of Commons. The English Speaker is noted for his impartiality—a moderator whose duty it is to enforce, impartially, the rules and maintain order and decorum in debate.[1] Indeed, the theory of the American Speakership, as one writer put it, was " introduced into the American system, under the Constitution, as a distinct American conception." [2] And as such it still remains, though there have been changes both in the power and influence of the Speaker since the " revolution " of March 19, 1910—changes which will be discussed elsewhere in this treatise.

The status of the Speaker of the House is undefined under the Constitution. The " founding fathers " at the Philadelphia Convention in fact wasted little time over the question of the Speakership,[3] and therefore left practically no

introduced by Gorham, allowing one member of the House to represent every 30,000 inhabitants. He said: "Athough his situation has hitherto restrained him from offering his sentiments on questions depending in the House, and it might be thought ought now to impose his silence on him, yet he could not forbear expressing his wish that the alternation proposed might take place." The amendment was adopted. Follett, *op. cit.*, pp. 24, 25.

[1] The impartiality of the English Speaker is based upon two grounds: "As regards his relation to the Crown, it is secured by the act of parliament which forbids his acceptance of any office of profit under the Crown, and by the adoption, about the same time as this act was passed, of the idea, now as matter of principle, that after resigning the chair he ought not to appear in the House either as one of the Government or as a private member. His impartiality within the House is guaranteed by a number of arrangements to which other parliaments provide no parallel. Above all, the member of the House of Commons who is elected to the chair ceases, from the moment of his election, to belong to any political party..." Redlich, *Procedure of the House of Commons* (London, 1908), vol. ii, p. 132.

However, the American Speaker is also forbidden to accept any office under the Constitution. See Article i, section 6.

[2] Brown, *The Leadership of Congress* (Indianapolis, 1922), p. 10.

[3] The Speakership was mentioned in a motion which provided that a

record for the enlightenment of their descendants. The influence and importance of the office depend upon the strength and personality of the man who is in the chair. While the "literary theory" of the office so vividly painted by Speaker Clay [1] is far from being realized, it is, nevertheless, noteworthy to observe that of the six Speakers since 1896 at least three were men of great strength and commanding influence. Speaker Reed, undoubtedly one of the greatest Speakers of the House, was the strongest personage in his party. To him, the Speaker of the House "had but one superior and no peer." [2] Two of the six Speakers were active candidates for the highest office of the nation, and one of them, Speaker Clark, almost had the nomination for the presidency within his grasp. Speaker Clark once declared in the House that "it is a great thing to be a Speaker of the House," and that he could have become Vice-President of the country if he so desired. [3] Later, in the Sixty-fifth

Privy Council of State be established "to consist of the President, the President of the Senate, the Speaker, the Chief Justice, and the heads of departments." The motion failed of passage. Follett, *op. cit.*, p. 25; also *cf.* Madison, *Journal of the Federal Convention* (Chicago, 1893), pp. 58, 70, 451, 701.

[1] "They (the duties of the Speaker) enjoin promptitude and impartiality in deciding the various questions of order as they arise; firmness and dignity in his deportment toward the House; patience, good temper, and courtesy toward the individual Members, and the best arrangement and distribution of the talent of the House, in its numerous subdivisions, for the dispatch of the public business, and the fair exhibition of every subject presented for consideration. They especially required of him, in those moments of agitation from which no deliberative assembly is always exempted, to remain cool and unshaken amidst all the storms of debate, carefully guarding the preservation of the permanent laws and rules of the House from being sacrificed to temporary passions, prejudice, or interests." Hinds, *Precedents of the House of Representatives*, vol. ii, section 1307.

[2] Alexander, De Alva S., *History and Procedure of the House of Representatives* (New York, 1916), p. 43.

[3] Speaker Clark said: "... I violate no confidence in stating that within

Congress, he declined to accept a Senatorial appointment by the Governor of his State to succeed the late Senator Stone.[1] It is also important to note that none of the three strong Speakers had ever sought either any other appointive office in the Federal Government or elective office in their respective States after leaving the Speaker's chair.[2]

By an Order in Council issued in 1919, it was ordained that the Speaker of the House of Commons "shall have, hold and enjoy place, preeminence and precedence, immediately after the Lord President of the Council," which makes him the seventh subject of the realm.[3] The Speaker of the House of Representatives, as has been said, has no such defined status. More than once he has been socially placed in a quandary. Speaker Cannon was invited in 1905 by President Roosevelt to a state dinner in honor of the justices of the Supreme Court. At the dinner the President asked Speaker Cannon if he would object to a seat below the Attorney-General. The Speaker objected. " Were it a

thirty minutes from now I could have been sworn in as Vice-President of the United States if I had wanted to be, but I preferred to stay with you [members of the House]." *Cong. Record*, 62nd Cong., 3rd Sess., p. 4855.

[1] In his letter to the Governor of the State of Missouri, Speaker Clark wrote: " In this awful crisis of our country's affairs—indeed, of the whole world's affairs—it is the imperative duty of every man to serve the people and uphold the Government to the best of his ability and in the position where he can do the most good. I believe that I can render more service in the Speaker's chair than in the Senate. Therefore I feel constrained to decline your tender of the Senatorship..." *Cong. Record*, 65th Cong., 2nd Sess., pp. 5664, 5665.

[2] Speaker Reed retired to practice law in New York city. Both Speakers Cannon and Clark returned subsequently to the House. But Speaker Gillett went to the Senate after serving three terms in the chair.

[3] The order runs as follows: Archbishop of Canterbury, Lord Chancellor, Archbishop of York, Prime Minister, Lord Chancellor of Ireland, Lord President of the Council and the Speaker. MacDonagh, *Pageant of Parliament* (London, 1921), vol. i, p. 136.

private dinner," the Speaker replied, " he would be content with any place the host might assign to him; and were he a private individual he would be equally pleased with whatever course the host might take, but he felt that in attending a state dinner as Speaker of the House, he might not waive the position to which he was entitled officially." [1] Rather than waive his official status the Speaker asked to be excused from the dinner.

The Constitution provides that " the House of Representatives shall chuse their Speaker." [2] Mr. McCall was disposed to think that the framers of the Constitution, " hav-

[1] Hinds, *op. cit.*, ii, 1309. A parallel case occurred when Robert C. Winthrop of Massachusetts was Speaker of the House. See Follett, *op. cit.*, pp. 296, 297. Lord Bryce wrote that Washington society was once agitated by a claim of the wife of a Speaker to take precedence over the wives of the justices of the Supreme Court, "a claim so ominous in a democratic country that efforts were made to have it adjusted without a formal decision." Bryce, *The American Commonwealth* (New York, 1923, abridged ed.), p. 107. Once at a public ceremony the carriage of Speaker Macon was placed almost at the end of the line. The Speaker, however, directed his driver to take his place next to the carriage of the President, so that he might not degrade his position as " the elect of the elect of the people." Hinds, " The Speaker and the House," *McClure*, vol. xxxv, p. 196.

[2] Article i, section 2. The office of the Speakership also occupies an inconspicuous place in the new constitutions of Europe. Article 26, section ii, of the new German constitution provides: " The Reichstag shall choose its own President, its Vice-President..." McBain and Rogers, *The New Constitutions of Europe* (New York, 1922), p. 182. Article 30, chapter ii, of the Austrian constitution provides: " The Nationalrat shall choose among its members its President and Second and Third President." *Ibid.*, p. 265. Article 35, section ii, of the Czechoslovakian constitution provides: " Each chamber shall elect its own chairman." *Ibid.*, p. 317. Article 77, section vii, of the Jugo-slavian constitution provides: " The National Assembly elects from its membership its officers for every session." *Ibid.*, p. 361. iv, article 43, of the Esthonian constitution: " The State Assembly elects the President ...at the first meeting after the elections..." *Ibid.*, p. 460. The Finnish constitution only mentions the office in Title iv, article 49. *Ibid.*, p. 477.

ing in mind, doubtless, the somewhat ambiguous relation of the ancient Speakership to the Crown and to the House of Commons," made the provision as it is.[1]   How far this is true is, however, difficult to determine, as the intents and purports of the framers are unknown to us.   The Constitution does not say whether the selection be necessarily confined to the membership of the House, though there has never been a case in which a Speaker was chosen from outside of the House.   Furthermore, it is silent on the manner of his election.   The Speaker of the House was first elected by ballot, but since 1839 he has been chosen by viva voce vote on roll call.[2]   Twice the House chose its Speaker by a plurality of votes and later confirmed the choice by a majority vote.[3]   In 1809 it was held that the Speaker should be elected by a majority of all present,[4] and in 1879 that he might be elected by a majority of those present, if a quorum,[5] thereby the custom requiring a majority of all members-elect was done away with.

The ceremonial conformity to the letter of the fundamental law with regard to the choosing and electing of the Speaker is but one of the many illustrations which show the discrepancy between the living reality of the instrument and its paper description.   In point of law, " the House of Representatives shall chuse their Speaker," but in point of fact, the House confirms the appointment — or rather the choice—which was already made in the party caucus or the conference as the Republicans sometimes call it.[6]   Contest for the Speakership culminates in the party caucus, but the

---

[1] McCall, *The Business of Congress* (New York, 1911), p. 21.

[2] Hinds, *op. cit.*, i, 187, 211.

[3] *Ibid.*, i, 211.

[4] *Ibid.*, i, 215.

[5] *Ibid.*, i, 216.

[6] For a discussion of the caucus, see *infra*, pp. 326 *et seq.*

preliminary skirmish for the contest actually commences long before the time of the caucus meeting. In times of hot contest, campaign managers of the several candidates opened up headquarters in Washington hotels, and for a time the civil war within the ranks of the majority party assumed a really belligerent air. It must be remembered that to capture the nomination for Speaker in the caucus meeting of the majority party is tantamount to election in the House, and it is but natural that the struggle is at its worst among the members of the majority party—and particularly at the time when the majority party has no outstanding leader. Speaker Reed who began, in the Fifty-fourth Congress, his second term as presiding officer, had practically no opposition in the Republican caucus. Neither Speaker Henderson nor Speaker Cannon encountered any serious opposition in winning the nomination. Speaker Clark was twice " unanimously " nominated in the Democratic caucus for Speaker, " a record no other [man] living or dead ever had." [1] But before the convening of the Sixty-sixth Congress a "stormy" contest for the Speakership had come to pass in the smooth water of the Congressional sea. As the House was Republican, the contest was between Mr. Gillett of Massachusetts and Mr. Mann of Illinois. Mr. Mann had been the Republican floor leader since the Sixty-second Congress and was the " logical " candidate for the office. In a statement issued by the " Gillett Committee " arguments against Mr. Mann were, however, advanced:

That he is " reactionary," that he is merely a parliamentarian rather than a statesman, that he would, in fact, if not in theory, abolish the selection of committees by the House itself, and that he would turn the clock back to the days when " Uncle Joe " Cannon was " Czar " and ruled the House with an iron hand

---

[1] *Cong. Record*, 63rd Cong., 2nd Sess., p. 4471.

until deposed. Cannon, by the way, is Mann's chief manager, and his mantle is said to have fallen on Mann's shoulders.

In selecting Gillett as their champion, the anti-Mann forces express faith in his liberal policies and confidence in his judgment and fairness. For two decades, Gillett has been one of the leading members of the junior chamber. . . . Gillett's war record is 100 per cent American, while Mann's falls far below that figure . . . and Gillett's record as floor leader in [during the] long absence of Mann is said to measure up fully to that of Mann.[1]

Several reasons were accountable for Mann's defeat for the nomination in the Republican caucus.[2] Mr. Mann was too closely identified with the Cannon régime. It was not that " reaction " was repulsive to the Republicans whose forefathers were the Federalists and Whigs, but rather due to the type of " reaction " imbued with " Cannonism." To nominate as Speaker a man who had been trained in the Cannon school was bad politics with the approaching Presidential election. Moreover, the disclosure of Mr. Mann's friendly relations with the Chicago packers alienated many of his lukewarm supporters. Mr. Mann admitted that once in 1907 he had received from the Swift packers " a choice piece " of beefsteak and an old horse for his "truck garden" in Chicago, " a magnificent animal " as he referred to it before the Senate Committee on Agriculture and Forestry.[3] This timely disclosure furnished the Gillett forces material for a campaign hymn:

> Can, Can,
> The Packers' Mann.

[1] The New York *Times*, January 20, 1919, p. 7.

[2] The vote stood: Gillett 138; Mann 69; Campbell of Kansas 13; Esch of Wisconsin 4; and Mondell of Wyoming 1. *Ibid.*, February 28, 1919, p. 1.

[3] *Ibid.*, January 16, 1919, p. 1.

Furthermore, the gods of the Republican party were at odds with Mr. Mann. Senator Penrose of Pennsylvania and Chairman Hays of the National Committee of the Republican party took an active part in securing the nomination of Mr. Gillett. As Mr. Sweet of Iowa has well described it: " The atmosphere of the caucus seemed to be getting hazy and ' penrosy.' " [1]

During the period under study the parliamentary experience of the six Speakers merits special attention. Speaker Reed was elected to preside over the House after twelve years of Congressional service, and Speaker Henderson after sixteen years of service. Speaker Cannon, who served longer than any other member ever entering Congress,[2] was elevated to the Chair in his thirty-first year in the House of Representatives. Speaker Clark was chosen in his sixteenth year of service in the House, Speaker Gillett in his twenty-seventh year, and the present Speaker, Mr. Longworth, at the time of his election was in his twenty-first year in the House. The total length of Congressional service of the six Speakers since 1896 amounts to one hundred and twenty years, with an average of twenty years for each of them— almost three times more than those who had been in the Chair before 1896. It is evident that the House, in electing a Speaker, gives weight to the length of Congressional service. Even if Henry Clay were alive today, he could hardly hope to be elected to the chair on the first day in which he made appearance in the House.[3] It also shows that the habit

[1] The New York *Times*, Jan. 16, 1919, p. 1.

[2] Mr. Cannon entered the House in the Forty-third Congress, and, with the exception of Fifty-second and Sixty-third Congresses, served through the Sixty-seventh Congress—totaling forty-six years of service in the House.

[3] Besides Clay, Pennington of New Jersey was also elected Speaker on his first appearance in the House. Before 1896 the average length of Congressional service before an election to the chair had been seven years. Follett, *op. cit.*, p. 34.

of reelecting a Speaker to the office seems to have taken a permanent hold upon the House.[1] Both Speaker Cannon and Speaker Clark were reelected consecutively for four terms, a distinction which has not yet been achieved by any other Speaker. Other Speakers—Reed, Henderson and Gillett—were reelected to the chair so long as their party remained in control of the House and so long as they were members of that body. Two of the Speakers, Cannon and Clark, were deprived of the honor on account of the change of party control, although still members of the House, while Speaker Reed and Speaker Henderson relinquished it because of reasons unknown to the nation at large.[2] Speaker Gillett could have been elected for the fourth time had he returned to the lower House of the Sixty-ninth Congress.

Furthermore, the right of succession to the Speaker's chair has not been exclusively granted to the floor leader.[3]

[1] For cases in which Speakers were not reelected before 1896, see *ibid.*, p. 34. The Speaker of the House of Commons is always reelected to the chair, but such reelection is not obligatory. Lord Russell said in 1835 that the House of Commons was under no obligation in a new Parliament to reelect the Speaker, unless he has won for himself the confidence and esteem not of his own party, but also of the general body of members. MacDonagh, *op. cit.*, vol. i, p. 125.

[2] *Cf. infra*, pp. 293-4. The retirement of Mr. Henderson was as mysterious as was his election to the Speakership. See Brown, *op. cit.*, p. 112.

[3] A contrast may be made with the House of Commons. The Speaker of the House of Commons has been "invariably" chosen from the ranks of the Ministerialists during the nineteenth century. Sir Henry Addington, Sir John Freemen-Mitford, Charles Abbot, Charles Manners-Sutton, James Abercromby, Charles Shaw-Lefevre, John Evelyn Denison, Henry Bouvrie Brand, Arthur Welseley-Peel and William Court Gully—all had mounted the Speaker's chair. So was James William Lowether, the first Speaker elected in this century. MacDonagh, *op. cit.*, vol. i, p. 123. Also ministers had been willing to give up their portfolios for the Speaker's chair. They were Spring Rice, Chancellor of Exchequer of the Melbourne administration, Lord John Russell and Sir Henry Campbell-Bannerman who was willing to lay down his portfolio as Secretary of State for War in 1895. *Ibid.*, p. 137.

Speaker Henderson had never held this position, although he had been chairman of the Committee on Judiciary and a majority member of the Committee on Rules. Speaker Gillett who before being inducted into the chair had been chairman of the Committee on Appropriations, was chosen by the Republican members of the House in preference over Mr. Mann, the Republican floor leader since the Sixty-second Congress. Both of them were, to be sure, far from being the strongest members on the Republican side of the House; but they were favored by the political conditions both within and without the House.

The " confirmation " by the House of the choice of the dominant party for Speaker takes place on the opening day of the first session of a new Congress. On this day the Clerk of the preceding House, by practice rather than by the force of law, calls the members-elect to order. The first performance of the congressional stage commences with prayer by the chaplain of the House, which if the House meets in a special session, is followed by the reading of the Proclamation of the President.[1] Then the Clerk proceeds to call the roll of members by states and, for the information of the House, announces the change and vacancies in the membership since the last general election. Upon the presence of a quorum, the Clerk declares that nominations for Speaker are in order.[2] The Clerk also appoints tellers, usually four in number, two of whom are from each of the two great political parties, to take their places at the Clerk's desk. It is at this moment the already-made choices of the

---

[1] Once the reading of the Proclamation of the President preceded the prayer of the House chaplain. *Cong. Record*, 67th Cong., 1st Sess., p. 77.

[2] Since the act of March 3, 1863, the election of Speaker has been given precedence over the question as to right of a member to his seat, and in 1876 it was held that, pending the election of Speaker, another question of privilege is not in order. Follett, *op. cit.*, p. 42.

different parties for Speaker are placed in nomination by
the chairman of the party caucus.[1]   A nomination speech is
usually short, not verbose, although several times lengthy
speeches were delivered by the Progressives who, in nominating candidates of their own, announced the purposes and
principles of their progressive stand.[2]   Nominations having

---

[1] In the Sixty-fifth Congress Thomas D. Schall of Minnesota, a
Republican, placed Mr. Clark of Missouri in nomination for Speaker.
The case should be regarded as exceptional, as it was during the time of
the European War. The President was a Democrat but in the House
no party appeared to have a majority. Mr. Mann, the Republican
nominee for Speaker, said to Mr. Kitchin of North Carolina, the
Democratic floor leader: "I deny that you are a majority until you
settle it by a roll call." *Cong. Record*, 65th Cong., 1st Sess., p. 117.
Out of patriotic motive, Mr. Schall appealed for "full cooperation between the President and the Congress." *Ibid.*, p. 107.
The political divisions in the House in the first session of the
Sixty-fifth Congress stood as follows:

Democrats	212
Republicans	213
Progressives	1
Independents	2
Socialists	1
Prohibitionists	1
Progressive Protectionists	1
Progressive Democrats	1
Vacancies	3
Total	435

[2] For the nomination of Mr. Murdock of Kansas and the declaration
of the principles of the progressive party, see *Cong. Record*, 63rd Cong.,
1st Sess., p. 63. For Mr. Brown's speech in nominating Mr. Cooper of
Wisconsin, see *Cong. Record*, 68th Cong., 1st Sess., pp. 7, 8. In the
Sixty-ninth Congress Mr. Cooper was again nominated by the Pro-
gressives in a long speech by Mr. Frear of the Wisconsin delegation.
Cong. Record, 69th Cong., 1st Sess., p. 6.. Only in a few cases has a
member ever made a seconding speech in support of a nomination. Mr.
Lenroot of Wisconsin seconded the nomination of Mr. Mann by Mr.
Greene of Massachusetts. *Cong. Record*, 65th Cong., 1st Sess., p. 108.
Mr. Nelson of Wisconsin, in seconding the nomination of Mr. Cooper
of Wisconsin, declared: "The demands of Mr. Longworth, candidate

thus been made, the Clerk calls the roll and members of the House answer as their names are called for whom they wish to vote.[1]   The announcement of the results of the votes received by the respective nominees is invariably greeted with " loud and continued applause " from the part.of the floor where a nominee's party associates sit.   To escort the Speaker-elect to the chair, the Clerk appoints a committee of three or four, consisting of the defeated candidates and, if there is only one defeated candidate, the majority floor leader and other party leaders are included.[2]   As a rule, the minority nominee introduces the newly-elected Speaker to the members of the House, but in the Sixty-seventh Congress Speaker Gillett was introduced by Mr. Mondell of Wyoming, the majority floor leader.   Customarily the Speaker-elect delivers a short inauguration speech appreciative of the honor conferred upon him, expressing his " aim," " duty " and " pleasure " to administer " impartially " the laws for the government of the House and ending with a plea for the cooperation of the members.[3]   The oath to support the Con-

for Speaker, and his threat that Progressives are to be tested by their votes on various matters commencing with the first vote for Speaker, are answered by the Progressives in their decision to vote for the Hon. Henry Allen Cooper, the Dean of the House, for Speaker." Mr. Nelson also declared, among other things, that the Progressives decided to vote against the Mellon tax plan. *Cong. Record,* 69th Cong., 1st Sess., p. 7.

[1] Formerly the House proceeded, on motion of a member, to vote *viva voce* for Speaker, but in recent years the House has proceeded at once to vote *viva voce* without the formality of a motion. Hinds, *op. cit.,* iii, 221. Since the Fifty-fourth Congress the House has twice, on a resolution of a member, elected the Speaker by *viva voce* vote. See *Cong. Record,* 56th Cong., 1st Sess., p. 4; also see *Cong. Record,* 57th Cong., 1st Sess., p. 44.

[2] According to Jefferson's *Manual,* " when but one person is proposed, and no objection made, it has not been usual in Parliament to put any question to the House; but without a question the members proposing him conduct him to the chair ..." Jefferson's *Manual,* ix.

[3] Speaker Clark made an inauguration speech of political importance upon his election to the Speakership in the Sixty-second Congress. See *infra,* p. 303.

stitution is usually administered by a member longest in continuous service in the House either named by the Clerk or at the request of the Speaker-elect himself, but very often of late the ritual has been performed by a member longest in discontinuous service or even by one not longest in continuous service.[1]

After the Thirty-sixth Congress there was no serious contest in the election of the Speaker on the floor of the House [2] until the Sixty-eighth Congress, when a party split caused trouble.   In the House the Republicans had 225 members, Democrats 205, Independents 1, Farmer-Labor 1, and Socialists 1.   The Progressives—numbering about twenty— who were nominally Republicans but were in fact diametrically opposed to the platform for which the Republican party stood, held the balance of power in the House.   The Democrats nominated Mr. Garrett of Tennessee for Speaker.   As for the Republicans, there were three candidates for the office, Mr. Gillett as the nominee of the Republican majority, Mr. Cooper of Wisconsin as that of the Progressive Republicans, and Mr. Madden of Illinois, who was, however, nominated

---

[1] Throughout Clark's Speakership (four terms altogether) Mr. Talbolt of Maryland was asked by Mr. Clark to administer the oath to him. Talbolt had only served nine discontinous terms in the House, while W. A. Jones of Virginia had eleven continuous terms to his credit. See *Cong. Record*, 62nd Cong., 1st Sess., p. 7; *Cong. Record*, 63rd Cong., 1st Sess., p. 64; *Cong. Record*, 64th Cong., 1st Sess., p. 6; *Cong. Record*, 65th Cong., 1st Sess., p. 108.   Twice Mr. Cannon administered the oath to Speaker Gillett. See *Cong. Record*, 66th Cong., 1st Sess., p. 8; *Cong. Record*, 67th Cong., 1st Sess., p. 80.   The member who is longest in continuous service, is called "the Father of the House." Mr. Cannon was not the Father of the House, although his service in the House was the longest of all members.   Cannon was on "involuntary vacation" during the Fifty-second and Sixty-third Congresses.

[2] For election contests for Speakership before the Thirty-sixth Congress, see Hinds, *op. cit.*, i, 222; v, 5356, 6647, 6649; also see Follett, *op. cit.*, pp. 50-63.

over his own protest. The Progressives presented the name
of Mr. Cooper, not because of the belief that they could elect
him but rather as a " protest to the rules that have grown up
in this body." [1] In nominating Mr. Madden, Mr. Reid of
Illinois said: ". . . . Acting upon my own initiative and
with a view to the future good of the Republican party in
the great Middle West from which I come, I place in nomination the name of Martin B. Madden of Illinois. . . ." [2]
On the first day, December 3, 1923, the House had four
roll-calls, and no one received a majority of the total votes
cast. [3] The next day four more roll-calls were taken with
no results. [4] The Progressives stood firm. Something had
to be done in order to end the deadlock. On the evening of
December 4, Mr. Longworth, then the Republican floor
leader, sought to have a conference with the representatives
of the Progressives and mutually agreed on a proposed program regarding the revision of the rules. This gentlemen's
agreement was made public, December 5, in a statement sub-

[1] *Cong. Record*, 68th Cong., 1st Sess., pp. 7, 8.
[2] *Cong. Record*, 68th Cong., 1st Sess., pp. 7, 8.
[3] *Ibid.*, pp. 8, 9, 10. The votes stood as follows:

Candidates	Votes received on each roll-call			
Gillett	197	194	195	197
Garrett	195	194	196	196
Cooper	17	17	17	17
Madden	5	6	5	5
Total	414	411	413	415

[4] *Ibid.*, pp. 11, 12, 13.

Candidates	Votes received on each roll-call			
Gillet	197	195	196	197
Garrett	197	197	198	198
Cooper	17	17	17	17
Madden	5	5	5	5
Total	416	414	416	417

mitted to the House by Mr. Nelson, and as a result, Mr. Gillett was elected on the first roll-call.[1]

Since March 4, 1925, the compensation of the Speaker has been at the rate of $15,000 per annum,[2] in addition to mile-

[1] The provisions of the gentlemen's agreement were: (1) that the rules of the preceding House be adopted for the rules of the present House for thirty days only; (2) during these thirty days amendments to the rules might be offered by any member to be referred to the Committee on Rules; (3) within such thirty days the Committee on Rules should report such amendments and rules which should be subject to "reasonable" discussion, amendment and record votes of the House; (4) any member should have opportunity to offer amendment to any rule of the House, be it reported or not, and might call for a record vote thereon; and (5) one motion to recommit should be in order. The result of the election was: Gillett, 215 votes; Garrett, 197 votes; and Madden, 2 votes. *Ibid.*, pp. 11, 12.

[2] The compensation of the members of both the House and Senate has been $10,000 per annum each since March 4, 1925. The Speaker receives the same amount of compensation as the Vice-President and the Cabinet members of the several departments. See 44 *Statutes at Large*, 1150. Also see *Cong. Record*, 68th Cong., 2nd Sess., pp. 3957, 4077, 4261.

The circumstances under which the salary bill was passed, merit consideration. The bill originated in the Senate in an amendment to a legislative appropriation bill, which had "twenty-odd or perhaps thirty pages" with no "less than fifteen amendments," and was passed in "ten or twelve or fifteen minutes." While in the House, a point of order was raised to the effect that under Rule viii those members who were elected to the Sixty-ninth Congress, should not be entitled to vote on the Senate amendment in question. However, Speaker Gillett overruled the point of order and held that "that provision of the Constitution [Rule] is in conflict with the other provision of the Constitution which says that the House shall fix its own salaries." *Cong. Record*, 68th Cong., 2nd Sess., p. 4266.

In opposing the bill, Senator Borah of Idaho said in the Senate: "The Congress fixes the salaries of its own members. That is an extraordinary privilege, and it ought to be dealt with in the most open and candid and deliberate way. We all know that there was no discussion of the subject either at the time of the passage of the bill or previously. We know there was no discussion of it at any time during the last campaign. We know the matter had never come to the public press or before the country... We shall never raise our salaries until we have so declared our intention to those who send us here." *Ibid.*, p. 4974.

age at the rate of 20 cents per mile " to be estimated by the nearest route usually traveled in going to and returning from each regular session." [1]   The office of the Speaker, under the act for the Legislative Branch of Government passed in February, 1927, has a secretary to the Speaker with a salary of $4,200 per annum; a parliamentarian, who was formerly called the Clerk to the Speaker's table, with $4,000; an assistant parliamentarian with $2,500; a Clerk to the Speaker with $1,940; a messenger to the Speaker's table with $1,520; and a messenger to the Speaker with $1,440. [2]   Besides, the Speaker of the House, in his capacity as a member, receives $4,000 per annum for hire of clerks " necessary employed " by him for office work, [3] and about $125 annually for stationery. [4]   As a member of the House, he is also entitled to the " franking privilege," that is, he may send free through the mail any mail matter or correspondence upon official or departmental business. [5]   More than once unsuccessful attempts were made to appropriate a small sum for the Speaker to maintain an automobile and its incidental expenses.   Thus in the Sixty-first Congress the Senate offered an amendment to a legislative appropriation bill providing for $2,500 for

[1] The mileage clause was written in the compensation act of July 28, 1866, which fixed the salary of Senators and Representatives at $5,000. On March 3, 1873, Congress passed another compensation act which increased the salary of the Senators and Representatives to $7,500 but retained the mileage clause. Hinds, *op. cit.*, ii, 1148.

The question is: Whether the passage of a later act which amounted to a repeal of the former act, repealed that act in its entirety or only a part of it. The compensation act of March ,3, 1873, just referred to virtually superseded that of July 28, 1866, and therefore the continuing existence of the mileage clause is of doubtful validity.

[2] 44 *Statutes at Large*, p. 1150.

[3] See *ibid.*, p. 1153; also *House Manual*, section 88, 69th Congress.

[4] *Ibid.*, section 87; also 44 *Statutes at Large*, p. 1154.

[5] 33 *Statutes at Large*, p. 441.

such purposes.[1] The House under the lead of Mr. Clark
of Missouri, however, voted to disagree to this amendment.
Whether this was done from the standpoint of economy or
from that of personal dislike to the incumbent of the
Speaker's chair (who was then Mr. Cannon), only the opponents of the bill knew.[2] The fact that Speaker Cannon had
to appear on the floor defending his course of action and
denying that he had ever " inspired," " encouraged," or
" approved " of the appropriation for the maintenance of
an automobile,[3] was most degrading to the dignity of the
Speakership, which members of the House, in their pursuit
of " picayunish and peanut politics," occasionally failed to
uphold. In the second session of the Sixty-third Congress
the Senate offered another amendment to the legislative,
executive and judicial appropriation bill providing for the
purchase of two automobiles, one for the use of the Vice-
President and the other for the use of the Speaker. The
amendment was disagreed to by the House.[4] It was not,

[1] *Cong. Record*, 61st Cong., 2nd Sess., p. 4526.

[2] *Ibid.*, p. 4527.

[3] *Ibid.*, p. 4527.

[4] *Cong. Record*, 63rd Cong., 2nd Sess., p. 11194. It seems that the
generosity of the House with regard to pensions and other petty claims
does not extend to the dignity of the Speakership. The appropriations
for pensions in the Sixty-first Congress amounted to $153,000,000. 36
Statutes at Large, p. 1085.

Nothing can be more profitable than to draw a contrast from the
Speaker of the House of Commons. The English Speaker receives an
emolument of £5,000 " to be paid, free of all taxes, out of the Consoli-
dated Fund direct, without having to be voted every year by the House
of Commons. Besides, a sum of £1,000 equipment money is given to
the Speaker on his first appointment. He could have a secretary, with
a salary of £500. The Speaker has a residence furnished by the State
and free of rent, rates, taxes, with coal and light supplied. His residence
is in that conspicuous wing of the Palace of Westminister . . ."
MacDonagh, *op. cit.*, vol. i, pp. 135, 136. The Speaker also receives

however, until the following session, the third session of the Sixty-third Congress, that a sum of $1,500 was finally appropriated " for driving, maintenance, and operation of an automobile for the Speaker of the House of Representatives." [1] This sum was several times increased and at the present time it amounts to $3,000.[2]

The Speaker has a dual personality. He is the presiding officer of the House, and is also the active Representative of a particular Congressional district of a State. In England the Speaker of the House, upon his election to the chair, actually, though perhaps not theoretically, forfeits his rights and privileges as the representative of a constituency in the House. His constituents have to choose between the honor of returning the Speaker and the disadvantage of being practicaly unrepresented in the Parliament. During the election he is prohibited by the force of usage from making political speeches or discussing issues

---

a pension of £4,000 a year. Upon resignation he is usually made a peer. This custom began with Speaker Charles Abbot, who, on retiring in 1817, was made Baron Colchester. *Ibid.*, p. 139.

On the royal attributes of the English Speaker, Redlich wrote: the Speaker "lives in a royal palace. He has his own court, his own civil list, his own public household. He is approached and addressed with a ceremony and deference such as is shown to royalty . . . He represents in his proper self the rights and privileges of all his subjects. In his own sphere his word is law, and, should that law be broken, he keeps his own officers to convey offenders to his own prison. His functions, multifarious as those of sovereignty itself, include many of a stately and ceremonial kind. He wears his own robe which it is not lawful for other man to don. His sceptre is borne before him—the mace of the most honourable House over which he rules, upon his head reposes his peculiar Crown, the Speakers wig, and just where the throne stands in the House of Lords we find in the House of Commons the Speaker's " chair ". "Who shall deny that the Speaker is, in every sense in which it were not treason to call him so, a king?" Redlich, *op. cit.*, vol. ii, p. 137.

[1] 38 *Statutes at Large*, p. 1004.

[2] 44 *Statutes at Large*, p. 1154.

along party lines.[1] The English Speaker neither participates in debate nor votes, except in the case of a tie. Quite the contrary, however, is the case with the American Speaker. In the first place he, as a member of the House, is elected upon a political platform either of his party or of his own formulation. The chance of his getting reelected from his district to the House is partly dependent upon the hold of his party but largely dependent upon his own personal strength in the district. Commenting on the eighty-fifth birthday of Mr. Cannon who had up to that time served in the House for more than forty-three years, Mr. Clark of Missouri said: ". . . . In the first place, the politics of his district must remain the same. In the second place, he must be a man of force and ability. In the third place, he must remain as faithful [to both the party machinery and his constituents] as the North Star." [2]

Like any other member of the House, the Speaker has to nurse his constituents. He freely introduces pension bills or bills for the relief of individuals or corporations or bills in favor of claims against the Government, or appears before the several departments to secure favors of one kind or another for his people " at home," "doing the chores," as it is

---

[1] See MacDonagh, *The Speaker of the House* (London, 1914), pp. 19-26.
Speaker Lowther addressed the electors of Penrith in the General Election of 1906: " More than ten years ago I was unanimously adopted by the House of Commons to preside over its deliberations in Committee as Chairman of the Committee of Ways and Means; during the two Parliaments it was my privilege and good fortune to discharge the duties of that office, and on June 8, 1905, I was unanimously elected to be Speaker of the House of Commons . . .

" I trust that you will consider my record and qualifications to be of such a character as to justify you in continuing to return me as your representative . . . The Speaker, as you know, has no politics, and I forebear therefore from entering upon a discussion of any of the current topics of political controversy . . . " *Ibid.*, pp. 25, 26.

[2] *Cong. Record*, 66th Cong., 3rd Sess., p. 794.

called.[1] He also introduces bills and resolutions of public nature and presents petitions and papers on behalf of individuals, societies and associations. Strictly speaking, however, the distinction between bills of public nature and those of private nature,[2] such as were introduced by the Speaker, is generally negligible. A pension bill is of private nature. A public building is in theory of public nature. But, as a matter of fact, those public building bills which the Speaker introduced were for the erection of buildings in his district of the State at the expense of the Federal Government: they are of local character. As will be shown in the following table,[3] more than ninety-five per cent of the bills and resolutions introduced by the Speaker since the Fifty-fourth Congress are of private and local nature. Once in a long while the Speaker presents a bill or resolution which is of general national character. Even so, it is usually of little importance. For instance, Speaker Clark introduced in the first session of the Sixty-second Congress a bill authorizing the Secretary of Labor to collect statistics relating to war. Speaker Gillett introduced for three consecutive Congresses a resolution proposing an amendment to the Federal Constitution prohibiting polygamy, and for two consecutive Congresses a bill which provided " for the world-wide extension of education by the cooperation of the national governments."

[1] This phase of work of the members of the House was described by Mr. Hardy of Colorado. See Guy U. Hardy, "Looking in on Congress —A Congressman's Day," *Cong. Record*, 67th Cong., 2nd Sess., p. 12419.

[2] The term "private" bills should be construed to mean all bills for the relief of private parties, bills granting pensions, bills removing political disability and bills for the survey of rivers and harbors. 28 *St. L.*, p. 609.

[3] Since the Fifty-fourth Congress the Speaker has freely introduced bill and resolutions of both private and public nature:

Sometimes the Speaker may request a member of the House

TABLE I

CONGRESSES

Nature of Bills and Resolutions.	54 No. of Bills Introduced.	55 No. of Bills Introduced.	56 No. of Bills Introduced.	57 No. of Bills Introduced.	58 No. of Bills Introduced.	59 No. of Bills Introduced.
Appointments	......	......	......	......	1	......
Bridges	......	......	1	......	......	......
Collecting Statistics Relating to War........................	......	......	......	......	......	......
Compensation to Individuals	......	......	......	......	......	......
Conferring Jurisdiction on Court of Claims.....................	......	......	......	......	......	......
Constitutional Amendment	......	......	......	......	......	......
Conveying Certain Lands	......	......	......	......	......	......
Donating Condemned Cannons...	......	......	......	......	......	......
Establishing Drainage	......	......	......	......	......	......
Establishing Fish-cultural Stations	......	......	......	......	......	......
Incorporating Carnegie Institute in Washington	......	......	......	1		
Increasing Cadets at West Point..	......	......	......	......	......	......
Inspection of Battlefields	......	......	......	......	......	......
Issuing Medal of Honor	......	......	......	......	......	......
Investigations...................	......	......	......	......	......	......
Keeping Railroads in Operation..	......	......	......	......	......	......
Pensions.......................	4	4	12	20	54	57
Preventing Unauthorized Wearing of Elks Badges	......	......	......	......	......	......
Prohibiting Exporting Wines into Africa	......	......	......	......	......	......
Purchasing Quarantine at Portland, Oregon	1					
Public Buildings	......	......	1	......	......	......
Raising Level of Dykes	......	......	......	......	......	......
Reappointment of Representatives of the House	......					
Reliefs and Claims..............	2	3	1	1	7	7
Transferring Military Reservations	......	......				
World-wide Extension of Education	......	......	......	......	......	....
Special Tax on Wine Manufacturers	......	......	......	......	......	
Withdrawing Certain Papers	......	......	......	......	......	......

to offer a resolution in which he is interested. This occurred

60	61	62	63	64	65	66	67	68	69
No. of Bills Introduced.	No. of Bills Introduced.	No. of Bills Introduced.	No. of Bills Introduced.	No. of Bills Introduced.	No. of Bills Introduced.	No. of Bills Introduced.	No. of Bills Introduced.	No. of Bills Introduced.	No. of Bills Introduced.
....	....	....	......	......	1	......	......	2	
....	....	2	1	......	......	1			
....	....	1							
....	....	......	......	......	......	1	1		
....	....	......	......	......	......	1	1	1	
....	....	......	......	......	......	1	1	1	
....	....	......	......	......	......	......		1	
....	....	......	1	1	4	6			
....	....	......	2	1					
....	....	......	1	1					
....	....	......	......	1					
....	....	......	.....	......	....	....	.....	1	
....	....	......	......	......	......	....	1	1	
2	....	......	......	......	......	....	1		
....	....	......	.....	......	......	....	1		
99	125	88	82	87	26	8	5	7	19
1									
....	....	......	......	......	......	1			
....	....	......	......	1	......	1	1		
....	....	......	......	1	1				
....	....	......	......	.....	.....	......	.....	1	
11	15	25	25	28	7	2	6	7	2
....	......	......	......	......	......	....	1		
....	....	......	......	......	......	1	2	1	
....	....	......	......	1					
1									

in the second session of the Sixty-ninth Congress, in which Mr. MacGregor of New York introduced a resolution for the creation of the office of an assistant parliamentarian at a salary of $2,500 per annum. Speaker Longworth thought it was " incumbent " upon him " to say just a word about this resolution, because it was introduced by the gentleman from New York at my request." [1]

Since the Fifth-fourth Congress there has been only one case in which the Speaker introduced a resolution of great political significance. In the first session of the Sixtieth Congress Speaker Cannon introduced, April 2, 1908, a resolution directing the Attorney-General to transmit to the House certain information concerning wood pulp and print

TABLE II

The following table shows the number of bills and resolutions which were introduced by the Speaker since the Fifty-fourth Congress, and which were enacted into laws:

Congresses.	Number of Bills and Resolutions Introduced.	Number of Bills and Resolutions Enacted.
54	7	1
55	7	
56	15	6
57	22	11
58	62	7
59	64	21
60	114	44
61	140	62
62	116	
63	112	1
64	122	
65	39	
66	23	1
67	20	
68	23	2
69	21	10

[1] *Cong. Record*, 69th Cong., 2nd Sess., p. 2622.

paper.[1]   Dissatisfied with the Attorney-General's action, Speaker Cannon introduced on April 20 another resolution which provided for the appointment by the Speaker (that is, by Mr. Cannon himself) of a select committee to investigate the wood-pulp and print-paper industries.[2]   The resolution was referred to the Committee on Rules, of which Mr. Cannon was chairman.   The following day Mr. Dalzell of Pennsylvania, the majority ranking member of the Committee on Rules, brought in a report for the appointment of a committee of six to conduct the said investigation.   Commenting on the course of action on the part of Speaker Cannon, Mr. Fitzgerald of New York said:

. . . The Speaker introduced a resolution, which passed this House, calling upon the Attorney-General to let him know just what had been done.   The Attorney-General made a reply which satisfied him, pleased the " Big Stick " up in the White House, but was not particularly pleasing to the " Big Gun " in the House of Representatives.   Then the Speaker said, " Why, they have me again."   So he fixed up a resolution, which recites a great many things in the " Whereases."   Then he provided that the Speaker shall appoint a committee of six to investigate the matter.

" Why have a committee waste the time of its members in this investigation when the Speaker has outlined the whole programme?   He knows what he is going to permit the House to do, why not direct the Speaker to investigate and ascertain what facts are?   And after he has done that, under the direction of the House, why not permit to frame another resolution and then call the Committee on Rules together and tell them what he wants done, bring in a report, tell those on that side of the House that he wants it adopted and then do it?   Why go

---

[1] *Cong. Record*, 60th Cong., 1st Sess., p. 4338.

[2] *Ibid.*, p. 4994.

through the farce of having a committee of six lose their vacation to keep back a report until after the election, and then drop the whole business?

. . . I have been in communication with some persons who imagine that they are [experts on wood pulp and print paper.] I have told them it was useless to write me about this matter, that the Speaker has abrogated all rules of the House; he is the whole business here now.   (Laughter on the Democratic side.) . . .[1]

Furthermore, the Speaker exercises his right, as a member of the House, to object to requests for unanimous consent— a topic which will receive fuller consideration at a later place.[2]   Finally, he debates and votes as a member of the House.

Though the Speaker may of right speak on matters of order and be first heard, he is, nevertheless, " restrained from speaking on any other subject, except where the House have occasion for facts within his knowledge; then he may, with their leave, state the matter of fact." [3]   There was a time, prior to 1896, when a Speaker asked leave to address the House even on a question of order,[4] but there were also times when the Speaker made brief explanations or statements from the chair without asking the assent of the House.[5]   Recent practice evidences an apparent absence of restraint, on the part of the Speaker, from speaking from the floor. Speaker Clark did not see " why the Speaker has not as much right to make speeches as any body else, if he

---

[1] *Cong. Record,* 60th Cong., 1st Sess., p. 5029.

[2] See *infra,* pp. 179 *et seq.*

[3] Jefferson's *Manual,* xvii.

[4] Hinds, *op. cit.,* iv, 3043.

[5] See *ibid.,* ii, 1373, 1374.

feels like it." [1] Speaker Reed participated from the chair in a debate on the quorum rule of the House,[2] for which he achieved great distinction as a parliamentarian.[3] Speaker Henderson strenuously defended himself from the chair in consequence of a newspaper story which intimated that he had threatened a member with coercion.[4]

Speaker Cannon who had been in the chair for eight consecutive years, spoke no less than fourteen times, four times from the Speaker's chair, four on the floor of the House and six in the Committee of the Whole House on the state of the Union. From the Speaker's chair he twice defended the rules of the House [5] and, with unanimous consent, argued from the chair the right of the Speaker to issue warrants of arrest.[6] He asked " indulgence " to address the House from the Speaker's chair after the passage of the Norris resolution, March 19, 1910.[7] On the floor of the House he refuted the " insinuation " pertaining to the " attempt " of members of one legislative body " to traffic in legislation " with those of the other body; [8] debated with Mr. Clark of Missouri on a tariff bill; [9] debated on the " controversy " touching an automobile in connection with the

[1] *Cong. Record*, 62nd Cong., 2nd Sess., p. 3705.

[2] *Cong. Record*, 54th Cong., 1st Sess., p. 579.

[3] See Follett, *op. cit.*, pp. 190, *et seq.*

[4] *Cong. Record*, 57th Cong., 1st Sess., pp. 2876, 2877.

[5] *Cong. Record*, 60th Cong., 1st Sess., pp. 8, 9; *Cong. Record*, 61st Cong., 2nd Sess., pp. 8488, 8489.

[6] *Cong. Record*, 59th Cong., 1st Sess., pp. 7625, 7626.

[7] *Cong. Record*, 61st Cong., 2nd Sess., p. 3436.

[8] *Ibid.*, p. 8529.

[9] *Cong. Record*, 61st Cong., 1st Sess., pp. 216, 217, 218.

office of the Speaker;[1] and urged the passage of a pension bill.[2] In the Committee of the Whole House on the state of the Union he denied the charge by Mr. Shackleford of Colorado of the one-man power of the Speaker of the House of Representatives;[3] spoke on the question of order,[4] on tariff,[5] on railroad legislation,[6] on a river and harbor appropriation bill,[7] and on appropriations of traveling expenses for the President.[8]

By far the most active in debate of all the six Speakers was, without question, Speaker Clark. Like Speaker Cannon, Speaker Clark presided over the House of Representatives for eight consecutive years. In frequency of debates, Speaker Clark exceeded his predecessor. During his eight years of Speakership, he participated exactly sixty-three times in various debates, eighteen of which times he spoke from the floor of the House and forty-five times in the Committee of the Whole House on the state of the Union.[9] However,

---

[1] *Cong. Record*, 61st Cong., 2nd Sess., p. 4527.

[2] *Ibid.*, 3rd Sess., p. 746.

[3] *Cong. Record*, 59th Cong., 1st Sess., p. 4355.

[4] *Cong. Record*, 60th Cong., 2nd Sess., p. 2713.

[5] *Cong. Record*, 61st Cong., 1st Sess., p. 1171.

[6] *Ibid.*, 2nd Sess., p. 4581.

[7] *Ibid.*, pp. 1873, 1874.

[8] *Ibid.*, p. 6945.

[9] Speaker Clark participated in debate on the veto message of the President on the wool tariff, *Cong. Record*, 62nd Cong., 1st Sess., pp. 4168, 4169; on the same question, *ibid.*, pp. 2207, 2208, 2209, 2210; on the Homestead bill, *ibid.*, 2nd Sess., p. 3705; on "political subjects," *ibid.*, p. 11840; on Tariff Board, *ibid.*, pp. 6186, 6187; on the Democratic caucus rule, *Cong. Record*, 63rd Cong., 1st Sess., p. 5157; on currency problem, *ibid.*, p. 5006; on disarmament, *ibid.*, p. 5832; on public buildings, *ibid.*, p. 4269; on Tariff Board, *ibid.*, pp. 769, 770, 779; on tariff conference report, *ibid.*, p. 5272; on tariff legislation, *ibid.*, p. 1368; on "industrial conditions," *ibid.*, 2nd Sess., pp. 1171, 1172, 1173; on Panama canal toll, *ibid.*, pp. 6055-6060; on the Philippine

he never debated from the Speaker's chair. As the number indicates, his oratorical activities extended to a wide range of subjects—from tariff and " industrial conditions " to the Democratic caucus rule and " political subjects," on which

Islands, *ibid.*, p. 16088; on Porto Rico regiment, *ibid.*, p. 4107; on a river and harbor appropriation bill, *ibid.*, p. 15925; on rules of the House, *ibid.*, p. 1796; on a relief bill, *ibid.*, pp. 13087, 13088; on a private bill on a bridge over the Missouri River, *ibid.*, p. 4928; on District of Columbia appropriation bill, *ibid.*, 3rd Sess., p. 4658; on public building, *ibid.*, p. 3437; on ship-subsidy bill, *ibid.*, p. 3965; on the adjournment of the Senate for more than three days, *Cong. Record,,* 64th Cong., 1st Sess., pp. 9267, 9268; on agricultural appropriation bill, *ibid.*, p. 6461; on Army increase, *ibid.*, pp. 4408, 4409, 4410; on publicity of campaign contributions, *ibid.*, p. 11073; on the creation of a Committee on Flood Control, *ibid.*, pp. 2089, 2090; on construction of battleships, *ibid.*, pp. 2220 *et seq.*; on "color" question in Juvenile Court, *ibid.*, pp. 6753, 6754; on Lincoln Memorial, *ibid.*, pp. 2594, 2595; on Merchant Marine, *ibid.*, pp. 8257, 8258; on Midshipmen at Navy Academy, *ibid.*, pp. 2240, 2241; on Mississippi River and Sacramento flood control, *ibid.*, pp. 7786, 7787, 8144, 8145, 8202-8203; on the Court of International Peace, *ibid.*, p. 9144; on revenue bill, *ibid.*, pp. 10661, 10662; on rural credits, *ibid.*, pp. 7926, 7927; on wool industry, *ibid.*, pp. 10518, 10519; on agricultural bill, *ibid.*, 2nd Sess., p. 966; on Army appropriation bill, *ibid.*, pp. 3717, 3833, 3834, *et seq.*; reading a letter from Samuel Gompers, *ibid.*, p. 2701; on the retirement of Asher C. Hinds, *ibid.*, p. 5025; on Navy appropriation bill, *ibid.*, pp. 2583 *et seq.*; on public buildings, *ibid.*, pp. 1557 *et seq.*; on pension bill, *ibid.*, p. 2099; on vocational education, *ibid.*, p. 168; on Army increase, *Cong. Record*, 65th Cong., 1st Sess., p. 297; on Army-Selective Draft bill, *ibid.*, pp. 1119, 1524-1525; on bond issue, *ibid.*, pp. 6580, 6581, 6645, 6684-6689; on copper companies, *ibid.*, p. 2842; on censorship, *ibid.*, p. 1761; on Government buildings, *ibid.*, pp. 3008, 3009; on enlargement of Interstate Commerce Commission, *ibid.*, pp. 4380, 4381; on rivers and harbors appropriation bill, *ibid.*, p. 3658; on soldiers and sailors insurance, *ibid.*, pp. 6889, 6890; on urgent deficiency bill, *ibid.*, p. 7248; on holidays during Christmas vacation, *ibid.*, 2nd Sess., p. 29; on removal of garbage in the District of Columbia, *ibid.*, p. 5465; on pension to State Militia, *ibid.*, pp. 7327 *et seq.*; on the resignation of Fitzgerald of New York, *ibid.*, p. 318; on diplomatic and consular appropriation, *ibid.*, 3rd Sess., pp. 1878 *et seq.*; on fortification appropriation, *ibid.*, p. 3816; on agreement to the time for consideration of Military Academy appropriation, *ibid.*, p. 2622.

he dwelt for thirty minutes by unanimous consent, and from here he arrived at " a bridge over the Missouri River," a private bill. In one Congress, the Sixty-fourth, he spoke twenty-three times, and it seemed that his popularity was enhanced each time he spoke. Very often he took the floor " amid general applause, the Members rising to their feet." [1] On the debate over the tariff legislation he commenced with the old hymn:

" This is the way I long have sought."
(Applause on the Democratic side.) [2]

And on the tariff conference report he rose to " make one of the longest and hardest fights in American politics." [3]

It is difficult to presage whether future Speakers will surpass Speaker Clark on this score. Speaker Gillett fell far short of the mark set up by his predecesor: he spoke no more than five times [4] in the course of his six years of Speakership—four times from the floor of the House and once in the Committee of the Whole House on the state of the Union. Like his predecessor, Mr. Gillett never debated from the Speaker's chair.

Speaker Longworth spoke once, in the first session of the Sixty-ninth Congress, from the floor of the House on the birthday of the Republican majority floor leader, Mr. Tilson of Connecticut. [5] In the second session of the Congress he

[1] *Cong. Record*, 63rd Cong., 1st Sess., p. 1368.

[2] *Ibid.*, p. 2368.

[3] *Ibid.*, p. 5272.

[4] Speaker Gillett spoke on the deficiency appropriation, *Cong. Record*, 66th Cong., 1st Sess., p. 5652; on a question of privilege, *ibid.*, pp. 3663 *et seq.*; on a relief bill, *ibid.*, 3rd Sess., p. 779; on Springfield Armory Military Reservation bill, *Cong. Record*, 67th Cong., 2nd Sess., p. 12731; on breach of privilege by Senate, *Cong. Record*, 68th Cong., 1st Sess., p. 4813.

[5] *Cong. Record*, 69th Cong., 1st Sess., p. 6692.

spoke three times: the first time he put forth his views, in the form of a question, on a Navy appropriation bill in the Committee of the Whole House on the state of the Union; [1] the second time he spoke, from the floor of the House, in favor of a resolution for the creation of the office of an assistant parliamentarian; [2] and the third time he pleaded, from the floor of the House, for " a powerful and adequate Navy." [3]   Speaker Longworth is much more partisan than his immediate predecessor, and the chances are that he will very likely exceed the latter in frequency of debate.   Already he has announced that in the Seventieth Congress which will convene on the first Monday of December, 1927, he would '' take an important part in the discussion of the naval question." [4]

Under the rules the Speaker " shall not be required to vote in ordinary legislative proceedings, except where his vote would be decisive, or when the House is engaged in voting by ballot; and in the case of a tie vote the question shall be lost." [5]   To vote in the case of a tie is called the Speaker's " casting vote."   But, as matter of fact, in the House of Representatives the question as to the right of the Speaker to " vote in ordinary legislative proceedings " has never been raised. [6]   The first Speaker who cast his vote in ordinary

[1] *Cong. Record,* 69th Cong., 2nd Sess., p. 1244.

[2] *Ibid.,* pp. 2672-2673.

[3] *Ibid.,* pp. 4703-4704.

[4] The New York *Times,* September 16, 1927, p. 6.

[5] Rule i, 6.

[6] The question was for the first time raised, December 4, 1803, on an amendment to the Constitution to change the form of voting for the President and Vice-President.   The vote in the House was 83 to 42, and it needed one more vote to make a two-thirds majority in the affirmative to have the amendment passed.   Speaker Macon voted in the affirmative, and the right of the Speaker to vote in such cases has not since been questioned.   Follett, *op. cit.,* p. 149.

proceedings probably was Henry Clay.[1] Speaker Clay claimed that he had a right to vote as an ordinary member of the House. But still this right was not then conclusively established. In 1824 a bill to make a money grant to General Lafayette was before the House, and Speaker Clay, "having been precluded, by the place he held, from the expression of his sentiments," felt it necessary to ask permission of the House to record his vote on the bill.[2] Before 1896 Speakers had, as a whole, sparingly exercised their right to vote " at pleasure," [3] partly, perhaps, due to the conscientious effort of some of the Speakers to retain a semblance of the judicial character of the office and partly because of the fact that some of them were not as active political leaders as others. In upward of a hundred years before 1896, votes cast by the Speaker with the minority to make an even division totaled more than twenty; with the majority to make a two-thirds vote, less than ten; and " unnecessary " votes, less than ten.[4]

The Speaker's name is not on the roll from which the yeas and nays are called,[5] and is not called unless on his request. At the end of a roll call, the Speaker, if he wishes to vote, orders the Clerk to read his name.[6] It has been held that

---

[1] The occasion was when the House in 1817 passed the Internal Improvement bill over the President's veto. *Ibid.*, p. 152.

[2] Hinds, *op. cit.*, v, 5968.

[3] If a Speaker may vote at any time, the effects of his vote will be: " He can, like any other member, help either the affirmative or the negative. What his privilege as Speaker then amounts to is that he can give or withhold such help and not be censured, unless, he not having voted, the House is evenly divided, in which case he is usually expected, and often required, to go on record, effectively if he votes with affirmative, uselessly if he votes with the negative." Luce, *op. cit.*, p. 452.

[4] The casting-votes cast by the Speaker during this period numbered more than ninety. See Follett, *op. cit.*, appendix F.

[5] Hinds, *op. cit.*, v, 5970.

[6] Speaker Clay once demanded that his name should be called first when

the Speaker can give his casting-vote after the intervention of other business or after the announcement of the result or on another day, if a correction of the roll shows a condition wherein his vote would be necessary and decisive.[1] He can, if he so wish, also withdraw his vote in case a correction shows that his vote appears to be unnecessary.[2] In the Sixtieth Congress the House voted on the passage of the Conspiracies against Aliens Bill. The vote was 101 to 100. As the vote was so close, a recapitulation was ordered. But, no sooner had the Clerk proceeded to recapitulate the vote, than Speaker Cannon ordered the Clerk to read his name. He answered in the affirmative—a casting vote. Immediately Mr. De Armond of Missouri raised the point of order that the Speaker could not vote after the roll call. Speaker Cannon, however, held the contrary and ruled:

. . . Years ago . . . there is a precedent of this kind, that where there is a mistake in a vote taken today, or say, on one day, and that mistake is corrected on another legislative day so as to make a tie, the Speaker in that case votes the day after. In other words, it [the recapitulation of the vote] is an ascertainment of the vote. Under the rule and practice such ascertainment shows that the vote was a tie upon recapitulation, and the Speaker is very clear as to the question of practice as well as the question of right that he is entitled to vote, and therefore votes " aye ".[3]

the Internal Improvement bill of 1817 was before the House. Miss Follett was of the opinion that there have, probably, been other instances which might not have come under her observation. Follett, *op. cit.*, p. 158.

[1] Hinds, *op. cit.*, v, 5969, 6061, 6063.

[2] *Ibid.*, 5971.

[3] Mr. De Armond appealed from the rule, but the appeal was laid on the table by a vote of 170 to 98. *Cong. Record*, 60th Cong., 2nd Sess., pp. 173, 174.

Just as the Speaker's share in debate has been enlarged since 1896, so has been his share in voting. During the Fifty-fifth Congress Speaker Reed voted seven times,[1] only one of which was a casting vote, which was given on a motion to limit debate.[2] Speaker Henderson, presiding over the House from the Fifty-sixth to Fifty-seventh Congress, cast fourteen votes,[3] on two of which he answered "present" merely for the purpose of making a quorum.[4]

Never has there been a Speaker (Speaker Clay included) who was more partisan, more active and more jealous of his right and privilege both as presiding officer and member of the House than both Speaker Cannon and Speaker Clark. In frequency of debate Speaker Clark, as has been shown,

[1] Votes cast by Speaker Reed were on the passage of the bill regulating imported duties, *Cong. Record*, 55th Cong., 1st Sess., p. 557; on the Dingley tariff conference report, *ibid.*, p. 2650; on urgent deficiency bill for national defence, *ibid.*, 2nd Sess., p. 2620; on the joint resolution recognizing independence of Cuba, *ibid.*, p. 3820; on conference report on independence of Cuba, *ibid.*, p. 4064; "nay" on payment of the U. S. bonds in standard silver dollars, *ibid.*, p. 1309.

[2] For the casting-vote, see *ibid.*, p. 519.

[3] Speaker Henderson's votes were as follows: he voted "nay" on motion to strike out the provision for Civil Service Commission, *Cong. Record*, 56th Cong., 1st Sess., p. 1905; on a substitute for trading with Puerto Rico bill, *ibid.*, p. 2428; on an election contest case, *ibid.*, p. 2793; on minority substitute in an election contest case, *Cong. Record*, 57th Cong., 2nd Sess., p. 2726.

He voted "yea" on the passage of the trade with Puerto Rico bill, *Cong. Record*, 56th Cong., 1st Sess., p. 2429; on a relief bill, *ibid.*, p. 3255; on the Senate amendment to the bill providing revenue for relief of Puerto Rico, *ibid.*, p. 4071; on a joint resolution relating to trusts, *ibid.*, p. 6426; on resolution extending thanks to John Hay, *Cong. Record*, 57th Cong., 1st Sess., p. 6194; on the Military Academy appropriation, *ibid.*, p. 7140; on extension of charters to National Bank, *ibid.*, p. 3810; on the demand of previous question, *ibid.*, 2nd Sess., p. 2727.

[4] He answered "present" on a motion to go the Committee of Whole. *Cong. Record*, 56th Cong., 2nd Sess., p. 1199; on call of no quorum. *Ibid.*, p. 1202.

took the lead; but in the number of votes cast the honor goes to Speaker Cannon. During his eight years of Speakership Mr. Cannon had cast his vote no less than one hundred and twenty-one times,[1] and, in addition, he was recorded as

[1] Speaker Cannon voted "yea" on a resolution for special order for Cuba convention bill, *Cong. Record*, 58th Cong., 1st Sess., p. 258; on an election contest case, *ibid.*, p. 1866; on an election contest case, *ibid.*, 2nd Sess., p. 1867; on the deficiency appropriation bill, *ibid.*, p. 5051; on the order of business, *ibid.*, p. 5807; on resolution concerning pension, *ibid.*, p. 4589; on bond issue for municipal improvement in Philippine Islands, *ibid.*, p. 4818; on resolution for special order for the Statehood bill, *Cong. Record*, 59th Cong., 1st Sess., p. 1507; on the passage of the Statehood bill, *ibid.*, p. 1587; on the eight-hour law on the Isthmus of Panama, *ibid.*, p. 1629; on Railroad Rates bill, *ibid.*, p. 2303; on an amendment to an amendment abolishing the office of Lieutenant-General of the U. S. Army, *ibid.*, p. 3934; on ordering the previous question, *ibid.*, pp. 4122, 4123; on adoption of resolution for special order, *ibid.*, pp. 4127, 4128; on the question to take recess, *ibid.*, p. 5353; on bill to increase pension to one Saunderson, *ibid.*, p. 7461; on compulsory education in the District of Columbia, *ibid.*, p. 7584; on adoption of conference report on the Commerce Act, *ibid.*, p. 9085; on passage of the coastwise pilotage bill, *ibid.*, 2nd Sess., p. 153; on motion to reconsider, *ibid.*, p. 4375; on a substitute to the Ship Subsidy bill, *ibid.*, p. 4376; on the third reading of the same bill, *ibid.*, p. 4377; on the passage of the same bill, *ibid.*, p. 4377 (Speaker Cannon voted five times out of the six roll calls on this bill); on motion to suspend rules and pass the Employers' Liability Act, *Cong. Record*, 60th Cong., 1st Sess., pp. 4438-4439; on motion to take recess, *ibid.*, pp. 4895, 4896; on conference report on the Senate bill for registration of all causes of tuberculosis in the District of Columbia, *ibid.*, p. 5767; also *ibid.*, p. 5768; on the passage of Vreeland currency bill, *ibid.*, p. 6295; on Senate amendments to a pension bill, *ibid.*, pp. 6369, 6370; on motion to disagree to Senate amendments, *ibid.*, p. 6375; on bill on additional Federal judges, *ibid.*, p. 6937; on motion to suspend rules and pass transportation of explosives, *ibid.*, p. 7010; on motion to suspend rules and pass the resolution on the estimates for clerical service, *ibid.*, p. 7012; on conference report on Post-Office appropriation bill, *ibid.*, p. 6761; on motion to suspend rules and pass the publicity of campaign contribution bill, *ibid.*, p. 6767; on motion to recede from disagreement to Senate amendment to Post-Office appropriation bill, *ibid.*, p. 6861; on motion to suspend bill and pass Fort Peck Indian Reservation bill, *ibid.*, p. 7213; on conference report to establish a

Footnote 1, page 53—*Continued.*

Bureau of Immigration and Naturalization, *ibid.*, p. 7216; on motion to take recess, *ibid.*, p. 7216; on motion to take recess, *ibid.*, p. 7218; on motion to suspend the rules and pass the joint resolution on clerical service, *ibid.*, p. 7278; on motion to take recess, *ibid.*, p. 7279; on motion to suspend the rules and pass life-saving apparatus bill, *ibid.*, p. 7282; on motion to take recess, *ibid.*, p. 7099; on bill on agricultural land in Forest Reserves, *ibid.*, p. 7143; on motion to suspend the rules and pass a bill relating to Baltimore and Washington Transit Co., *ibid.*, p. 7146; on motion to take recess, *ibid.*, p. 7152; on conference report on Vreeland currency bill, *ibid.*, p. 7077; on motion to suspend the rules and pass Washington and Maryland railroad bill, *ibid.*, p. 7090; on conference report on bill authorizing a survey of certain townships in Wyoming, *ibid.*, p. 7092; on motion to suspend the rules and pass the bill for a Memorial University in the State of Iowa, *ibid.*, p. 7284; on motion to suspend the rules and agree to conference report on a public building bill, *ibid.*, p. 7290; on resolution to amend rules on call of committees of the House, *ibid.*, 2nd Sess., p. 3572; on relief of certain discharged soldiers, *ibid.*, p. 3400; on bill acquiring national forest in Southern Appalachian and White Mountains, *ibid.*, 3566; on legislative, judicial, etc., appropriation bill, *ibid.*, p. 3033; on the same bill, *ibid.*, p. 3034; on the same bill, *ibid.*, p. 2638; on bill to amend ocean mail service act, *ibid.*, p. 3694; on order of business, *ibid.*, p. 2597; on resolution to modify rules relative to vote on motions to suspend the rules, *ibid.*, p. 3311; on the same resolution, *ibid.*, p. 3312; on bill to reduce salary of the Secretary of State, *ibid.*, p. 2403; on the same bill, *ibid.*, p. 2415; on resolution for special order for the same bill, *ibid.*, p. 2409; on engrossment and third reading of the conspiracies against aliens bill, *ibid.*, pp. 173, 174; on resolution on adoption of the House rules, *Cong. Record*, 61st Cong., 1st Sess., p. 20; on the same resolution, *ibid.*, p. 21; on agreeing to Fitzgerald amendment, *ibid.*, p. 33; on resolution for special order for revenue bill, *ibid.*, pp. 1118, 1119, 4384, 4385; on amendment on "hides" to tariff bill, *ibid.*, p. 1298; on passage of tariff bill, *ibid.*, p. 1301; on order of business, *ibid.*, p. 2723; on conference report on tariff bill, *ibid.*, pp. 4754, 4755; on joint resolution enlarging the scope of inquiry of schedules relative to population, *ibid.*, 2nd Sess., p. 3288; on joint resolution celebrating anniversary of Emancipation Act, *ibid.*, p. 8600; on motion to take recess, *ibid.*, p. 3308; on motion to adjourn, *ibid.*, pp. 3323, 3324; on motion to take recess, *ibid.*, pp. 3388, 3415; on motion to postpone, *ibid.*, p. 3417; on motion to suspend the rules and pass bill on leasing coal lands in Alaska, *ibid.*, 3rd Sess., p. 3242; on motion to recommit reciprocity with Canada bill, *ibid.*, p. 2563; on legislative, judicial, etc., appropria-

" not voting " three times,[1] answered " present " ten times,[2] made a tie vote once,[3] and recorded a casting-vote twice.[4]

tion bill, *ibid.*, p. 3592; on passage of bill on payment of officers and enlisted men of militia, *ibid.*, p. 3801.

Speaker Cannon voted "nay" on minority amendment to an election case, *Cong. Record*, 58th Cong., 2nd Sess., p. 1865; on Senate amendment to a Navy appropriation bill, *Cong. Record*, 59th Cong., 1st Sess., p. 8888; on amendment to a Navy appropriation bill, *ibid.*, 2nd Sess., p. 3069; on motion to lay on table to consider votes on a ship subsidy bill, *ibid.*, p. 4347; on amendment to agricultural appropriation bill, *Cong. Record*, 60th Cong., 1st Sess., pp. 4323, 6294, 6295; on amendment on "barley" in tariff bill, *Cong. Record*, 61st Cong., 1st Sess., p. 1296; on amendment on lumber in tariff bill, *ibid.*, pp. 1294, 1294, 1295, 1295; on timber, *ibid.*, p. 1293; on petroleum, *ibid.*, pp. 1299, 1300; on motion to recommit the tariff bill, *ibid.*, pp. 1301, 4755; on resolution to increase membership of the Committee on Rules, *ibid.*, 2nd Sess., pp. 3436, 3437; on bill to create Court of Commerce, *ibid.*, p. 7577; on universal transfer over street railways in the District of Columbia, *ibid.*, pp. 5350, 5351; on promotion of a certain retired officer of the Army, *ibid.*, p. 4761; on resolution for special order for reciprocity with Canada bill, *ibid.*, 3rd Sess., pp. 2562, 2564; on payment of officers and enlisted men of militia, *ibid.*, p. 3710.

[1] Speaker Cannon was recorded as "not voting" on bill to erect National Forest Reservation Commission, *Cong. Record*, 61st Cong., 2nd Sess., pp. 9026, 9027; on motion to recommit bill establishing postal saving depositories, *ibid.*, p. 7767.

The author undertook to write Mr. Fess, Parliamentary Clerk of the House, and asked him to explain the recording of the Speaker's name as "not voting." Mr. Fess replied, April 5, 1926, that "after consultation with the official reporters of debates," he was "convinced that the inclusion of the name of the Speaker among those not voting is by error."

[2] Speaker Cannon answered "present" on question of consideration on bill abolishing the office of Lieutenant-General of the U. S. Army, *Cong. Record*, 59th Cong., 1st Sess., pp. 3930, 3931; on amendment to a pension bill, *ibid.*, pp. 7079, 7098, 7100, 7101, 7102; on motion of no quorum, *ibid.*, pp. 7089-7105 (there were ten roll calls on motions of no quorum. Speaker Cannon answered "present" four out of the ten calls) ; also *ibid.*, 2nd Sess., p. 4304.

[3] Speaker Cannon cast a tie vote on the demand of previous question. He voted "yea." The vote stood—yeas 107 and nays 107. *Cong. Record*, 58th Cong., 2nd Sess., p. 385.

[4] The casting-votes were on the passage of the conspiraries against

On the other hand, Clark had voted ninety-six times,[1] not

aliens bill. Speaker Cannon voted "aye." The vote stood—yeas 101 and nays 100, *Cong. Record*, 60th Cong., 2nd Sess., pp. 172, 173. On a motion to strike out the enacting clause of the Cheyenne Indian Reservation bill Speaker Cannon voted "nay." The vote stood—yeas 117 and nays 118. *Cong. Record*, 61st Cong., 2nd Sess., p. 3288.

[1] Votes cast by Speaker Clark as follows: he voted "yea" on joint resolution to Constitutional amendment on popular election of Senators, *Cong. Record*, 62nd Cong., 1st Sess., p. 243; on bill on publicity of campaign contributions, *ibid.*, pp. 267, 268, 269; on reciprocity with Canada bill, *ibid.*, p. 559; on bill to repeal duties on agricultural implements, *ibid.*, p. 112; on bill to reduce duties on wool, *ibid.*, p. 2356; on bill to reduce duties on manufactures of cotton, *ibid.*, p. 3584; on conference report to reduce duties on wool, *ibid.*, p. 3919; on the same bill over the President's veto, *ibid.*, pp. 4170, 4174; on resolution on special order for bill to reduce duties on manufactures of cotton, *ibid.*, p. 4314; on a pension bill, *ibid.*, 2nd Sess., p. 284; on joint resolution terminating the treaty of 1832 with Russia, *ibid.*, p. 353; on bill to fix duties on chemical schedule, *ibid.*, p. 2295; on order of business, *ibid.*, p. 2370; on bill repealing duties on sugar, *ibid.*, p. 3457; on excise tax bill, *ibid.*, p. 3637; on passage of bill repealing duties on wool, *ibid.*, pp. 4141, 4142; on bill establishing Children''s Bureau, *ibid.*, p. 4226; on bill regulating the granting of injunction, *ibid.*, pp. 6470, 6471; on order of business, *ibid.*, p. 7520; on order of business, *ibid.*, pp. 8715-8716; on passage of bill reducing duties on manufactures of cotton, *ibid.*, p. 10117; on conference report on bill reducing duties on wool, *ibid.*, p. 10153; on order of business, *ibid.*, p. 10748; on an election case, *ibid.*, pp. 10781, 10781; on bill reducing duties on wool, *ibid.*, p. 10845; on bill to revise duties on iron and steel, *ibid.*, p. 10942; on legislative, judicial, etc., appropriation bill, *ibid.*, p. 11035; on Post-Office appropriation bill, *ibid.*, p. 11042; on legislative, judicial, etc., appropriation bill, *ibid.*, p. 11478; on call of no quorum, *ibid.*, p. 11761; on call of the House, *Cong. Record*, 63rd Cong., 1st Sess., p. 1458; on passage of Underwood tariff bill, *ibid.*, p. 1387; on the currency bill, *ibid.*, p. 5129; on conference report on the tariff bill, *ibid.*, p. 5274; on motion to recommit national banking bill, *ibid.*, 2nd Sess., p. 16956; on conference report on currency bill, *ibid.*, p. 1464; on joint resolution justifying employment by the President of armed forces in Mexico, *ibid.*, p. 6957; on resolution favoring suspension for one year of naval construction programs, *ibid.*, p. 480; on order of business, *ibid.*, pp. 13070, 16955; on motion to recommit bill amending Panama Canal toll act, *ibid.*, p. 6088; on bill for more autonomous government of Philippine Islands, *ibid.*, pp. 16628,

including, however, the vote of " present " once,[1] a tie vote

16629; on bill making deficiency appropriation for army, *Cong. Record,* 64th Cong., 1st Sess., p. 5022; on bill for families of men in draft force in the service of the U. S. militia, *ibid.,* p. 10356; on joint resolution authorizing draft of National Guardsmen into military service, *ibid.,* p. 9892; on joint resolution to appoint members of Board of Managers of National Home for Disabled Volunteers, *ibid.,* p. 3313; on passage of bill increasing Army, *Cong. Record,* 65th Cong., 1st Sess., pp. 1557, 7104; on election of officers of the House, *ibid.,* pp. 109, 110, 110, 111; on resolution adopting the House rules, *ibid.,* p. 112; on bill for emergency bond issue, *ibid.,* p. 690; on amendment to bill punishing espionage, *ibid.,* p. 1816; on deficiency appropriation bill, *ibid.,* p. 1693; on joint resolution declaring war upon Austria-Hungary, *ibid.,* 2nd Sess., p. 99; on order of business, *ibid.,* p. 9035; on motion of reconsideration, *ibid.,* p. 4801.

Speaker Clark voted "nay" on joint resolution on Constitutional amendment relating to popular election of Senators, *Cong. Record,* 62nd Cong., 1st Sess., p. 241; on motion to recommit bill reducing duties on wool, *ibid.,* p. 2356; on motion to adjourn, *ibid.,* p. 3612; on amendment to agricultural appropriation bill, *ibid.,* 2nd Sess., p. 3236; on motion to recommit bill reducing duties on sugar, *ibid.,* p. 3456; on motion to recommit bill reducing duties on wool, *ibid.,* pp. 4140, 4141, 9913, 9914; on motion to concur in Senate amendment to excise bill, *ibid.,* pp. 9916, 9918; on motion to concur in Senate amendment to bill reducing duties on sugar, *ibid.,* p. 9922; substitute to bill reducing duties on manufactures of cotton, *ibid.,* p. 10116; on an election case, *ibid.,* p. 10780; on bill for additional judge in Eastern District of Pennsylvania, *Cong. Record,* 63rd Cong., 1st Sess., p. 2271; on order of business, *ibid.,* 2nd Sess., p. 16898; on amendment relating to appointment and compensation of an assistant to Secretary of State, *ibid.,* p. 11210; on order of business, *ibid.,* 2nd Sess., pp. 14110, 16898; on bill amending Panama Canal Tolls Act, *ibid.,* pp. 6087, 6089, 5618, 5619; on bill for development of water power, *ibid.,* pp. 14181, 14182; on conference report on bill increasing efficiency of military establishment, *Cong. Record,* 64th Cong., 1st Sess., p. 7615; on motion to recommit bill relating to amendment to armor-plate factory, *ibid.,* p. 9189; on bill to increase army, *Cong. Record,* 65th Cong., 1st Sess., pp. 1555, 2215; on motion to recommit resolution on adoption of the House Rules, *ibid.,* p. 113; on motion to adjourn, *ibid.,* 2nd Sess., p. 10955; on minority substitute in an election case, *ibid.,* 3rd Sess., pp. 4800, 4802, 4803.

[1] Speaker Clark answered "present" on amendment to House joint resolution on appointment of members of Board of Managers of National Home for Disabled Volunteers. *Cong. Record,* 64th Cong., 2nd Sess., p. 3313.

once,[1] " not voting " twice,[2] and a casting-vote twice.[3]   All in all, he voted one hundred and two times.   It is improbable that any future Speaker would ever attempt to participate in debate and voting to such an amazing extent as did Speaker Cannon and Speaker Clark.   For instance, Speaker Gillett, who was the immediate successor of Speaker Clark, and who had been in the chair for no less than six years, recorded his vote only eighteen times.[4]   Some of his votes, as will be seen, were made for the purpose of making a quorum.   The present Speaker, Mr. Longworth of Ohio, did not record a single vote during the Sixty-ninth Congress in which he served his first term as presiding officer of the House.

[1] On motion to table motion declining to receive communication from Postmaster General.   The vote stood — yeas 165, nays 165.   Speaker Clark voted " yea."   The question was therefore lost.   *Cong. Record*, 65th Cong., 2nd Sess., p. 4975.   *Cf.* Rule i, 6.

[2] On motion to adjourn, *Cong. Record*, 63rd Cong., 3rd Sess., p. 3833; also on motion to adjourn, *Cong. Record*, 64th Cong., 1st Sess., p. 9509.

[3] On motion to agree to conference report on bill making appropriations for Post-Office Department.   The vote stood—yeas 150, nays 149. Speaker Clark voted " yea," *Cong. Record*, 65th Cong., 2nd Sess., p. 8386; on resolution for special order for bill establishing sanatorium for disabled soldiers and sailors.   The vote stood—yeas 152, nays 151. Speaker Clark voted " yea," *ibid.*, 3rd Sess., p. 49.

[4] Speaker Gillett voted " yea " on motion to table a motion for the relief of one Carey, *Cong. Record*, 66th Cong., 1st Sess., p. 3167; on passage of a pension bill, *ibid.*, p. 3170; on amendment relating to delivery of special-delivery mail matter, *ibid.*, 3rd Sess., p. 3721; on order of business, *Cong. Record*, 67th Cong., 1st Sess., p. 4325; on call of no quorum, *ibid.*, pp. 4326, 4327; on demand of previous question, *ibid.*, 2nd Sess., pp. 556, 557, 558, 600; on motion to go to the Committee of whole, *ibid.*, p. 603; on demand of previous question, *ibid.*, p. 7081; on conference report on District of Columbia appropriation bill, *ibid.*, pp. 9286, 9288; on motion of no quorum, *ibid.*, p. 9289; on passage of reinstatement of certain land officers, *ibid.*, p. 9640; on resolution on the adjournment of the House, *ibid.*, p. 9878.
He voted " nay " on motion to recommit Treasury and Post-Office Departments appropriation bill.   *Cong. Record*, 68th Cong., 2nd Sess., p. 1028.

Under the rules of the House the Speaker is " required " to vote on two conditions only—where his vote is decisive and when the House is engaged in voting by ballot. But, as the House has since 1896 never voted by ballot, so the Speaker has never had any occasion to vote under the latter part of the rule.[1] To vote to break a tie, to complete a two-thirds vote and to make a tie, in which case the question is lost—these are the cases where the Speaker's vote is decisive. Since 1896 there were only five occasions upon which the Speaker voted to break a tie [2]—five casting-votes; on two occasions the Speaker's vote was needed to make a tie; [3] and not once was the Speaker's vote really needed to complete a two-thirds vote, although several times the Speaker voted with the majority on questions which under the rules required a two-thirds vote. In other words, since 1896 there were only seven occasions upon which the Speaker was " required " under the rules to vote.

Occasionally, but not frequently, a Speaker, as a member of the House, casts his vote either to make a two-thirds vote or on a call of no quorum.[4] But in both of these cases the aggregate number of the votes thus far recorded is, however, insignificant as compared with the bulk of the votes cast for political and personal reasons — the " unnecessary votes," [5] as Miss Follett called them. The Speaker freely

---

[1] The last election by ballot seems to have occurred in 1868 in the impeachment case of President Johnson. See Hinds, *op. cit.*, v, 6003.

[2] *Cong. Record*, 55th Cong., 2nd Sess., p. 519; *Cong. Record*, 60th Cong., 2nd Sess., pp. 173, 174; *Cong. Record*, 61st Cong., 2nd Sess., p. 6067; *Cong. Record*, 65th Cong., 2nd Sess., p. 8386; *Ibid.*, 3rd Sess., p. 49.

[3] *Cong. Record*, 58th Cong., 2nd Sess., p. 385; *Cong. Record*, 65th Cong., 2nd Sess., p. 4975.

[4] See *supra*, pp. 52-58 on the Speaker's share in vote.

[5] Follett, *op. cit.*, appendix F.

votes, in his capacity as a private member of the House, on measures vital to the political fortune of his party, to the National welfare or to the interests of corporations, individuals and his home district. He votes on a tariff bill, a currency bill, an appropriation bill, and in fact on any public bill that is before the House. So, also, he votes on pension or other bills of a private nature, if thereby he can build his political fences in his district. To say that the Speaker is more a member than the presiding officer of the House, is by no means an exaggeration. To say that the Speaker of the House has been more of a political than of a non-partisan moderator, seems to be an undeniable fact. Only time can tell when the pendulum will swing to the other extreme.

CHAPTER II

The Speaker and the Committee System

As the character of the Speakership of the House of Representatives has its origin in that of the colonial assemblies, so has the method of committee appointment by the Speaker.[1] The first rule which was adopted, April 7, 1789, by the House of the First Congress, provided that the Speaker should appoint all the committees "except such as consisted of more than three members, which was [were] to be chosen by ballot."[2] But, soon, difficulties incidental to balloting presented themselves, and the Speaker appointed all the committees, each of which consisted of no more than three members.[3] In the second session of the First Congress the House adopted, January 13, 1790, a rule extending the Speaker's power of appointment to all committees "unless otherwise specially directed by the House, in which case

[1] See McConachie, *Congressional Committees* (New York, 1898), chapter i.

[2] Hinds, *op. cit.*, iv, 4448.

[3] The reason for the small size of the committees was explained by Mr. McConachie: "Business of the earlier Houses went to a host of select committees. At least three hundred and fifty were raised in the Third Congress [in which there were only 106 Representatives in the House]. A special committee had to be formed for every petty claim. A bill founded on the report of one small committee had to be recommitted to, or carefully drafted by another committee..." But the number of the select committees declined very rapidly. From 1813 to 1815 the number dropped to 70. From 1833 to 1835 the number was 35. There were 22 from 1853 to 1855, and 20 from 1873 to 1875, the Forty-third Congress. McConachie, *op. cit.*, pp. 124, 125. The Committee on Enrolled Bills of three members was the only standing committtee in the House during the first Congress. Hinds, *op. cit.*, iv, 4350, 4416. In the Sixty-ninth Congress there are 61 standing committees in the House (if we count the three Election Committees as one).

they shall be appointed by ballot." [1]   But as the standing committees increased in number, another rule provided that at the commencement of each session of Congress the Speaker be authorizd to appoint the regular standing committees.[2]   Since 1861 the life of the committees has been prolonged from one session to one whole Congress.[3]   Were it not for the fact that the Speaker could not appoint those committees in whose report he might have personal interest,[4] his power of appointing committees prior to 1911 would have been complete.

In principle, committees were originally created as impartial boards.[5]   But, in the nature of things, party interests were in evidence even in the First Congress, and committees were thus from the outset so constituted as to mirror the political division of the House.   In the First Congress Speaker Muhlenberg appointed to a committee relating to the slave-trade members of the House who were either pro-slavery or neutral on the question,[6] and the anti-slavery members were not appointed.   " It has been in fact," Miss Follett writes, " all but universally acknowledged that the Speaker's first thought in the construction of the committees should be the interests of his party." [7]

[1] Hinds, *op. cit.*, iv, 4448.

[2] *Ibid.*, 4448. For several times it was debated whether the rules of the House of one Congress could bind on the succeeding House. On March 19, 1860, the House adopted a rule: " These rules shall be the rules of the House of Representatives of the present and succeeding Congresses, unless otherwise ordered." This rule remained in force through the Fiftieth Congress. See *ibid.*, v, 6743-6755.

[3] Follett, *op. cit.*, p. 218.

[4] The Speaker could not appoint the committee before which the Speaker's seat as a member was to be contested or when charges were made against him. In these cases the committee was appointed by the Speaker *pro tempore*, by ballot or by a resolution of the House. Hinds, *op. cit.*, i, 809; ii, 1286, 1360-1362, 1364.

[5] Follett, *op. cit.*, p. 220.

[6] *Ibid.*, p. 221.   [7] *Ibid.*, p. 221.

Custom has established certain well-defined principles, unwritten rules, governing the appointment of committees by the Speaker. Seniority rule, that is, promotion in accordance with the length of service on a committee, geographical distribution and party regularity—all these were taken into consideration in making up committees. Moreover, as the committees are bi-partisan, the Speaker was not only expected to apply these unwritten rules to the members of both the majority and minority parties in their committee assignments, but also to give the minority party a fair representation both in number and strength. The dominant party in the House has always a majority on every committee. The ratio between the different parties on the committees is generally in proportion to the strength of the different parties in the House.[1] Chairmanships of the committees are held

[1] The following table shows the ratio of party representation on the committee on Ways and Means in proportion to the strength of the parties in the House since the Fifty-fourth Congress. This committee gives an index to party representation on the House Committees.

PARTY REPRESENTATION ON THE COMMITTEE ON WAYS AND MEANS AS COMPARED WITH THE PARTY MAJORITY IN THE HOUSE

Congress	Proportion on the Committee	Party Majority in the House	Total Number of Representatives
54	11 to 6	133	357
55	11 to 6	56	357
56	11 to 7	13	357
57	11 to 6	40	357
58	11 to 6	29	386
59	12 to 6	114	386
60	12 to 7	58	386
61	12 to 7	47	391
62	14 to 7	65	391
63	14 to 7	145	435
64	14 to 8	21	435
65[2]	13 to 10	..	435
66	15 to 10	39	435
67	17 to 8	167	435
68	15 to 11	25	435
69	15 to 11	59	435

[2] In the Sixty-fifth Congress the political divisions of the House stood

by the members of the majority party. The last time in which members of the minority party were given chairmanships was 1855.[1] Since that time not a single case of this kind has ever happened.

The Speaker was not bound to follow the unwritten rules. In fact, there have been cases in which he appointed persons to represent his own views or removed persons for political reasons. In 1801 Speaker Macon appointed one of his favorites in preference over William B. Giles of Virginia and Samuel Smith of Maryland.[2] In 1857 Speaker Orth removed Mr. Giddings, the oldest member of the House, from the Committee on Territories, a very important committee at that time, in order to be sure that the Kansas bill be reported out.[3] Indeed, toward the end of the last century there had grown up the " theory " that " the Chair has the right to have and to pursue a policy of its own." [4] To quote the same writer further:

The importance of the Speaker's appointment of the committees is greatly increased by the fact that it is an absolute power. There is no provision which requires that the committees be approved, and as a matter of fact, the House never questions an appointment. And the Speaker, in spite of the restrictions on his prerogatives, has many opportunities to constitute the committees so that he may to a great extent procure or prevent what legislation he wishes: he may give a good committee to a poor chairman; or he may satisfy the general feeling

—Republicans, 216; Democrats, 210; and Third party, 9. The Democrats were allowed to organize the House. Mr. Clark of Missouri was elected Speaker. *Cf. supra*, p. 30 (footnote 1).

This table is modeled upon a similar one made by Mr. Hinds up to the Fifty-ninth Congress. See Hinds, *op. cit.*, iv, 4477 (foot-note).

[1] See Follett, *op. cit.*, pp. 226, 227.

[2] *Ibid.*, p. 223.

[3] *Ibid.*, pp. 226, 227.

[4] *Ibid.*, p. 222.

in the appointment of a chairman, and then give him a committee which reflects the Speaker's, not the chairman's view, and with which, therefore, the chairman can not act.[1]

The outcry against the Speaker's power of committee appointment had been of long standing,[2] but it became loudest during the Speakership of Mr. Cannon. The first thing he did upon his elevation in the Fifty-eighth Congress to the Speakership was to appoint Mr. Hemenway of Indiana, instead of Mr. Bingham of Pennsylvania, the Republican ranking member, to succeed himself as chairman of the Committee on Appropriations. The action of the Speaker was a breach of the time-honored principle of seniority rule under which Mr. Bingham, being ranked second, but not Mr. Hemenway, who was in the third place on the committee prior to his appointment,[3] should have become chairman of this great committee. In the Fifty-ninth Congress Mr. Hemenway was elected to the Senate, and Speaker Cannon appointed Mr. Tawney of Minnesota to succeed the former to the chairmanship. Mr. Tawney had never served on the Committee on Appropriations.[4] For the second time Mr. Bingham was passed over. Curiously enough, this occurrence was little heeded by the critics of Canonism. It may

[1] See Follett, *op. cit.*, p. 228.

[2] For attempts to remove the power of committee appointment from the Speaker, see *ibid.*, pp. 235-240. By the nineties of the last century the Democratic party in a number of the States went on record to attack the rules of the House and particularly Speaker Reed. Atkinson, *The Committee on Rules and the Overthrow of Speaker Cannon* (New York, 1911), pp. 71 *et seq.*; also see *The Outlook*, vol. lxxxxi, pp. 512-513.

[3] See *Cong. Record*, 57th Cong., 1st Sess., p. 182.

[4] Before becoming chairman of the Committee on Appropriations Mr. Tawney stood third on the Committee on Ways and Means, second on the Committee on Insular Affairs, and was chairman of the newly created Committee on Industrial Arts and Expositions. See *Cong. Record*, 58th Cong., 1st Sess., pp. 222, 531.

be that Mr. Bingham, then an old man, was reluctant to take upon himself the strenuous chairmanship of that committee, and therefore Speaker Cannon's action can hardly be taken as a penalty upon him. In the Sixty-first Congress Mr. Mann of Illinois was made to outrank Irving P. Wangner of Pennsylvania by becoming chairman of the Committee on Interstate and Foreign Commerce, and Mr. Weeks of Massachusetts was made chairman of the Committee on Post-Office and Post-Roads, upon which he had never served. Both of these cases [1] were unnoticed.

Speaker Cannon was, however, very pointedly censured by the " outrageous " changes which he made in other cases. In the Sixtieth Congress J. W. Wadsworth of New York, chairman of the Committee on Agriculture, retired, and in his place C. F. Scott of Kansas was appointed in preference over E. S. Henry of Connecticut and Gilbert N. Haugen of Iowa, both of whom ranked ahead of Mr. Scott on the Republican side of the committee. It was stated that this was because of Mr. Henry's views on the meat-inspection bill, pure food bill and other reform legislation ran counter to those of Speaker Cannon.[2] In the same Congress Speaker Cannon made E. B. Vreeland of New York chairman of the Committee on Banking and Currency [3] to replace C. N. Fowler of New Jersey who had refused to report a currency bill

[1] See *Cong. Record*, 60th Cong., 1st Sess., pp. 426, 427, 428; *Cong. Record*, 61st Cong., 1st Sess., pp. 5901, 5902.

[2] *Arena*, vol. xxxix, p. 618. The reason why Mr. Haugen was overlooked has never been known. Another case: C. R. Davis of Minnesota was removed by Speaker Cannon from the Committee on Agriculture, because the former defied the advice of the Speaker to drop the scheme for the Government to establish agricultural high schools throughout the country. *Ibid.*, p. 618.

[3] Mr. Vreeland had never served on the Committee on Banking and Currency prior to his appointment to the chairmanship. See *Cong. Record*, 59th Cong., 1st Sess., pp. 297-299.

agreed upon by the Republican majority in the caucus. Other members of the House who incurred the displeasure of the Speaker were either removed or demoted, namely, Mr. Cooper of Wisconsin, removed from the chairmanship of the Committee on Insular Affairs; Mr. Norris of Nebraska from the membership of the Committee on Public Buildings and Grounds, the Committee on Elections and the Committee on Invalid Pension; Mr. Murdock of Kansas was demoted to the foot of the Committee on Post-Office and Post-Roads; and Mr. Gardner of Massachusetts removed from the chairmanship of the Committee on Industrial Arts and Expositions. The Gardner case was worth mentioning. Speaker Cannon, before the announcement of the appointments of the committees, had informed Mr. Gardner that he could retain the chairmanship of the Committee on Industrial Arts and Expositions if he " chose to do so." But Mr. Gardner said in reply:

. . . Whether I wish to or not, in the future I should have to continue to be an insurgent on all matters in order to prove my good faith to the insurgent body and . . . under those circumstances, I should prefer not to be chairman of the Committee on Industrial Arts and Expositions.[1]

So Speaker Cannon removed Mr. Gardner. As reasons for the removal or demotion of other members, Speaker Cannon explained that these members

Failed to enter and abide by a Republican caucus, and this being a government through parties, for that as well as for other sufficient reasons, the Speaker of the House, being responsible to the House and the country, made the appointment with respect to these gentlemen as he conceived to be his duty in the execution of the trust reposed in him.[2]

[1] *Cong. Record*, 61st Cong., 2nd Sess., p. 3320.
[2] *Cong. Record*, 61st Cong., 2nd Sess., p. 3321.

Speaker Cannon threw no light on the " other sufficient reasons " regarding the demotion of those members. It is, however, questionable whether the Speaker is, constitutionally speaking, responsible to " the country." He is elected, not as Speaker but as member of the House from a district of a State, and, as Speaker of the House, receives no mandate from the nation at large. He is elected to the Chair by his party associates to whom only he is, strictly speaking, responsible. He is not like the President of the country, the " standard bearer " of his party, and has no status under the Constitution. Broadly speaking, it may be true that, as a matter of unwritten law, this country is a government through parties. But the point is that in regard to the House, which is not like the executive branch of the Government over which is an official directly elected by the vote of the people, each of its members is equal to any other, and when a Representative votes for one of his fellow members for Speaker, he does not delegate his rights and privileges as representative of his constituency. This was precisely the view which the insurgent Republicans took during the progressive movement in the Sixty-first Congress as well as in the recent Congresses.

In order to ascertain the extent of the Speaker's power over committee appointments, ten important committees during the Speakership of Mr. Cannon are taken for study. These are the committees through which nearly all of the important legislation is reported to the House; and since the Sixty-second Congress the practice has been that no member should serve on more than one of these ten committees,[1] the

[1] However, there are exceptions to the rule. In the Sixty-seventh Congress the Democratic minority elected Mr. Riordan of New York to the Committee on Rules and the Committee on Naval Affairs, and Mr. Sabath of Illinois to the Committee on Foreign Affairs and the Committee on Immigration and Naturalization. Mr. Mondell, the

ten " exclusive " or " key " committees as they are sometimes called.[1] Two facts will be shown in the following
table, facts which have a direct bearing upon the extent of
the Speaker's power over committee appointments—(1) the
number of vacancies on each of the ten committees on the
Republican side in each Congress, and (2) the number of
transfers to each of the ten committees on the Republican
majority side during the same period. In other words, the
table is an attempt to show the number of appointments
which Speaker Cannon actually made during his eight years
of administration:

Republican majority floor leader, objected to Mr. Sabath's being on two
such "exclusive" committees, but made no objection in Mr. Riordan's
case "for reasons, to a certain extent, ... personal," and for further
reasons "presented strongly from the minority side from sources that
I (Mr. Mondell) felt entitled to consideration." However, both Mr.
Sabath's and Mr. Riordan's names were withdrawn. *Cong. Record,*
67th Cong., 1st Sess., pp. 408-411. But finally both Mr. Riordan and
Mr. Sabath were allowed to remain on those committees without any
change.

[1] They are Committees on Ways and Means, Appropriations, Banking
and Currency, Rivers and Harbors, Military Affairs, Naval Affairs,
Interstate and Foreign Commerce, Judiciary, Agriculture, and Post-
Offices and Post-Roads.

The number varies in different Congresses between the two majority
parties. For example, in the Sixty-second Congress there were twelve
such "exclusive" committees—Appropriations, Judiciary, Interstate and
Foreign Commerce, Rivers and Harbors, Agriculture, Foreign Affairs,
Military Affairs, Naval Affairs, Post-Office and Post-Roads, Insular
Affairs, the District of Columbia, and Merchant Marine and Fisheries.
In the following Congress changes were again made. See Page, *Con-
gressional Hand-Book* (Washington, D. C., 1913), pp. 31, 32.

Committees [1]	58th Congress			59th Congress			60th Congress			61st Congress		
	M.[2]	V.[3]	Tr.[4]	M.	V.	Tr.	M.	V.	Tr.	M.	V.	Tr.
Agriculture	11	4	...	11	1	1	13	4	3	12	6	
Appropriations	11	3	....	11	3	1	11	1	..	11	1	2
Banking & Currency	11	1	3	12	4	1	12	1	..	12	3	4
Judiciary	11	2	1	12	3	..	12	4	1	12	5	1
Interstate & Foreign Commerce	11	6	..	12	1	..	12	1	1	12	2	
Military Affairs	11	..	2	12	1	2	12	3	1	13	2	1
Naval Affairs	11	3	1	12	2	1	12	..	2	12	2	
Post-Offices & Post-Roads..	11	2	5	12	..	..	12	2	..	13	3	5
Rivers & Harbors	11	3	....	12	..	..	13	2	..	12	6	
Ways & Means	11	4	....	12	1	1	12	5	1	12	2	
Total	110	28	12	118	16	7	121	23	9	121	32	13

As was shown, the number of vacant committee places on the Republican side was rather small. This is particularly true of these ten important committees where strong members of the House sit. From the Fifty-eighth Congress to the Sixty-first Congress there were altogether four hundred and seventy places on these ten major committees on the Republican majority side, out of which Speaker Cannon made forty-one changes or removals and appointed ninety-nine members to fill seats left vacant by former members either because of resignation, death or defeat at the polls. In other words, Speaker Cannon availed himself of less than one-fifth of the chances for the exercise of the power of

[1] Only the committee places on the Republican majority side are considered, and those on the minority side will be dealt with in connection with the minority floor leader.

[2] M. means membership of the committee on the Republican majority side in that particular Congress.

[3] V. means vacancies occurring in the committee.

[4] Tr. means transfers made from other committees by the Speaker.

appointment over these ten of the most important committees of the House, whereas more than four-fifths of the members of these committees were appointed under the seniority rule. Of these forty-one changes or removals, certainly not all were arbitrarily made by the Speaker; some were made at the request of the members themselves. A member of the Committee on Military Affairs may have agreed to change place with one on the Committee on Public Lands. If agreement of such changes was reached before the announcement of the appointment, the parties concerned requested the Speaker to make the changes, and usually such request was granted if it did not affect the " geographical " plan of the committee distribution. If, however, the request was made after the announcement of the committees, the Speaker submitted it to the House for unanimous consent. Thus in the Fifty-ninth Congress Mr. Mondell of Wyoming and Mr. Miller of Kansas having agreed to change committee places between them, Speaker Cannon put the following question before the House:

These gentlemen desire to exchange committee places, and if there be no objection, Mr. Mondell will go unto the Committee on Public Lands and retire from the Military Affairs, taking the place in the Committee on the Public Lands that he held in the last Congress, and Mr. Miller, if there be no objection, will go off from the Committee on the Public Lands unto the Committee on Military Affairs. Is there objection?

There was no objection.[1]

The power of appointing committees by the Speaker was a " real issue "[2] in the attempts to reform the House. In the eyes of the insurgents no change would be of any real and permanent value to the country if that change did not

[1] *Cong. Record,* 59th Cong., 1st Sess., p. 344.
[2] *Cong. Record,* 61st Cong., 2nd Sess., p. 6278.

take away from the Speaker the power of appointing standing committees.[1]   The insurgents therefore insisted on this change.   During the opening days of the Sixty-first Congress some of them were even inclined to deprive the Speaker of the power of appointing the Committee on Ways and Means at the risk of postponing the tariff legislation until December.   The attempt was only thwarted at the request of one of the insurgent members, who stated that "the manufacturers in his district were becoming demoralized over the uncertainty of business conditions and that they were talking panic on Wall Street,"[2] should the tariff be not soon revised.   The movement was thus halted until the Sixty-second Congress, in which the Democratic party was returned to power.   During the campaign in 1910 the Democratic party in its platform had pledged itself to reform the rules of the House.[3]   As the campaign progressed, Congressional candidates of the Democratic party declared in favor of the plan to make either the Committee on Ways and Means or the Committee on Rules, preferably the former, a Committee on Committees with power to appoint the House committees for the majority in the forthcoming Congress. This proposed Committee on Committees, as it was then advocated, was to be constituted on a geographical basis and its members were not to be on any other committee.   Mr. Clark of Missouri, the Democratic floor leader of the House, fell in line with the suggested plan.[4]   He did it, undoubtedly,

---

[1] *Cong. Record*, 61st Cong., 2nd Sess., p. 6279.

[2] Atkinson, *op. cit.*, p. 97.

[3] It has been generally referred to as the Denver platform adopted in 1908.

[4] His own plan was that the Democratic caucus should elect the Committee on Ways and Means and also an enlarged Committee on Rules, and then empowered one of these committees to select all other committees, with the proviso that no member of the committee which was to select all other committeemen be a member of any other committee. See *The Outlook*, vol. lxxxxvi, p. 987.

out of his desire to catch the wind of public sentiment which took a favorable turn over the idea of the " election " of the committees by the House, and which, as he said, seemed to blow strongest " in those debatable States " where the Democrats " must get the votes to elect the President and the House of the Sixty-second Congress in 1912. In all these States the independent vote is decisive and the independent votes appear to favor the election of the committee by the House. So let it be." [1]

The plan, as outlined, was adopted by the Democratic caucus on the eve of the commencement of the Sixty-second Congress.[2] At the caucus meeting Mr. Foster of Illinois introduced a resolution providing that the Committee on Ways and Means be authorized to name the standing committees of the House, subject to the Democratic caucus ratification and that the majority members of the Committee on Ways and Means should not be eligible to serve on any other standing committee.[3] Mr. Underwood of Alabama was unanimously nominated for chairman of the Committee on Ways and Means, which position made him the majority leader of the House. Referring to the importance of Mr. Underwood's nomination, the New York *World* records: " It is significant of the control of the party situation still held by the leaders under the new arrangement that this nomination was made by the Hon. Champ Clark who had previously been made the choice of the caucus for Speaker." [4]

Under this new arrangement the Committee on Ways and

---

[1] *Ibid.*, p. 988. Mr. Clark wrote: "As far as I was concerned, the fight was made for two reasons: First, because the rules, in my opinion, need liberalizing; second, for political advantage." Clark, *My Quarter Century of American Politics* (New York, 1920), vol. ii, p. 259.

[2] See the New York *World*, January 20, 1911, p. 2.

[3] The New York *World*, January 20, 1911, p. 2.

[4] *Ibid.*, p. 2.

Means on the Democratic side acted as the Committee on Committees with the duty to organize the House, to be subject, however, to the formality of the Democratic caucus ratification. After the ratification Mr. Underwood, as majority leader, submitted the Democratic list of the committee selections to the House and thereupon moved its adoption.

No definite ruling was made as to whether nominations by individual members made on the floor are in order,[1] although, under the rules, it is provided that committees are elected by the House at the commencement of each Congress.[2] Since 1911 there has been only one case in which a nomination by an individual member was made on the floor. This occurred in the second session of the Sixty-second Congress in which Mr. Madison of Kansas, a Republican member of the Committee on Rules, died, and in his place Mr. Mann, the Republican minority leader, having appointed "upon his own suggestion," Mr. Campbell of Kansas, requested Mr. Underwood to move his selection. Thereupon Mr. Norris of Nebraska placed Mr. Murdock of Kansas, a Republican Progressive, in nomination. A debate ensued during which Mr. Underwood pleaded with the Democratic members of the House not to take any part in the quarrel over the question, as it was a family dispute among the Republican members.[3] The question was decided by a roll-call by which Mr. Campbell, being nominated by his party leader, was elected.

The Democratic party was at the helm of the ship of state

---

[1] See *Cong. Record*, 63rd Cong., 1st Sess., p. 1871. It was, however, held that the majority leader or any other member of the House can at any time move the previous question to the motion on the adoption of the committee elections. *Ibid.*, p. 1914.

[2] Rule x.

[3] *Cong. Record*, 62nd Cong., 2nd Sess., pp. 854-865.

in the House from the Sixty-second to the Sixty-fifth Congress. During this time the Democratic members of the Committee on Ways and Means appointed the House committees on the Democratic side.[1] But with the commencement of the Sixty-sixth Congress in which the Republicans became the majority in the House, the Committee on Committees, while retaining its name, was framed on a different model. This committee was established upon the motion of Mr. Mann of Illinois at the Republican caucus, on February 28, 1919, at which Mr. Mann was defeated by Mr. Gillett of Massachusetts for Speaker.[2] It consists of one member from each State having Republican representation in the House. The members are nominally elected by the Republican caucus but actually the caucus elects the persons nominated by the State delegation. The small States having small Republican representation in the House usually choose their

[1] During the Sixty-third Congress the Progressive Party consisting of about twenty insurgent Republican members was the third party in the House. Referring to the methods of making committee selections by the three parties of the House, Mr. Murdock, leader of the Progressive Party, said: "... Under the system here in the House there are three ways of selecting committees. The Republicans empower the gentleman from Illinois (Mr. Mann) the minority floor leader, to designate the Republican members of a committee. The Democrats empower the Ways and Means Committee to make the selections.

"In the Progressive Party, it is true we are few in numbers, but we get together with open doors and agree on committee assignments. All the committee assignments made in the Progressive Party are made openly. All of them are voted upon. Every one has a full chance for discussion, and there is a complete agreement in the conference before the nominations are made.

"Now, so far as this manner of making nominations is concerned, there is only one way in which I can make nominations. After the members of the Progressive Party have determined whom they want upon committees, then I submit the nominations to the gentleman from Alabama (Mr. Underwood) and he comes before the House and makes his nomination." *Cong. Record*, 63rd Cong., 2nd Sess., p. 478.

[2] *Searchlight*, vol. iv, no. 1, p. 4.

representative by a system of rotation, but the general practice is to nominate the senior member of the State and keep him on the committee, since the longer he has served and the greater his influence the better will be his chance to secure good committee spoils for members from his State. The majority floor leader is chairman ex-officio of the committee and is invariably the representative from his State, in which case he can vote at the committee meetings. Each member of the committee casts as many votes as there are Republicans in the House from his State. As has been said, one of the functions of the committee is to select the Republican membership on all standing committees in the House and determine the ratio of the committee representation between the Republican majority and the Democratic minority. The committee elects its own secretary, who is usually a member of the sub-committee of five or six whose duty it is to parcel out the vacancies on the unimportant committees to the new and unimportant Republican members and whose action is always adopted by the full committee. The other important function of the committee—the full committee—is to select the Steering Committee, the floor leader and the whip.[1] All actions taken by the committee are subject to the formality of Republican caucus approval.

Commenting on the system of committee selection inaugurated in the Sixty-second Congress, Mr. McCall, a leading Republican in the House during the Speakership of Mr. Cannon, wrote:

. . . With a committee of the usual size sitting behind closed doors, with responsibility dissipated among a dozen or more members, each one of them distracted by personal importunity and the demand of his own locality, which ordinarily he could not resist, a result would be reached, of which no single member of the committee would be likely to approve. Combinations

[1] *Searchlight*, vol. iv, no. 1, p. 6.

between members and between groups of States would be inevitable. . . .[1]

Mr. McCall's dread of dissipation of responsibility " among a dozen or more members " was comparable to the horror entertained by Speaker Reed of appointing committees by a board. In 1882 Mr. Orth of Indiana offered a resolution to amend the rules that the House, after its organization at the commencement of each Congress, should proceed to elect, by *viva voce* vote, a board of eleven members to select the House committees. Mr. Reed was opposed to the amendment, and argued:

. . . Whatever complaint can be made against the appointment of the committee as the result of the pressure on the Speaker can be made with redoubled force against the appointment by a board elected by this House. Think of the Speakership of this House going into commission! Think of the log-rolling there would be in order to get such a board as would favor various measures that might be presented.[2]

The forces or the principles, for weal or woe, determining the awarding of committee spoils, which have been in operation since 1911, had long been at work. They were at work even in the days when the committees were appointed nominally by a " responsible single agent," the Speaker of the House, but actually by a coterie from the Speaker's party " sitting behind closed doors." In the Fifty-fourth Congress Speaker Reed sent for Mr. Dingley of Maine to assist him in making up the committees.[3] So, also, was it with Speaker Cannon, who " consulted " Mr. Mann of Illinois on committee organization.[4] Indeed, much of the making up

---

[1] McCall, *The Business of Congress* (New York, 1911), p. 134.

[2] *Cong. Record*, 47th Cong., 1st Sess., p. 465.

[3] Dingley, *op. cit.*, p. 391.

[4] In criticising Mr. Longworth of Ohio for his support of Mr. Gillett

of committees was — and still is — done behind the veil of secrecy. Moreover, the Speaker was not free of outside influence in the appointment of committees. Speaker Blaine's experience was indeed very revealing. "Your father," wrote a member of the Speaker's family, "left for New York. . . . He had cotton and wool manufacturers to meet in Boston, and, over and above all, pressure to resist or permit. As far as he gets his committees organized, just so far some after-consideration comes up which overtopples the whole list like a row of bricks." [1]   Later, during the Speakership of Mr. Reed, Jonathan B. Dolliver of Iowa secured his appointment to the Committee on Ways and Means through the influence of his wife. Mr. Clark tells us, in his *My Quarter Century of American Politics,* that the Reeds and Dollivers were on "very friendly footing." Both Mr. Dolliver and his wife were in hopes that Mr. Reed would place him on the committee on Ways and Means. When Mr. Dolliver learned that his name was not on the list of this important committee, he "sorrowfully" communicated the fact to his wife, "who immediately proceeded to Reed's office, and when she returned, her husband was on the Ways and Means Committee." [2]

Since the introduction of the "election" method in the

of Massachusetts, instead of Mr. Mann of Illinois, for Speaker, Mr. Cannon said in the Republican caucus, February 28, 1919: "Before I selected my committee when Speaker in the first term of Mr. Longworth, I spoke to Mr. Mann and consulted with him as to what course I should take respecting Messrs. Burton, Keifer, and Mr. Longworth. He suggested that Mr. Burton be made chairman of Rivers and Harbors; Keifer chairman of Appropriations, and that young man (Mr. Longworth) should be appointed to Ways and Means. That was done. The only thing I got for it was when he got down to Oyster Bay he issued a statement that he would not support me if I were the caucus nominee for Speaker." The New York *Times*, March 1, 1919, p. 3.

[1] Alexander, *op. cit.,* p. 70.

[2] Clark, *op. cit.,* vol. ii, pp. 315-316.

Sixty-second Congress little has ever come to the surface to sustain the charge that " combinations between members and groups of States would be inevitable." On the other hand, the evils attendant upon the system of committee appointment by the Speaker were in evidence. To some extent the defeat of Speaker Blaine for the Presidential nomination in 1876 was said to have been due to the opposition of Mr. Tyner of Indiana who claimed that Blaine, when candidate for Speaker, had promised him the chairmanship of the Committee on Post-Office and Post-Roads in exchange for Tyner's support of him for the Speaker. But Blaine failed to keep his word; consequently Tyner " knifed the Plumed Knight." [1] Mention has already been made of Speaker Blaine's conference with the cotton and wool manufacturers in Boston before the House committees were appointed. It was charged that chairmanships were bargained between the Speaker and members of the House. In 1883 Speaker Carlisle, before appointing A. H. Buckner, of Missouri, chairman of the Committee on Banking and Currency, and Richard P. Bland, also of Missouri, chairman of the Committee on Coinage, obtained personal assurances that the former would not attack the national banking system and the latter would drop his scheme for the unlimited coinage of silver. [2]

Essentially the system—the committee system—has been what it was before 1911 with both its good and bad points. In its outward form the system is changed in that before the Sixty-second Congress it was the Speaker who announced to the House the committee selections of both parties, whereas since then the majority floor leader or the minority floor leader, as the case may be, presents, either by way of a

[1] Clark, *op. cit.*, vol. i, p. 205.
[2] Follett, *op. cit.*, pp. 228-229.

motion or a resolution the list of chairmen and members of the committees to the House that they " be . . . . and are hereby, *elected* chairmen and membership of the standing committees of the House." [1] Immediately the previous question is demanded, and the House confirms the " election." In a public statement Mr. Longworth, whose opinion commands serious consideration, contrasted the fruits of the Republican Committee on Committees with those of Cannonism :

The performance of the Republican Committee on Committees of its important duty, that of selecting the Steering Committee, the Floor Leader and the Whip, was exactly what ought to have been expected from the men and under the methods controlling. Its net result was to make Mr. James R. Mann the dominating figure in the next House of Representatives. It is the most complete sort of triumph for reactionism. Even the final effort of some of us to enlarge and liberalize the Steering Committee, so as to secure representation upon it of the progressive sentiment of the West, of the States on the Southern border, which substantially contributed to the Republican majority, and of labor, was defeated by the usual vote. If it had been deliberately planned to restore the conditions existing in the House ten years ago, as a result of which the Republican majority became a minority, the plan could not have been more successfully consummated. Then the leadership was held by Mr. Cannon, assisted by Mr. Mann of Illinois,

[1] *Searchlight*, vol. iv, no. 1, pp. 6, 7. In the same place Mr. Mann's influence over the House organization was analyzed. On the Committee on Committees the Mann adherents were numerically in majority. As a result, the floor leader, Frank W. Mondell of Wyoming, the Whip, Harold Knutson of Minnesota, nine of the ten important committee chairmanships were Mann adherents.

However, with regard to the chairmanships, there were some other conditions in favor of Mr. Mann,—conditions which generally govern the committee selections, and which will be discussed in the following pages.

Mr. Dalzell of Pennsylvania and Mr. Tawney of Minnesota, together with Mr. Payne of New York acting as chairman of the Ways and Means Committee. Under today's arrangement the real leadership is held by Mr. Mann, assisted by Mr. Cannon of Illinois, Mr. Mondell of Wyoming and Mr. Moore of Pennsylvania, together with Mr. Fordney of Michigan acting as chairman of Ways and Means Committee.

As I gaze upon these two pictures, I find it impossible to differentiate between them. If there is any real difference it might lie in the views of the chairmen of the Ways and Means Committee. After service on that committee with both for a good many years I am inclined to think that, as compared with Mr. Fordney, Mr. Payne was a rather advanced tariff reformer.[1]

The principles governing the committee assignments have remained almost as constant as the " northern star." In the first place, seniority in service still receives preference in the allotment of the House committees. Speaking to the "Baby Congressmen " on " The Making of a Representative," Speaker Clark said: "A man has to learn to be a Representative just as he must learn to be a blacksmith, a carpenter, a farmer, an engineer, a lawyer, or a doctor." And " as a rule," he continued, " the big places [on the committees] go to old and experienced members " of the House.[2] From the

[1] *Searchlight*, vol. iv, no. 1, p. 7.

[2] Mr. Clark added that during his first eight years in the House he "never advanced a peg, so far as committees went." *Cong. Record*, 64th Cong., 1st Sess. (appendix), p. 559. Speaker Cannon also said: "A man comes here for his first term, and although he may be a man of great ability and high character, how is any one to know it? He must prove it, and until he does prove it he must serve his probation and be put, not on the Ways and Means Committee to frame a tariff bill or on the Appropriations Committee, but on an unimportant committee, where he can show what he has in him and learn the business of government; for there is much to learn here ... It is not all as simple as many people think." *Cong. Record*, 61st Cong., 1st Sess. (appendix), p. 108.

Sixty-second to Sixty-fifth Congresses only one exception occurred in one of the " big places " in the Sixty-third Congress in which James Hay of Virginia, who had never served on the Committee on Military Affairs, was selected to its chairmanship in preference over W. J. Fields of Kentucky. From the Sixty-sixth to Sixty-ninth Congress the seniority rule governing the promotion to the chairmanship of the ten " key " committees was only once broken in the Sixty-seventh Congress, and that occurred in the newly enlarged Committee on Appropriations after the passage of the budget bill.   In a sense, this committee had to be reconstructed, with the increase of its membership and the corresponding increase of its importance pertaining to appropriations.   Mr. Good of Iowa, chairman of the committee, having resigned from the House, Martin B. Madden of Illinois, who, in the preceding Congress was the Republican ranking member of the Committee on Post-Office and Post-Roads, was transferred and made chairman of the Committee on Appropriations.   The fact that only two such cases have ever happened with the important committees since the Sixty-second Congress indicates that this time-honored rule has been of late strengthened.   Even if John Randolph were alive today, he could not have become chairman of the important Committee on Ways and Means in his first term in the House.[1] Statistics show that from the Sixty-second Congress to the Sixty-ninth Congress the minimum length of service of the chairman of the ten important committees of the House has been three terms and the maximum length has been fifteen.

In the second place, the division of committee spoils must have a geographical basis.   One State must not be given more than two places on an important committee.   In the Fifty-fourth Congress Mr. Dingley of Maine wrote, December 4, 1896, in his diary that " I am probably to be

---

[1] See Follett, *op. cit.*, p. 223.

chairman of the Ways and Means Committee," but he added that Speaker Reed might fear that the many prominent places which the State of Maine had already held in the House might prevent the Speaker from appointing him to the position.[1] Certain States have been regularly represented on certain committees since 1896. Thus the States of New York and Pennsylvania are invariably represented on the Committees on Ways and Means and on Appropriations. This fact, furthermore, shows that territorial claims as a basis for committee allotments are grounded on economic and agricultural interests. On the Committee on Agriculture on the Republican side the States of Iowa, Kansas, Illinois and New York have been represented in every Congress at least since the Fifty-eighth Congress,[2] and since the Sixty-seventh Congress the State of North Dakota, the birthplace of the Non-Partisan League in 1920, has received recognition on the committee.[3]

Then comes the principle of party regularity. To follow the party leaders and to support the party organization in the House — these are the duties which members of the House must perform in order to get promotion in their committee assignments or to retain their seats on the important committees. Speaker Cannon, let it be remembered, de-

[1] Dingley, Jr., *op. cit.*, p. 391. The State of Maine had four members in the House. They were Thomas B. Reed, Nelson Dingley, Charles A. Boutelle and Seth L. Milliken. Reed was Speaker of the House; Dingley chairman of the Committee on Ways and Means; Boutelle chairman of the Committee on Naval Affairs; and Milliken chairman of the Committee on Public Buildings and Grounds. All these committees are important committees in the House. See *Cong. Record*, 54th Cong., 1st Sess., p. 284.

[2] In the Fifty-eighth, Sixty-sixth and Sixty-ninth Congress Illinois had two Representatives on the committee, while New York had two on the committee in the Sixty-seventh and Sixty-eighth Congresses.

[3] North Dakota, however, had one Representative on the committee in the Sixty-first Congress.

moted the insurgent Republicans to the back places of insignificant committees, because these members " failed to enter and abide by a Republican caucus " and " other sufficient reasons," [1] which, in the judgment of the Speaker, warranted their removal from their important committee positions to the unimportant ones.

Prior to 1911, when the Speaker exercised the power of committee appointment, party regularity was one of the determining factors in the allotment of the spoils of the committee places. Since 1911, when the House " elects " the committees, this principle has been as important as ever before. In the Sixty-eighth Congress, Mr. Wefald of Minnesota, of the Farmer-Labor party, was asked before the announcement of the committee assignments: " If you are given assignments with Republicans, will you support the Republicans, will you support the Republican organization?" Mr. Wefald replied: " I shall support the Republican organization whenever it is right, and I hope it will be right all the time so that I can support it all the time." [2] Wefald was finally assigned to the Committees on Invalid Pensions, on Patents, and on Woman Suffrage, all of which are insignificant committees. Still more recently, in the Sixty-ninth Congress, the Republican members from Wisconsin were deprived of their places in the " key " committees for having supported the late Senator La Follette of Wisconsin for President on the Third Party ticket in 1924 and repudiated the nominee of the Republican party. Mr. Longworth, the Speaker-elect for the Sixty-ninth Congress, declared in a Chicago speech, November 2, 1925, with regard to the Wisconsin members:

[1] See *supra*, p. 67.
[2] *Searchlight*, vol. ix, no. 7, p. 7.

. . . Some of them, eleven or twelve, under the Wisconsin leadership, showed their true colors at the election. They not only had their own Presidential candidate but worked harder against the Republican candidate than the Democrats did.

And, lo and behold! In Congress they asked to be restored to full membership in the councils of the party which they had done their best to destroy. They wanted high positions in the key committees. We said no, that they had to start over if they wanted to be Republicans. . . .[1]

Mr. Longworth made repeated assertions to the same effect before the convening of the Sixty-ninth Congress, December 7, 1925. The significant point to be noted is that he was the only Republican leader of the House who went on record to the country that the Wisconsin members were to be ousted from the " key " committees in the House. And ousted indeed they were from their former committee places in the Sixty-ninth Congress, a fact which warrants apprehension of the relation of the Speaker to committee assignments. True, he has no direct voice in the making of the assignment, but his influence, both personal and official, must be recognized.

The leader of the minority party had the power of appointing the minority members to and of removing them from committees, sometimes with and sometimes without the formality of approval of the party caucus. This power was acquired when Mr. Cannon was elevated to the Speaker's chair in the Fifty-eighth Congress.[2] Prior thereto the minority leader had not been given such power. The effectiveness of this power may be shown by a case occurring in the Fifty-eighth Congress. The Democratic caucus decided to report and support the Davey bill on rate-making. Mr.

[1] The New York *Times*, November 2, 1925, p. 6.
[2] McCall, *op. cit.*, p. 133.

Lamar of Florida and Mr. Shackleford of Missouri, both of whom were Democratic members of the Committee on Interstate and Foreign Commerce, reported the so-called Hearst bill, which had not been considered in the Democratic caucus and was therefore not supported by the other four Democratic members of that committee. In the following Congress, the Fifty-ninth, Mr. Williams, leader of the Democratic party, removed both Mr. Lamar and Mr. Shackleford from the Committee on Interstate and Foreign Commerce. In defense of his action, Mr. Williams said on the floor:

> I had one of [the] two things to do, either to appoint two men in place of the two who could agree with the four or to leave the four and appoint four men who could agree with the two. I did not believe that the four men were so much inferior, intellectually or as statesmen, [to] either of the two gentlemen. . . . I was led all the more to the conclusion by the fact that the Democratic caucus, whose action was defied by the gentleman (Mr. Lamar), had voted upon the two bills and overwhelmingly adopted the bill advocated by the four Democratic members of the committee.[1]

Usually the Speaker accepted assignments made by the minority leader, with no material changes, unless they interfered with the "geographical plan." However, in the Sixty-first Congress Mr. Clark of Missouri, then the minority leader, declined to organize the minority in committee assignments, for "he would not organize the minority unless the organization he offered should not be written in without the dotting of an 'i' or the crossing of a 't'."[2] The cause of this controversy was that Mr. Clark intended to retain Mr. Heflin of Alabama on the Committee on Agriculture, but, as Mr. Heflin's stand against grain and cotton

---

[1] *Cong. Record*, 59th Cong., 1st Sess., pp. 349-359.

[2] *Cong. Record*, 62nd Cong., 1st Sess., p. 165.

speculation antagonized Mr. Cannon, the Speaker objected to his being on that committee, which had jurisdiction over this legislation.[1]   In the same Congress the Republican party caucus, in choosing members to the select Committee on the Investigation of the Department of Interior and the Bureau of Forestry, attempted to select the Democratic members on the committee and have the Democratic caucus confirm the choices.   The attempt was unsuccessful, due to the effort of Mr. Cooper of Wisconsin, who protested against the action of the Republican caucus and finally made the latter accept Mr. James of Kentucky and Mr. Graham of Illinois, both of whom were nominated to the select committee by the Democratic caucus.[2]

Since 1911 the leader of the minority party has still retained the power of organizing the minority committees, with " certain restrictions."   The Democratic majority in the Sixty-second Congress held that the minority could not select but " recommend " its own committee members to the majority leader.[3]   Mr. Underwood, the Democratic floor leader, even went so far as to state to the leader of the Republican minority that the latter could not make certain appointments to a committee.   Once Mr. Underwood told Mr. Mann, the minority leader, that " for delicate personal reasons " he could not appoint a certain Republican minority member to a certain committee.[4]   " In one Congress," Mr. Mann said, " as I recall—although I may be mistaken about that—the Democratic majority themselves selected certain members of the Committee on Rules." [5]

The difficulty of the committee system in the House of

---

[1] *Cong. Record*, 61st Cong., 2nd Sess., pp. 1092-93.

[2] *Ibid.*, pp. 3322-3233.

[3] *Cong. Record*, 62nd Cong., 2nd Sess., p. 860.

[4] *Cong. Record*, 67th Cong., 1st Sess., p. 409.

[5] *Ibid.*, p. 409.

Representatives can be attributed, in no small measure, to the irregularity of the procedure in the committee and the overcrowded conditions which the committees are confronted with—two causes, or two defects, whose existence is independent of the fact whether the committees be appointed by the Speaker or " elected " by the House. These causes were in existence long before the inception of Cannonism and have been at work ever since the March revolution, 1910. Most of the committees have never kept any record of proceedings of the executive sessions in the committee rooms whose four walls are impenetrable.[1] Nor have they ever disclosed to the public a record vote on measures under consideration. The rules of the House are silent on the question of the committee quorum, although it is provided in Jefferson's *Manual* that " a majority of the committee constitutes a quorum for business." [2] It was once claimed that " most " of the committees call the roll of the committee to ascertain whether a quorum is present,[3] but such claim has not been generally

[1] In the House it is entirely within rule and usage for a committee to conduct its proceedings in secret. Hinds, *op. cit.*, iv, 4558-4564. The House itself may not abrogate the secrecy of the committee's proceedings except by suspending the rules. *Ibid.*, 4565.

[2] Jefferson's *Manual*, xxvi; also see Hinds, *op. cit.*, iv, 4540, 4552. With regard to the Committee on Rules see *infra*, pp. 151-152.

[3] *Cong. Record*, 67th Cong., 2nd Sess., p. 8928. To the ornamental committees, that is, those which never met to legislate in the House, the question of quorum was of little importance. The eleven Committees on Expenditures in the different Departments which were abolished in the Seventieth Congress, might be classified under this head.

In the Fifty-ninth Congress, with the exception of the Committee on Expenditures in the Department of Agriculture, these committees never functioned and their members could not even locate the respective committee rooms. One of the members who had been on the Committee on the Levees of the Mississippi River for two years, said that he could not remember whether the committee had ever met once during two years. When asked if he knew where the committee room was located, he

substantiated. Frequently a committee takes action without a formal meeting of its members. In the Sixty-second Congress the Committee on Interstate and Foreign Commerce, consisting of twenty-one members, " authorized " one of its members to take from the Speaker's table a Senate bill for consideration when only eleven members of the committee gave their assent. And what was all the more important was that these eleven members, all of whom were Democrats, never met as a committee to sanction the authorization.[1]

Perhaps what is the most serious question in respect of the committee system in the House of Representatives is that of pigeonholing bills by the committees. When a bill " goes from the Clerk's desk to a committee room," writes Mr. Wilson, not, however, without exaggeration, " it crosses a parliamentary bridge of sighs to dim dungeons of silence whence it will never return." [2] Prior to 1911 when the Speaker wielded the power of committee appointments, the burden of responsibility for the burial of bills in the committee rooms see-sawed to and fro between the Speaker and the members of the House—neither end of the beam was inclined to take upon itself the responsibility for the performance of the work. Thus, at the members' end Mr. Norris of Nebraska writes:

replied that he " walked in front of the door once, but never darkened it." See *Cong. Record*, 59th Cong., 2nd Sess., p. 227.

Alvan T. Fuller of Massachusetts wrote in his letter of resignation from the membership of the Committee on Expenditures in the Interior Department that the committee " has had no meeting during the present Congress excepting one short smoke talk ... " *Cong. Record*, 65th Cong., 2nd Sess., p. 2743. Charles L. Abernethy of North Carolina, a member of the Committee on Expenditures in the Navy Department said that the committee has never met in eight years, and yet it has a clerk and a secretary. *Cong. Record*, 68th Cong., 1st Sess., p. 1237.

[1] *Cong. Record*, 62nd Cong., 2nd Sess., pp. 11398-9.

[2] Wilson, *op. cit.*, p. 69; also *cf. infra*, p. 115 relating to the number of bills and resolutions introduced to the House in each Congress and the number of bills and resolutions reported from the House committees.

At the very first meeting of one of the important committees of the House, to which a new member had been assigned, he was astounded to hear one of the older members of the committee inquire of the chairman if he had seen the Speaker in regard to a particular bill that was then under consideration. He was still more astounded when, at that meeting, a motion was actually made and passed instructing the chairman to have a conference with the Speaker and to ascertain whether he would permit the passage of the bill in question.[1]

But, on the other hand, Mr. Gardner of Massachusetts, states:

There can be no manner of doubt that the suppression of many a bill is due rather to the timidity of Congressmen than to any rooted objection on the part of the Speaker. . . . It is an open secret that many a member who favors a measure, and, if necessary, would vote for it, privately expresses to the Speaker his hope that it will not be brought up for action.   Two cases in point are the Immigration Bill of 1906 and the Littlefield Bill relative to the transportation of liquor.   Many a member was well aware that he would offend constituents, no matter which way he votes on those measures.[2]

[1] *Cong. Record*, 61st Cong., 2nd Sess., p. 6278.

[2] Gardner, "Rules of the House of Representatives," *North American Review*, vol. clxxxix, p. 239.

On the Littlefield Bill Speaker Cannon wrote that Mr. Littlefield "had a majority of members on both sides of the House to support his bill, but when he wished them to support his demand for the regular order, set aside an appropriation bill, and go to the call of the committees that his bill might be brought forward under that order, his majority melted away..." Cannon, *loc. cit., Century*, vol. lxxviii, p. 309. Mr. Cannon cited another case. In the Sixtieth Congress a member from Missouri introduced a pension bill for members of the Missouri militia. The bill was referred to the Committee on Military Affairs which had eleven Republican and seven Democratic members. "The bill was never considered in the full committee or in the sub-committee," and in fact "no one ever made any effort to have it considered." In January, 1908, Mr. Cannon was, however, called to the attention of this bill by a constituent

In 1911 the Speaker was deprived of the power of appointing the committees, but this innovation has brought forth no light to the bills in the "dim dungeons." Thousands of bills,[1] some of which are resolutions, lie at rest in the dockets of the House committees in each Congress. While it is undoubtedly true that of these bills a considerable number are unworthy of consideration,[2] there are, however, among the dead ones some good bills entitled to a hearing before the House. Elsewhere it is pointed out that the Speaker, as a political leader, and the controlling forces, which have been developed since 1911, have been exercising control over legislation as much as they had been before. And one of the main causes which renders such control possible is due to the immensity of the business in the House. Unfortunately, during the recent years of reform agitation no legislative device has ever been advanced from the mem-

of a Democrat in the House who enclosed the following letter which he received from that Democrat: "Mr. Russell will do the best he can; and the Democrats on the committee would all vote for the bill, as would all the Democrats in the House, I am sure, on my request; the trouble is that the Republicans have a majority of the committee and they will not vote to report it to the House. Even if they did so vote, the Speaker would not allow it to come up in the House for a vote." *Ibid.*, p. 309.

Mr. Hinds gave another case. Once a majority of the members of the House signed a petition asking Speaker Reed to bring the Nicaragua bill before the House. On several occasions when members of the House who had signed the petition, happened to be in the Speaker's room, Mr. Reed asked their opinion of the Nicaragua bill. "I signed a paper asking its consideration," one member told the Speaker, "because powerful influences in my district favor it, but my judgment approves your position, that the problem needs further examination and discussion before we commit ourselves and posterity to the Nicaragua route." Hinds, "The Speaker of the House," *MacClure*, vol. xxxv, p. 201.

[1] See *infra*, p. 115, relating to the number of bills and resolutions introduced since the Fifty-fifth Congress.

[2] See *infra*, p. 116 (footnote) where reference to these unworthy bills is made.

bers of the House to check the menacing flood of the myriad petty private bills, thereby facilitating the work of the committees and lessening the opportunity for the few powerful House leaders to control legislation.

The Speaker has not been divested of all of his appointing power. He appoints the chairman of the Committee of the Whole House on the state of the Union,[1] who is not only a faithful party man but whose appointment is often based upon his known disposition to rule in favor of the bill under consideration.[2] The chairman of the committee recognizes for debate,[3] but in this respect he has little, if any, discretion or direct exercise of power over recognition.[4] Miss Follett-thought that the custom of going into the Committee of the Whole is " peculiarly felicitous to the system of directorship," for " the Speaker is thus able to influence legislation in two ways, directly and indirectly." [5] Directly, he leads his party on the floor, and indirectly, he appoints one of his trusted lieutenants in the chair who " handles

[1] Rule xxiii, 1.

[2] If the bill "is to be stoutly contested, he usually knows in advance the points upon which he must rule, and his decisions not infrequently are prepared before his appointment." Alexander, *op. cit.*, p. 263.

[3] Hinds, *op. cit.*, v, 5003. Debates held in the committee are of two kinds, one is the general debate, and the other is the five-minute rule for the purpose of explaining any amendment that a member may offer. Rule xxiii, 5.

[4] The time for the general debate, usually two hours in length, is agreed upon by the order of the House. And in the absence of such an order by the House it may be made by unanimous consent in the Committee of the Whole. Hinds, *op. cit.*, v, 5232. The time for the general debate is equally controlled by the two leaders representing both sides of the bill. *Cong. Record*, 67th Cong., 3rd Sess., p. 143.

A member who has spoken once on an amendment under the five-minute rule can speak once more on the same by offering one and only one pro-forma amendment. Hinds, *op. cit.*, v, 5778, 5222.

[5] Follett, *op. cit.*, p. 294.

measures as he wishes." [1]   The importance of the chairmanship of the Committee of the Whole can be readily seen
from the nature of the measures considered therein.   They
include " bills raising revenue, general appropriation bills,
and bills of a public character, directly or indirectly appropriating money or property." [2]   One hundred members of
the House constitute the quorum of the committee. [3]   It was
stated that in the Committee of the Whole the House does
ninety-five per cent of all the business that is done during
the life of a Congress and casts ninety-five per cent of the
vote in the committee in which, under the rules, no roll-call
is made. [4]

The Speaker also appoints the managers of a conference
committee on the part of the House [5] on occasions of disagreement in amendments to bills between the Senate and
the House or " in all cases of difference of opinion between

---

[1] Nowadays the Speaker debates and votes whenever he sees fit—in
the Committee of the Whole or in the House, and can exert both his
direct and indirect influence over the House at any time.   See chapter
i on the Speaker's share in debate and vote.

[2] Rule xiii, 1; also Rule xxiii, 3.

[3] Rule xxiii, 22.

[4] *Cong. Record*, 68th Cong., 1st Sess., p. 8.   The progressive Republicans protested against the " secret ballot " in the Committee of the Whole.
Their attempt to reform the rules in the Sixty-eighth Congress has been,
or will be, dealt with elsewhere.

The absence of roll call has provoked criticism.   One writer considers
the committee as the "safety valve" of the Congressional Government,
"the darkest, most devious spot in the whole procedure of the House
of Representatives."   See *Searchlight*, vol. i, no. 9, p. 4.

Mr. Luce, however, defends that "the absence of the roll call conduces
to judgment disinterested, without an eye to the effect on party standing or the chance of reelection."   Luce, *op. cit.*, p. 90.   But it must not
be forgotten that each member of the House is bound by oath to perform
"well and faithfully . . . the duties of the office" "without any mental
reservation or purpose of evasion."   Hinds, *op. cit.*, i, 128.

[5] Rule x, 2.

the two Houses." [1]   Under the practice of the House the Speaker usually appoints three managers,[2] the chairman, the majority ranking member and the minority ranking member of the committee from which the measure was reported. On several occasions the practice was, however, not adhered to.   It was in fact held that the Speaker decides the size of a conference committee.[3]   In 1897 Speaker Reed once appointed seven managers on a revenue bill.[4]   At other times the Speaker appointed five managers while the Senate named three, or vice versa.[5]   Once in the Sixty-third Congress Speaker Clark appointed three managers when the Senate had nine.   A motion to instruct the Speaker to appoint a greater number of managers was made but was held out of order.[6]   So long as the managers of the two Houses constitute two separate committees each of which votes separately and acts by a majority,[7] the discrepancy in the size of the membership between the two is of little importance.   The important question therefore lies in the political color of the committee which it reflects and the latitude of the Speaker's power in the appointment of the managers.   But before taking up this question a discussion of the power of the committee both in its theoretical and practical aspects is in order.

There are two general principles governing the managers

[1] Jefferson's *Manual*, xlvi.

[2] Hinds, *op. cit.*, v, 6336.

[3] *Ibid.*, v, 6336.

[4] *Cong. Record*, 55th Cong., 1st Sess., p. 2512.   For earlier cases see Hinds, *op. cit.*, v, 6335.

[5] *Cong. Record*, 57th Cong., 1st Sess., pp. 7524, 7525; *ibid.*, 2nd Sess., pp. 2868, 2949; *Cong. Record*, 58th Cong., 3rd Sess., pp. 805, 806, 826.

[6] *Cong. Record*, 63rd Cong., 2nd Sess., p. 1316.

[7] Hinds, *op. cit.*, v, 6334, 6336.

of a conference committee. The one is that managers cannot inject into a bill any absolutely new legislation, and the other is that what they do inject into a bill must be germane.[1] Actually, however, managers, to quote Speaker Clark, tend to " reach out and to do things that they have no business to do." [2]   In case conference managers transcend the power granted to them, a member may raise either a point of order against their report, in which case the Speaker may rule out or sustain it,[3] or a member may offer a motion to recommit if the Senate has not discharged its managers [4] and if—and this is important — he can obtain recognition from the Speaker.   On November 21, 1921, when Mr. Fordney of Michigan called up the conference report on the Fordney revenue bill, Mr. Garner of Texas rose to ask the following parliamentary inquiry:

Mr. Garner.   Mr. Speaker, a parliamentary inquiry.

The Speaker pro tempore.   The gentleman will state it.

Mr. Garner.   Mr. Speaker, a motion to recommit to the conferees with instructions to the managers on the part of the House can be made, if I understand it, at the conclusion of the consideration of the conference report.   Or must it be made at this time?   I want to save all my rights.

The Speaker pro tempore.   The motion can not be made at this time.   The report has not yet been read.   The gentleman from Michigan (Mr. Fordney) is entitled to the floor.   *The motion can be made if recognition is secured before final action on the report.*[5]

---

[1] Hinds, *op. cit.*, v, 6409, 6410, 6414-6416; also see *Cong. Record*, 65th Cong., 1st Sess., p. 7427.

[2] *Ibid.*, p. 7427.

[3] Hinds, *op. cit.*, v, 6409, 6410, 6414-6416.

[4] See *House Manual*, section 543, 69th Congress.

[5] *Cong. Record*, 67th Cong., 1st Sess., p. 8068.

The conference report on the Fordney-McCumber tariff bill in the second session of the Sixty-seventh Congress furnishes one of the striking examples of the power of the conference managers. The House Committee on Ways and Means put in the bill a provision on dye embargo, which was, however, struck out by the House. Then the bill went to the Senate. The Senate Committee on Finance restored the dye-embargo provision, but when the bill came before the Senate for passage, that provision was again voted out. It was clear that a majority of members in both Houses were opposed to an embargo on dye industry. Nevertheless, when the bill went to the conference committee, managers on the part of both Houses again inserted that provision in the bill. In the House a point of order was made against the report but was overruled by Speaker Gillett. Mr. Fish, of New York, a regular Republican, deplored on the floor of the House that the report was " the worst example of the workings of so-called invisible government " [1] he ever witnessed since he became a member of the House. After a lengthy debate Mr. Garner of Texas moved to recommit the report to the committee of conference with instructions to strike out the provision on the dye embargo. The motion was carried by a vote of 177 to 130.[2]

Meetings of conference committees are generally held in the Senate end of the Capitol behind closed doors, and only in rare cases are members of the House (or the Senate) and others admitted to present arguments.[3] Under such circumstances the managers on the part of the House adjust the differences with the managers on the part of the Senate on

[1] *Cong. Record*, 67th Cong., 2nd Sess., p. 12496.

[2] *Ibid.*, p. 12531. The motion to recommit also provided that the House conferees agree to the Senate amendment putting fertilizer potash on the free list.

[3] Hinds, *op. cit.*, v, 6254, 6263.

disagreeing amendments to a bill, and report their results to the House. As early as 1852 it was held by Speaker Boyd that a conference report must be acted on as a whole.[1] This ruling was strengthened by two decisions of Speaker Henderson who held, in 1901 and 1902 respectively, that a conference report could not be voted on separately and that it " must be adopted as an entirety or voted down as an entirety." [2] Again, on June 23, 1906, when Mr. John S. Williams of Mississippi proposed an amendment to a bill to amend the interstate commerce law and to enlarge the powers of the Interstate Commerce Commission, Speaker Cannon held the Williams amendment out of order and said that ". . . a conference report . . . stands as a unit. The effect of the report is to dispose of all matters of disagreement between the House and Senate, and there is but one possible disposition to be made of it. . . . And that is to reject it or agree to it. . . ." [3] The consequences of these rulings are the strengthening of the power of conference managers who are appointed by the Speaker. Managers can leave out or put in legislation into a bill either for partisan purposes or sectional interests—and at the behest of party leaders. In such cases members of the House can do two things: they may raise a point of order to be sustained or ruled out by the Speaker; they may offer a motion to recommit if recognition by the Speaker can be secured and if the Senate has not discharged its managers.

Sometimes a conference report is brought up under a special order from the Committee on Rules.[4] To show how this is done, the Payne tariff bill may be cited. This bill had

[1] Hinds, *op. cit.*, v, 6530.

[2] *Ibid.*, v, 6531-6533.

[3] *Ibid.*, v, 6534.

[4] The system of special order will be discussed in the following chapter.

801 Senate amendments which were referred *in toto* to the conference committee for adjustment.[1]   After an agreement was reached between the House and Senate managers and the House managers made their report to the House, the Committee on Rules brought in a special order which provided that " none of the provisions of said [conference] report shall be subject to a point of order." [2]   The bill was passed as it was reported out from the conference committee. Thus in practical effect the managers on the part of the House had the absolute power to pass judgment upon the entire body of Senate amendments.   Moreover, it must be remembered that the Speaker was then chairman of the Committee on Rules.

Customarily the Speaker appointed conference managers who mirror the party divisions of the House.   Nevertheless, in the Fifty-fourth Congress Speaker Reed once appointed members entirely from his own party to a conference committee on a bill for the maintenance of a free public library and reading room in the District of Columbia.[3]   The Speaker is also at liberty to select members who, in his opinion, are in sympathy with the prevalent sentiment of the House; and to this end he appoints managers from a committee other than that which has reported the bill.[4]   With regard to tariff measures or appropriation bills of importance, it has

[1] See *Cong. Record*, 61st Cong., 1st Sess., p. 4364 where the Committee on Rules reported a special order providing for nonconcurrence in gross in the Senate amendments and for the appointment of a conference committee.

[2] *Ibid.*, p. 4688.   Several hours of general debate were provided for the bill, but speeches during the general debate were made for home consumption.   One motion to recommit the bill was made but rejected by a vote of 186 against 191.

[3] *Cong. Record*, 54th Cong., 1st Sess., p. 3698.

[4] *Cong. Record*, 56th Cong., 2nd Sess., p. 1033; *Cong. Record*, 57th Cong., 1st Sess., pp. 6118-6119.   Also see Rogers, " Conference Committee Legislation," *North American Review*, vol. ccxv, p. 302.

been the practice for the chairman of the Committee on Ways and Means or of the Committee on Appropriations to suggest to the Speaker members of his committee to be appointed as conference managers.[1]

The Speaker should let the minority leader or the ranking minority member of the committee know in advance of the minority appointment, especially if the appointment is a case of departure from precedent. Failure to do so provokes objection from the minority side. To give a concrete illustration. In the first session of the Sixty-ninth Congress Mr. Elliott of Indiana, chairman of the Committee on Public Buildings and Grounds, asked, May 7, 1926, unanimous consent for a conference on a public building bill. Speaker Longworth appointed Mr. Elliott, William E. Kopp of Iowa, Charles Brand of Ohio, Frank Oliver of New York and John H. Kerr of North Carolina as managers on the part of the House. Oliver was ranked third and Kerr fourth on the minority side. Mr. Garrett of Tennessee, the minority leader, protested against the appointment and said:

. . . What I complain about is this: If the Speaker or the ranking Republican member (Mr. Elliott) had notified this side of the House they did not intend to place on the conference committee the gentleman from Texas (Mr. Lanham), the ranking Democratic member, we would have had notice of that fact, we could have adapted ourselves to whatever remedy we may have in order to carry out what we think ought to be the policy of the

[1] *Cong. Record,* 62nd Cong., 1 Sess., p. 1279 where Mr. Henry of Texas said: " When the Ways and Means Committee is to go into conference with the Senate on a great tariff bill, a great revenue measure, how are the conferees selected? Are they really, in fact, selected by the Speaker, as the rule provides shall be the case? Every intelligent Member knows that the chairman of the Ways and Means Committee suggests those conferees. The same is true with respect to the great Appropriations Committee ... Frequently, and, I imagine, in almost every instance, the chairman of that committee suggests the conferees ... "

House with reference to representation of our side. In this instance the gentleman (Mr. Elliott) asked and obtained unanimous consent to send the bill to conference, and then, without the slightest notice, the Speaker appointed some one entirely out of line with the usual procedure of the House. I do not believe that is entirely fair to this side of the House, because no notice was given.[1]

Mr. Lanham of Texas, the ranking minority member of the committee, was not appointed to the conference committee on account of his opposition to the bill. It is also important to notice that in this case J. W. Taylor of Tennessee, the majority ranking member, and Daniel A. Reed of New York, who was third on the majority side of the committee, were not appointed to the conference committee. Kopp was ranked fourth and Brand sixth on the majority side. Speaker Longworth, " not having been apprised in advance that this appointment would meet with opposition from the leader of the minority party," withdrew the appointment. Finally, however, the Speaker appointed three managers to the conference, consisting of Elliott, Kopp and Lanham.[2] This case is indicative of the limitations upon the Speaker in the appointment of conference managers.

Finally, the Speaker appoints all the select committees,[3] which are either political or non-political. To the latter class belong those committees which are appointed by the Speaker either on occasions of celebration or in the performance of social functions. In such cases, the Speaker appoints the member senior in service from each State, and if two or more members from a State are of the same length of service, he appoints the eldest.[4] A perfunctory duty indeed it is.

[1] *Cong. Record*, 69th Cong., 1st Sess., p. 8833.

[2] *Ibid.*, p. 8847.

[3] Rule x, 2.

[4] *Cong. Record*, 63rd Cong., 2nd Sess., p. 13456.

The point of importance lies, however, in the power of appointing select committees of political nature. Formerly custom dictated that the Speaker should appoint the member having moved a select committee, as chairman of the committee,[1] but the practice has been of late disregarded by the Speakers.[2] Prior to 1880 the House had on several occasions wrested the power from the Speaker and proceeded to select such committees itself.[3] And since then similar cases occurred.

In the second session of the Sixty-first Congress a resolution was introduced to investigate the Department of Interior and the Bureau of Forestry. Under the rules the resolution was referred to the Committee on Rules, from which Mr. Dalzell offered a report providing for a special committee of twelve members, six of whom were to be appointed by the President and six to be "designated" by the Speaker from the members of the House to "make a thorough and complete investigation of the administration and conduct of the Interior Department . . . and the Bureau of Forestry." Immediately objection was raised from the floor. Mr. Fitzgerald of New York charged that "this entire proceeding has not been originated or perfected in either House of Congress, but apparently it has been arranged in the White House." Mr. Norris of Nebraska rose to offer an amendment to the report of the Committee on Rules that the proposed special committee be appointed by the House. The amendment was passed by a close vote of 149 to 146.[4]

Another case occurred in the first session of the Sixty-second Congress in which the Democrats were returned to

---

[1] Hinds, *op. cit.*, ii, 1275; iii, 2342; iv, 4514-4516.

[2] *Ibid.*, iv, 4517-4523, 4671.

[3] *Ibid.*, iv, 4448, 4470, 4471-4476.

[4] *Cong. Record*, 61st Cong., 2nd Sess., p. 384.

power in the House of Representatives after a lapse of sixteen years.[1] On May 9, 1911, Mr. Henry of Texas, chairman of the Committee on Rules, brought in House resolution 157 which provided that a committee of nine be elected
by the House to make an investigation of violations of the
anti-trust act of 1890 by the American Sugar Refining
Company.[2] On May 16, Mr. Henry submitted an identical
resolution for the investigation of violations of the same act
by the United States Steel Corporation.[3] House resolution
157 introduced by Mr. Stanley of Kentucky originally provided that the committee to investigate the American Sugar
Refining Company be " selected " by the Speaker. Speaker
Clark shrank from the responsibility. " The Speaker had a
conference with me," Mr. Henry said, " and stated that for
reasons satisfactory to himself he preferred the Committee
on Rules should so amend the Stanley resolution and provide
for the election by the House, and I yielded to his wishes." [4]
" For personal reasons," too, Mr. Underwood of Alabama,
floor leader of the Democratic majority, " did not desire
these resolutions to go to the Ways and Means Committee," [5]
which was the Committee on Committees with powers to
make committee appointments.

As provided in the resolutions reported from the Committee on Rules, the two investigation committees were to
be *elected by the House.* The farce of this procedure was
brought to light during a debate on the floor of the House.
On May 16, 1911, Mr. Henry submitted a list of nine mem-

[1] Prior to Sixty-second Congress the Democrats were in majority for
the last time in the House of Representatives in 1894.

[2] *Cong. Record*, 62nd Cong., 1st Sess., p. 1143.

[3] *Ibid.*, p. 1230.

[4] *Ibid.*, p. 1277.

[5] *Ibid.*, p. 1257.

bers to constitute the committee for the investigation of the United States Steel Corporation, and moved their adoption. As to how these members were selected, let the *Congressional Record* tell the story:

Mr. Murdock. Will the gentleman yield to me for a question?
Mr. Henry of Texas. I will.
Mr. Murdock. This is the nomination of a committee to be elected by the House. Will the gentleman inform the House how the committee was nominated?
Mr. Henry of Texas. The committee was nominated *by several Members* who were interested in the resolution. Any individual Member has the right to propose names.
Mr. Murdock. This is a new procedure, and one with which I am in hearty accord but I want to know how the gentleman arrived at the nomination.
Mr. Henry of Texas. I have nothing to withhold from the House. Those who are interested on this side of the House thought they were able to agree about the names, and did agree, and then I asked the minority leader on the other side to submit names, which he did, and we accepted them as suggested by him.
Mr. Cooper. Will the gentleman yield?
The Speaker. Does the gentleman from Texas yield to the gentleman from Wisconsin?
Mr. Henry of Texas. Yes.
Mr. Cooper. I am very much interested in the statement of the gentleman from Texas. As to a proposition to investigate the greatest trust in the world, the gentleman from Texas says that some of the gentlemen on that side of the House are interested in it. I had supposed that the whole House and the whole country are interested in the proposition.
Mr. Henry of Texas. They are, I will say to the gentleman.
Mr. Cooper. I had supposed the whole majority side over there and some of the people on this side were interested, in addition to the leader of the minority, of whom the gentleman

spoke. I shall not object, however. But I should think, if any proposition of investigation were a matter for the consideration of the whole House, this would be it, and that it would be left to each side of the House to select its own members on the committee.

Mr. Henry of Texas. The gentleman is correct, and the whole country is interested. Does the gentleman desire to offer any amendment or suggest any other name?

Mr. Cooper. Not now; no.

Mr. Henry of Texas. Then, Mr. Speaker, I ask the adoption of the resolution.[1]

The resolution was agreed to.

Mr. Henry then called up the resolution which provided for the membership of the committee to investigate the American Sugar Refining Company. Here the tyranny of one-man power, not of the Speaker as was in days of Cannonism but of the chairman of the Committee on Rules, was in evidence. To quote the *Congressional Record* further:

Mr. Booher. Mr. Speaker, I would like to ask a question of the gentleman from Texas.

The Speaker. Does the gentleman from Texas yield to the gentleman from Missouri?

Mr. Henry of Texas. Yes.

Mr. Booher. I would like to know how many members of the committee [on rules] on this side of the House—the minority Members—were present when these nominations were made?

Mr. Henry of Texas. When the actual nominations were made, several Members; but I have talked with a number of Democrats on the subject and tried to confer with my party associates about the membership. The matter was submitted to the minority leader on the other side for suggestions as to his selections of committeemen.

[1] *Cong. Record*, 62nd Cong., 1st Sess., p. 1253.

Mr. Booher. How many members of the minority were present when the nominations were made on that side?

Mr. Henry of Texas. We did not have anything to do with that because the gentleman from Illinois (Mr. Mann) acts for the minority.

Mr. Booher. The leader of the minority answered for his entire side?

Mr. Henry of Texas. I presume the leader of the minority answered for his side. . . .

Mr. Fitzgerald. Will the gentleman yield?

Mr. Booher. I would like to ask what is the difference between the old and the new way of selecting committees? (Laughter and applause on the Republican side).

Mr. Henry of Texas. There is a great difference. Under the old rule the Speaker appointed. Under this new system the House elects . . .

Mr. Booher. No doubt the action of the gentleman is fair, but I, for one, have not been consulted in this matter. (Laughter). . . .[1]

Mr. Fitzgerald of New York, chairman of the important Committee on Appropriations, then rose to voice his opposition to the pending resolution:

. . . I know that no Speaker would select a committee of this character without consultation with Members on his own side of the House, at least. For my part, I am unable to see any distinction between the selection of a committee in this way . . . under the pretense of selecting a committee and the selection by the Speaker himself. My understanding was when the House was to elect a committee for any purpose, that—so far, at least, as the Democratic membership of the House was concerned— the selection would be nominated to the Democratic caucus, to be ratified by the caucus, and then submitted to the House, and at least we would have the pretense of having the party in control pass in advance upon the selection.[2]

[1] *Cong. Record*, 62nd Cong., 1st Sess., p. 1254.

[2] *Ibid.*, p. 1254.

Mr. Harrison of New York characterized this method of selecting committees like " letting a cat out of a bag " and as " equivalent to transferring from the Speaker's control into the hands of the chairman of the Committee on Rules this tyranny we heard so much about in the last Congress." [1] It was brought out during the debate that Mr. Henry had not consulted one-tenth of the majority membership of the House before he submitted to the House his resolutions for the election of the members to the two investigation committees. With the members of the Committee on Rules, he had consulted only a " small fraction " of them. At one place he argued that the nominations were made by " unanimous " choice of the members of the Committee on Rules. "As chairman of the Committee on Rules," he assured the House, " I desire to state that the responsibility was upon that committee." [2]   At another place, however, he informed his colleagues that:

The Committee on Rules did not, neither did the Democratic or the Republican membership, nor did any sub-committee of the Democrats or the Republicans make the selections. Therefore I make the candid statement to the House that as a Representative from the eleventh congressional district of Texas, not as the chairman of the Committee on Rules, not as a member of Committee on Rules, the responsibility of nominating these 10 Democratic Members should be charged against me.[3]

[1] *Cong. Record*, 62nd Cong., 1st Sess., p. 1254.

[2] *Ibid.*, p. 1257. He said further: "We have no ambition to select these men. The Committee on Rules does not aspire to do it. It is a large proposition to investigate the great trusts. The Committee on Rules have unanimously agreed upon two resolutions, and no one can raise his voice against a single member of this committee proposed..." *Ibid.*, p. 1257.

[3] *Ibid.*, p. 1278.

The action of Mr. Henry was not in accord with the spirit of the Democratic party in its effort to do away with the evils of one-man control.   For a fair criticism of Mr. Henry's action and as a proper procedure for him to pursue, we must quote Mr. Fitzgerald:

Let me say to the gentleman from Texas that his position will hardly square with what we are attempting to do.   He says that as the Representative from the eleventh district of Texas he nominates these men to the House; but when the late Speaker (Mr. Cannon) as Speaker of the House, as Representative of the eighteenth Illinois district, he nominated the committees to the House; the House then had the same right, under the rules, by resolution to have substituted other names for the committees named by him.

If we are to have committees elected by the House, if this side of the House is to allow that method, then one of the two things should be done, either opportunity should be given for men in the Democratic caucus to express preference without directly antagonizing some individual member for membership on the committees, or the committee on Ways and Means, the members of which under the Democratic caucus rules are prohibited from serving upon any other committee, should act as a nominating committee.   If that be done, it will save much controversy and much unnecessary discussion and will conduce very much to the success and harmony of the party in the House.[1]

The removal in 1911 of the power of the Speaker over committee appointment has not in effect rescued the House from the control of a few of the powerful and important leaders.   Nor has it removed the many defects which have impeded the progress of the work of the committees.   Indeed it is very unfortunate that the House has been thus far

[1] *Cong. Record*, 62nd Cong., 1st Sess., p. 1282.   For the debate on the resolution, see *ibid.*, pp. 1253-1258, 1277-1296.

mainly concerned with the political aspect of the ailment, that is, the question of the power over appointment, and has shown little, if any, inclination toward the internal improvement of the committee system, the legislative aspect of the question. Meticulous and meaningless bills of both private and public nature encumber the committee rooms. And as bills increase in intricacy, the difficulties of the committees increase accordingly. To get a bill out of a committee is not a hit-and-miss process; it is a selective one. There must be therefore some person or agent to do the selecting. Now as was ever before, the Speaker is not the sole agent who does the work. In the following chapter attempts will be made to show the ruling forces in the House and their relation to the Speaker.

CHAPTER III

The Committee on Rules

THE rules of the House of Representatives provide that bills, memorials and resolutions of a public nature may be " delivered, indorsed with the names of Members introducing them, to the Speaker, to be by him referred " to the committees having jurisdiction of the subject or subjects.[1] The rules and practice specify with considerable accuracy what subject each committee shall receive;[2] but not infrequently occasions arise when much is left to the Speaker's judgment. There are in the House more than sixty standing committees, and at times a bill may fall within the jurisdiction of several of these committees.[3] The importance of the power of the Speaker in this connection is that he may

[1] Rule xxii, 3; also see Rule xxiv, 2, regarding the disposal of business on the Speaker's table. The same procedure is prescribed for the introduction of petitions, memorials and bills of a private nature with the difference that reference to a committee is made by the member who introduces them. Rule xxii, 1.

[2] See Rule xi.

[3] On June 20, 1922, President Harding transmitted the report of the International Joint Commission relative to the improvement of the St. Lawrence River and navigation from the Great Lakes to the sea. The Committees on Foreign Affairs, on Interstate and Foreign Commerce and on Rivers and Harbors claimed jurisdiction over the report. The Committee on Ways and Means also made the same claim. Speaker Gillett held an "informal" hearing, in which members of each committee appeared to argue the question. Briefs were filed. Finally Speaker Gillett announced that the report be referred to the Committee on Interstate and Foreign Commerce. It was unusual for a Speaker to make an announcement from the chair as to reference of a bill. *Cong. Record*, 67th Cong., 2nd Sess., pp. 1457-1458, 1644-1650.

refer a bill, if he is interested in it, to a friendly committee to be acted upon, or, if he is opposed to it, he may refer it to an unfriendly committee from which no report will be made. The fact is all the more important when, prior to June, 1910,[1] a committee declined to report a bill, there was practically no possibility for a member on the floor to move to discharge the committee and to bring before the House the bill for consideration. In the first session of the Fifty-ninth Congress a bill providing for an appropriation of $423,000 for the purchase of about 100 acres of land in the District of Columbia to be added to the Rock Creek Park was introduced to the House, and was referred by the Speaker to the Committee on Public Buildings and Grounds,[2] from which the bill was not reported. In the second session of the same Congress this same bill was introduced in and passed by the Senate. And when it came to the House, Speaker Cannon again referred it to the same committee which reported it adversely.[3] However, in the first session of the Sixtieth Congress this bill again found its way to the Senate and was passed by that body. And when it came to the House, Speaker Cannon, who was interested in the passage of the bill, this time referred it to the Committee on Appropriations, which reported it with favorable recommendations. On May 26, 1908, Mr. Tawney of Minnesota, chairman of the Committee on Appropriations, moved to pass the bill. The motion was, however, defeated by the House by a vote of 57 against 164.[4]

[1] See chapter vi on the Discharge Calendar.

[2] See *Cong. Record*, 59th Cong., 1st Sess., p. 4069.

[3] *Ibid.*, 2nd Sess., p. 3155.

[4] See *Cong. Record*, 60th Cong., 1st Sess.., pp. 6998-7003. On the evening of March 3, 1909, a few hours before the session of Congress expired, Mr. Smith of Michigan moved to suspend the rules and pass this same bill. During the reading of the bill by the Clerk one member rose to ask if the special order of that day only applied to

The power of the Speaker in making reference of bills is a limited one. But with the House it is not so. On December 4, 1876, Mr. Springer of Illinois offered a resolution with the specific proviso that it be referred to the Committee on Judiciary. A point of order was made that under the rules of the House the resolution should be referred to the Committee on Elections. Speaker Randall overruled the point of order and held that it was competent for the House to refer any subject to any committee that it might choose.[1] This ruling thus established the precedent that the House itself may by vote refer any bill or resolution to any committee of the House without regard to the rules of jurisdiction.[2] In case of an erroneous reference with regard to a bill, memorial or resolution of a public nature, correction may be made, by the House, without debate, on any day immediately after the reading of the *Journal,* by unanimous consent, or on motion of a committee claiming jurisdiction, or on the report of the committee to which the bill has been erroneously referred.[3] Communications from the executive departments or from other sources should be addressed to the Speaker who refers them to the appropriate committees.[4]

Private Calendar and if this bill was on this calendar. The Speaker pro tempore replied that it was a motion to suspend the rules. So the Clerk continued to read the bill. However, the motion to suspend the rules was rejected by a vote of 31 against 192. See *ibid.*, 2nd Sess., pp. 3787-3788, 3792-3794.

[1] Hinds, *op. cit.*, iv, 4363.

[2] See *ibid.*, 4362, 4364, 4375; v, 5527. However, bills being now introduced by filing them at the Clerk's desk, the House does not often have the opportunity to express its wish as to reference, except by motion to change reference. See *ibid.*, iv, 3364.

[3] Rule xxii, 3. With regard to a private bill, memorial or petition, correction of erroneous reference may be made, without action by the House, at the suggestion of the committee in possession of it. Rule xxii, 2.

[4] Rule xli.

Messages—other than an annual message—from the President are referred either by the Speaker or by the House to the committee from which bills are to be originated,[1] while Senate bills are referred under the direction of the Speaker.[2]

The committees, either standing or select, are the means by which bills are examined in respect to content and form, a work which the House cannot do.[3] Usually a bill comes before a committee with no presumption in its favor. The committee may take evidence regarding it, may hear its friends and its opponents. The member who has introduced it may appear before the committee and state his case. The committee may also hear those who are interested in it. This is what is called a "hearing."[4] Hearings are sometimes public, sometimes *in camera*. Authority is conferred upon the committee to send for persons and papers in facilitating their search for further facts for deliberations.[5] And in the

[1] Hinds, *op. cit.*, iv, 4053; v, 6631, 6633, 6634. The annual message of the President is usually referred to the Committee of the Whole House on the state of the Union by the House on motion. From the Committee of the Whole it is distributed to appropriate standing committees by resolutions reported from the Committee on Ways and Means. *Ibid.*, v, 6621, 6622, 6631.

[2] *Ibid.*, iv, 3107, 3111.

[3] There have been, however, exceptional cases in which bills are never referred to appropriate committee before they are passed by the House. Cases of this nature will be referred to at a later place.

[4] It has been held in England that parties or petitioners have a right to be heard on private bills, but "in the matter of public bills there was developed no right of hearing akin to the right of petition, for the hearing of private parties adversely affected by a public bill was a privilege granted rather than a right recognized." In American no such right exists in any case, whether public or private. In 1888 the Committee on Ways and Means of the House of Representatives declined to hear certain tariff arguments. Luce, *Legislative Procedure* (New York, 1922), p. 143.

[5] Witnesses are summoned in pursuance and by virtue of the authority conferred on a committee by the House of Representatives to send for persons and papers. Hinds, *op. cit.*, iii, 1750.

case of important bills, such as revenue or interstate and foreign commerce bills, preparations are made by the committee—not to mention the parties interested—far ahead of the time of their introduction to the House. Much of the superficial criticism heaped upon the heads of the legislators would be spared if the public knew the amount of thought, time and labor bestowed upon the preparatory work of some of the important measures before they emerge to light of day.

Take the Payne tariff bill for instance. Cannonism was then at its height. The bill was introduced on March 17th, 1909,[1] and was reported back the following day from the Committee on Ways and Means. In the report the prolonged work done by the Committee on Ways and Means before the introduction of the bill was told:

The Committee [on Ways and Means] has, from time to time, during the past two years, been obtaining information for a revision of tariff, to have it in readiness . . . and especially since the resolution of May 16 last,[2] the committee has had an additional force of clerks at work, mainly of experts in tariff matters, detailed from the different departments by the order of the President, obtaining and properly tabulating the information that comes to the committee. They also prepared blanks early in the Summer, which were sent to all our consuls or consular agents seeking detailed information as to the cost of labor, manufacture, etc., in the foreign countries. . . . This information has been particularly useful for comparison with

[1] *Cong. Record*, 51st Cong., 1st Sess., p. 65.

[2] The resolution read: "*Resolved*, That the Committee on Ways and Means is authorized to sit during the recess of Congress and to gather such information through Government agents or otherwise, as to it may seem fit looking toward the preparation of a bill for the revision of the tariff; and said committee is authorized to purchase such books and to have such printing and binding as it shall require...to employ an additional stenographer, and to incur such expenses as may be necessary by said committee." *Cong. Record*, 60th Cong., 1st Sess., p. 6430.

the statements of wages paid abroad submitted in the public hearing before the committee. . . .

The committee has also obtained valuable information through the Department of Commerce and Labor [1] from special agents employed in that department who have reported from time to time on the industries abroad. . . .

The committee opened up hearings at Washington on the 10th day of November which continued daily until the 24th of December, and every one who desired an oral hearing up to that time was granted the privilege. Since then briefs have been invited and have been filed. This information has been printed for the use of the committee. . . .

The committee preparing the bill has been daily in session since the 24th of December. Each paragraph in the former tariff has been very carefully considered, and the hearings bearing upon the same have been carefully examined and read by the committee.[2]

It is a fact that due consideration is given to important bills by the committees either before or after they are introduced to the House. From these committees bills are reported [3] back to the House to be placed upon the calendars of the House [4] waiting for further action under the rules for the order of business.[5]   Bills thus placed upon the calendars may be called up by a committee under the call of com-

---

[1] The separate Departments of Commerce and Labor were not established until 1913.

[2] *Cong. Record*, 61st Cong., 1st Sess., p. 158.

[3] The following table shows the total numbers of bills and resolutions introduced to the House, reported from the committees and enacted into laws since the Fifty-fifth Congress. (For continuation of note see table, next page.)

[4] There are three calendars to which all business reported from committees are referred—a Union Calendar, a House Calendar and a Private Calendar. See Rule xiii, 1.

[5] See Rule xxiv.

mittees during the morning hour,[1] under the Unanimous-Consent Calendar,[2] under the suspension rule,[3] or under the rule for Calendar Wednesday.[4]

As was shown, the number of bills and resolutions introduced in the House of each Congress is enormous.[5] For

Note 3, preceding page, continued :

Congress	Number of Bills & Resolutions Introduced	Number of Reports	Public Laws & Resolutions	Private Laws & Resolutions	Total Laws & Resolutions
55.........	12,223	2,364	429	1,044	1,473
56..........	14,339	3,006	443	1,498	1,941
57..........	17,560	3,919	470	2,311	2,871
58..........	19,209	4,904	574	3,467	4,041
59..........	25,897	8,174	692	6,248	6,940
60..........	28,440	2,300	350	234	584
61.........	33,015	2,302	525	285	810
62..........	28,870	1,628	530	186	716
63..........	21,616	1,513	417	283	700
64..........	21,104	1,637	458	226	684
65..........	16,239	1,187	404	104	508
66..........	16,170	1,420	470	124	594
67..........	14,475	1,763	655	276	931
68.........	12,474	1,652	707	289	996
69..........	17,415	2,319	808	537	1,423

From " Calendars and History of Legislation of the House of Representatives " prepared under the direction of Mr. William T. Page, Clerk of the House. It must be noted, however, that these figures on the number of bills and resolutions introduced to the House are not complete, for they do not include bills and resolutions originated in the Senate and are subsequently introduced into the House.

[1] See *infra*, pp. 228 *et seq.*

[2] See *infra*, pp. 186 *et seq.*

[3] See *infra*, pp. 197 *et seq.*

[4] See *infra*, pp. 234 *et seq.*

[5] It is exceedingly easy for a member of the House to introduce a bill, be it a public or private bill. What he has to do is to leave the bill in the box at the Clerk's desk. See Hinds, *op. cit.*, iv, 3365.

Lord Bryce's criticism of the motives of the members of the House in introducing bills to the House may well be quoted: "... Few bills are brought in with a view to being passed. Most are presented in

instance, in the Sixty-eighth Congress there were introduced 12,474 bills and resolutions, out of which only 1,652 were reported from the committees. Of these 1,652 reported bills 996 were enacted into laws. The actual legislative days in session during this Congress amounted to 216.[1] To consider each and every one of these 1,652 reported bills during these 215 days would call for an average of between seven and eight bills and resolutions a day. That is impossible. There must be ways and means whereby a bill, when ready for passage and yet incapable of being reached in its regular order, can be selected and brought in for an " immediate " consideration in the House or in the Committee of the Whole House on the state of the Union as exigency demands. And here is where the Committee on Rules comes into play, a committee, as will be shown, had much to do with the rise and " fall " of the power of the Speaker.

order to gratify some particular persons or places, and it is well understood in the House that they must not be taken seriously. Sometimes a less pardonable motive exists. The great commercial companies, and especially the railroad companies, are often through their land grants and otherwise brought into relations with the Federal government. Bills are presented in Congress which purport to withdraw some of the privileges of these companies, to establish or favour rival enterprises, but whose real object is to levy blackmail on these wealthy bodies, since it is often cheaper for a company to buy off its enemy than to defeat him either by the illegitimate influence of the lobby, or by the strength of its case in open combat..." Bryce, *op. cit.*, p. 104. Sometimes bills are introduced without the knowledge of the introducers. On January 27, 1906, the *Record* bore the fact that Mr. Duzer of Nevada had introduced a resolution, but on the same day Mr. Duzer was recorded as absent and paired. On February 6, Mr. Williams read a letter from Mr. Duzer who denied that he ever introduced the resolution in question. Mr. Duzer wrote: "I never authorized, directed, or requested introduction of same; ... it was introduced without my knowledge or consent, and am as yet unacquainted with even its purpose or language." The resolution was ordered by the House to be destroyed. *Cong. Record*, 59th Cong., 1st Sess., p. 3067.

[1] If 15 days be deducted for organizing the House and the committees, the number of the legislative days would be reduced to 200.

In the early days of Congress when members of the House were few and business was small, the Committee on Rules occupied an unimportant place among the committees of the House, so much so that no appointment was made by the Speaker to the committee for several Congresses.[1] For many years the committee never made a report.[2] Its first advance towards the development of strength was made in 1811, in which year the status of the Previous Question was agreed upon by the House.[3] Yet still it was, as it had been, a select committee only to be authorized at the beginning of each Congress to report a system of rules,[4] and it remained so until 1880.[5] In 1841 it was held that, as the

[1] The Fifteenth, Sixteenth, Eighteenth, Nineteenth and Twenty-first Congresses. Alexander, *op. cit.*, p. 182.

[2] *Ibid.*, p. 182.

[3] The question had been a subject of heated debate during the Tenth, Eleventh and Twelfth Congresses. See Atkinson, *op. cit.*, pp. 11, 12. The formula devised to avoid passing judgment on a proposal was introduced in 1604 in the House of Commons: " Shall the main question be put? " Instead of " main," the adjective "previous" has come into use. In the Long and Short Parliament the word "now" was added which changed the nature of the motion: "Shall the main question be now put? " See Luce, *op. cit.*, pp. 270, 271. This form has, however, not been in use. *Cf.* Jefferson's *Manual*, xxxiv. In the modern practice of the House of Representatives the previous question is put as follows: "The gentleman from — demands the previous question. As many as are in favor of ordering the previous question say aye; as many as are opposed will say no." Hinds, *op. cit.*, v, 5443. If the question is answered in the affirmative, there will be no debate on the main proposition.

[4] Hinds, *op. cit.*, iv, 4321. As an outgrowth of the Speakership contest in 1849 the Committee on Rules became a standing committee consisting of nine members. The experience lasted through two Congresses. McConachie, *Congressional Committees* (New York, 1898), p. 192.

[5] In the revision of the rules of 1880 the Committee on Rules was changed into a standing committee of five "without any notice to that effect...although other changes were carefully commented upon." *Ibid.*, p. 194.

House had given the committee leave to report at all times, it might report at different times.[1]   On December 5, 1853, a resolution was adopted providing that the report of the committee " shall be acted upon by the House until disposed of, to the exclusion of all other business, anything in the rules hereby temporarily adopted to the contrary notwithstanding." [2]   Five years later a momentous innovation occurred, the importance of which was perhaps little realized at that time.   On June 14, 1858, Warren Winslow, of North Carolina, moved to appoint a committee on rules, of whom the Speaker was one, to revise the House rules and to report thereon at the next session.[3]   Then in 1880 came the revision of these rules.   The revised rules provided, among other things, that " all proposed action touching the rules and joint rules shall be referred to the Committee on Rules." [4]

Since then, in quick succession, one privilege after another was conferred by the House upon this all-powerful committee.   In the Fifty-ninth Congress it was decided that a special order from the Committee on Rules fixing a day for particular business was in order, in so far as the special order was in the nature of a change of rules to permit the

[1] Hinds, *op. cit.*, v, 6780. *Cf.* Atkinson and Beard, " Syndication of Speakership," *Political Science Quarterly*, xxvi, p. 382, where they said that on June 16, 1841, a resolution was adopted that the Committee on Rules " shall have right to report at all times." In 1891 the right to report at any time was conferred upon the committee. Hinds, *op. cit.*, iv, 4231. But, as a matter of fact, the committee had exercised the privilege of reporting at any time prior to 1891. See *ibid.*, 4621.

[2] Atkinson and Beard, *loc. cit.*, p. 382.

[3] Hinds, *op. cit.*, iv, 4321.

[4] It was held as early as 1876 that a proposition to change the rules might be referred only to the Committee on Rules. *Ibid.*, v, 6776. It was also held first in the Fifty-second Congress and again in the Fifty-ninth Congress that the committee had jurisdiction of all special orders providing for the consideration of bills or classes of bills. *Ibid.*, iv, 4326; also see *Congressional Journal*, 59th Cong.., 1st Sess., p. 1378.

committee to report it, under its leave to report at any time.[1] In the Fifty-second Congress it was held that, pending the consideration of the report from the Committee on Rules, the Speaker "may entertain one motion that the House adjourn; but after the result is announced he shall not entertain other dilatory motion until the said report shall have been fully disposed of."[2] Thus Speaker Crisp held, on September 20, 1893, that, pending the consideration of a report from the Committee on Rules, a motion to reconsider or a motion to appeal was dilatory within the meaning of the rule.[3] More than a year before Speaker Crisp had ruled, on March 7, 1892, that question of consideration could not be raised against a report from the Committee on Rules re-

[1] Hinds, *op. cit.*, v, 6774. In the same Congress authority was given to consider propositions relating to the hour of daily meeting and, in the Fifty-fifth Congress, the days on which the House shall sit. *Ibid.*, iv, 4325. On February 15, 1887, it was held that special orders must be referred to and reported back from the Committee on Rules alone. McConachie, *op. cit.*, p. 198. But, in the first session of the Sixtieth Congress, two special orders were reported from committees other than the Committee on Rules. On April 22, 1908, Mr. Mondell of Wyoming introduced, from the Committee on Public Lands, a special order for the consideration of a joint resolution on Oregon and California railroad land grants. "Immediately," upon its adoption, the resolution, so the order went, "shall be read in the House and one amendment thereto may thereupon be offered," and the general debate on the resolution should be "not exceeding three hours." Mr. Fitzgerald of New York asked: "Has the Committee on Rules been abolished?" In reply the Speaker pro tempore (Butler Ames of Pennsylvania) held that "the rules are such that a majority of the House can have its own way." The order was agreed to by a vote of 123 to 83. *Cong. Record*, 60th Cong., 1st Sess., pp. 5090, 5093. On April 27, 1908, Mr. Tawney of Minnesota presented a special order, from the Committee on Appropriations, for an immediate consideration of a sundry civil appropriation bill. The order was agreed to by a vote of 136 to 97. *Cong. Record*, 60th Cong., 1st Sess., pp. 5300, 5302.

[2] Follett, *op. cit.*, pp. 275, 276.

[3] Hinds, *op. cit.*, v, 5739.

lating to an order for the consideration of individual bills.[1] In the Fifty-third Congress the House gave the committee the right to sit during sessions of the House [2] and abandoned at the same time the provision that no rule or standing order should be changed without one day's notice, thus enabling the committee to report without previous notice.[3]

The practice of adopting by a majority vote a special order from the Committee on Rules began in 1883. In that year the Republicans wanted to enact a tariff bill, which was on the regular order of the calendar. To reach it for an earlier consideration would require a special order, the passage of which must be by a two-thirds vote, which the Republicans did not have. The Committee on Rules, therefore, brought in a resolution providing that, on its adoption by a majority vote, the rules should be suspended and the tariff bill be made a special order. The resolution was passed and the rule requiring a two-thirds vote for a suspension of the rules was thus set aside.[4]

---

[1] Hinds, *op. cit.*, v, 4961. On January 8, 1894, Speaker Crisp held the same way. But it is interesting to know that twice in 1891 Speaker Reed put the question of consideration against a report from the Committee on Rules before the House. The House decided by a vote to consider the question of consideration. See *ibid.*, 4962, 4963.

[2] See Rule xi, 62.

[3] Follett, *op. cit.*, p. 276. Also, orders relating to the use of the galleries of the House during the electoral count are within the jurisdiction of the Committee on Rules. Hinds, *op. cit.*, iv, 4327.

[4] *Ibid.*, iv, 3160. This method—the method of adopting a special order from the Committee on Rules by a majority vote—was not in favor during the following three Congresses. In 1887 it was regarded as a proceeding of "doubtful validity." It was not until after 1890 that this method had gained the favor of the House as an efficient means of bringing in bills out of their regular order for an immediate consideration. *Ibid.*, 3152. However, even as late as 1902 a point of order was made that a special order from the Committee on Rules was to be agreed upon by a majority vote. Speaker Henderson held that "The question has been fought out again and again, and is well settled that the Com-

Another power of the Committee on Rules is that of proposing amendment to a bill. In the Fifty-second Congress Mr. Dockery of Missouri introduced a resolution for the creation of a joint commission to examine into the conditions of the public service in the Executive Department of the Government at the national Capitol. The resolution was referred to the Committee on Rules from which a report was made authorizing the Committee on Appropriations "to insert in one of the general appropriation bills " a provision for the creation of such a commission. On February 7, 1893, when this paragraph of the bill was considered in the Committee of the Whole House on the state of the Union, a point of order was made. The chairman of the committee, however, overruled the point of order and ruled:

Here is a resolution . . . reported in an appropriation bill that is identically the language of the resolution considered by the House. The Committee on Rules reported the resolution and submitted a report instructing or authorizing the Committee on Appropriations to include these words in an appropriation bill. The Chair hardly thinks that it would be proper, or in order, for a committee of the House to undertake to say that it did wrong in instructing the Committee on Appropriations to report this provision. . . . The Chair overrules the point of order.[1]

Another case: On February 3, 1897, Mr. Henderson of Iowa reported a rule from the Committee on Rules providing for an amendment to an appropriation bill for the government of the District of Columbia. The amendment in

mittee on Rules can bring in a rule providing for the order of business in the House... There have been many decisions that a rule from the Committee on Rules which fixes the order of business with the approval of the House does not require a two-thirds vote." *Cong. Record,* 57th Cong., 1st Sess., p. 4820.

[1] Hinds, *op. cit.*, iv, 3839.

question was to repeal the jurisdiction of the Court of Claims for the settlement of all outstanding claims against the District of Columbia and was offered and ruled out on the preceding day in the Committee of the Whole on the ground that it was new legislation.[1] The rules of the House forbid amendment being made to an appropriation bill to change the existing law,[2] and this rule can be most effectively evaded by the adoption of a resolution from the Committee on Rules, neither a point of order nor a question of consideration against the resolution being in order. Several similar cases[3] occurred since 1896, and all of them were attempts to restore amendments which had been previously ruled out either in the House or in the Committee of the Whole, and to engraft them upon general appropriation bills. On February 20, 1907, the Committee on Rules went one step further. When reported several amendments to a Post-Office Department appropriation bill, it provided in the resolution that " the previous question shall be considered as ordered on said amendments immediately and on the bill to

[1] *Cong. Record*, 54th Cong., 2nd Sess., pp. 1502-1505.

[2] Rule xxi, 2, reads : " No appropriation shall be reported in any general appropriation bill, or be in order as an amendment thereto, for any expenditure not previously authorized by law, unless in continuation of appropriations for such public works and objects as are already in progress. Nor shall any provision in any such bill or amendment thereto changing existing law be in order, except such as being germane to the subject matter of the bill retrench expenditures by the reduction of the number and salary of the officers of the United States, or by the reduction of amounts of money covered by the bill: *Provided*, That it shall be in order further to amend such bill upon the report of the committee or any joint committee authorized by law or the House Members of any such commission having jurisdiction of the subject matter of such amendment, which amendment being germane to the subject matter of the bill shall retrench expenditures."

[3] See *Cong. Record*, 57th Cong., 1st Sess., p. 4894 ; also 2nd Sess., p. 2051 ; *Cong. Record*, 58th Cong., 1st Sess., pp. 1603-1608 ; *Cong. Record*, 59th Cong., 2nd Sess., p. 897.

its final passage without intervening motion or appeal." [1]
In presenting the resolution from the Committee on Rules,
Mr. Dalzell of Pennsylvania said: "There are certain paragraphs in the post-office appropriation bill which went out
on points of order. . . . The object of this rule is to restore to the bill the paragraphs which went out on points of
order." [2]

The bestowal of these privileges by the House upon the
Committee on Rules had a direct bearing upon the power of
the Speaker as chairman of the committee. For here is a
man who is the presiding officer of the House as well as the
titular head of his party in the House, and upon whom
rested the chairmanship of this powerful committee. He, as
presiding officer, enforced and interpreted the rules on questions relating to the jurisdiction and privileges of the committee of which he was chairman. The partiality of the
judgment upon the question is obvious. In fact, enough has
been shown as to the Speaker's rulings in favor of the Committee on Rules and a citation of further instances only lends
additional weight to the charge of the " omnipotence " of
this committee. For instance, it has been repeatedly decided
that under the rules [3] no business should be transacted before
the reading of the *Journal* [4] on any legislative day. In the
Fifty-second Congress Thomas C. Catchings of Missouri
once reported, before the reading of the *Journal,* a special
order from the committee for the consideration of the free

[1] *Cong. Record*, 59th Cong., 2nd Sess., p. 3942.

[2] *Ibid.*, p. 3943.

[3] Rule i, 1 read: " The Speaker shall take chair on every legislative
day precisely at the hour to which the House shall have adjourned at the
last sitting, immediately call the Members to order, and on the appearance of a quorum cause the *Journal* of the proceedings of the last day's
sitting to be read, having previously examined and approved the same."

[4] Hinds, *op. cit.*, iv, 2751-2756.

coinage bill. A point of order was made, but Speaker Crisp ruled that " it shall always be in order to call up for consideration a report from the Committee on Rules, and pending the consideration the Speaker may entertain one motion that the House adjourn." [1] Again, in the Fifty-third Congress Mr. Catchings brought in an order for the consideration of a pension bill. As the bill was not reported from the Committee on War Claims, Thaddeus M. Mahon of Pennsylvania raised a point of order, which was overruled by Speaker Crisp on the ground that the Committee on Rules had jurisdiction to report " a resolution fixing the order of business and the manner of considering a measure, even though the effect of its adoption would be to discharge a committee from a matter pending before it." [2]

Before March, 1910, the power of the Speaker was in part due to the increase of the power of the Committee on Rules. For the latter had privileges which were not accorded by the House to any other committee. Through a special order, the Committee on Rules regulated what should be considered, how long a debate on a bill should last, when a vote should be taken, or whether a bill should be voted with or without amendment. It proposed amendments to legislative bills over which other committees had jurisdiction. A special order from the committee suspending the regular business of the House for the time being took precedence over a motion to proceed under regular order.[3] When a special order set apart a day for a particular bill or of business from a particular committee, that order had precedence over a continuing order for the consideration of a bill or of

[1] Rule xi, 56; also see *Cong. Record*, 52nd Cong., 1st Sess., pp. 1818-1832.

[2] Hinds, *op. cit.*, v, 6771.

[3] *Ibid.*, iv, 3170-3172.

business from any other committee.[1] A bill, when reported under a special order, had prior right for its consideration over a report made privileged by the rules.[2] Even a motion to suspend the rules was held not in order during the consideration of a bill under a special order.[3] It was also held that a motion to postpone a special order providing for the consideration of a class of bills was not in order,[4] that the question of consideration could not be raised against a report from the Committee on Rules relative to the order for considering individual bills,[5] and that pending the consideration of a report from the committee, only one motion to adjourn was in order, whereas either a motion to reconsider or an appeal from the ruling of the Speaker was held as dilatory.[6] Indeed, "a report from the Committee on Rules, in the nature of a motion to suspend the rules, is in order at any time, and except for certain limitations [7] . . . may supersede and rescind any previous action taken by the House, whether by unanimous consent,[8] majority or two-thirds vote." [9]

But no sooner had the power of the Committee on Rules reached its zenith than the force of opposition was felt. At the commencement of the Fifty-sixth Congress Joseph N. Bailey of Texas said:

[1] Hinds, *op. cit.*, 3197, 3198.

[2] *Ibid.*, 3175, 3176.

[3] *Ibid.*, v, 6838.

[4] *Ibid.*, 4958.

[5] *Ibid.*, 4961-4963.

[6] *Ibid.*, 5739.

[7] A report from the Committee on Rules is not in order after the House has voted to go to the Committee of the Whole. *Ibid.*, 6781. A conference report has precedence of a report from the Committee on Rules, even after the yeas and nays and the previous question have been ordered. *Ibid.*, 6449. For other limitations under the rules since March, 1910, see Rule xi, 56.

[8] See *Cong. Record*, 60th Cong., 1st Sess., pp. 4349, 4350.

[9] From a letter, dated April 1, 1926, to the author from Mr. Lehr Fess, Parliamentarian of the House.

I feel certain that either the power of the Committee on Rules could [should] be curtailed or the membership of that committee could [should] be enlarged. . . . The three members who constitute a majority of that committee would . . . become a legislative triumvirate.   Under these rules the Committee on Rules not only decides what business the House must transact, but also what business the House must not transact.

It is enough to clothe the Speaker with the power of recognition and to supplement that by adding the power to appoint committees of the House; but to add to those powers, great almost to the point of being dangerous, the absolute control of the House through its Committee on Rules is giving greater power to the Speaker of the House than any one man in this free Republic ought to possess.   To say that the power still remains with the House is subterfuge, because the House can never pass upon a question until the Committee on Rules see [s] fit to report.   To say that the committee can be controlled by the majority is not candid, because the committee is considered the Speaker's official family, and no gentleman of the Speaker's party would serve upon it unless he could support the Speaker's policy.[1]

The scathing animadversion of Mr. Bailey explained the position of the opponents of the Committee on Rules.   The essential point to be remembered is that where the strength of the committee lay, there the attack from the opponents centered.   Rightly or wrongly, the opponents of the committee argued that the power of the committee had grown beyond the control of the House—and much less the majority of the House; that this power, enormous as it was, was due to the position of the Speaker as chairman of the committee; and that the Speaker exercised the " absolute control of the House through its Committee on Rules," that is, through the two majority members of the committee.   To curtail the power of the Speaker in his relation to the com-

[1] *Cong. Record*, 56th Cong., 1st Sess., p. 7.

mittee would necessarily mean two things, either to enlarge the membership of the committee, or to remove the Speaker therefrom.

The logic of this argument, however, warrants further examination. Had the power of the committee grown to the extent to be beyond the control of the House or of the majority of the House? Had the Speaker the " absolute control " of the House through the Committee on Rules? How far was the control by the Speaker through the committee justifiable? Did the House of Representatives succeed in gaining control over the committee by enlarging its membership and removing the Speaker therefrom? But, before answering these questions, it may be well to ask, in the first instance: Was the Committee on Rules, as it was then constituted, necessary, even though not indispensable, to the cumbrous procedure of the House?

The Committee on Rules was—and still is—necessary as a means of expediting legislation. To give a concrete case: President Taft wanted to make Senator Knox Secretary of State. The obstacle in the Senator's way was that the latter had voted in the Senate for the increase of the salary of Cabinet members and was therefore ineligible under the Constitutional prohibition.[1] To surmount the obstacle, the Senate passed by unanimous consent a resolution to restore the salary of the Secretary of State to $8,000. But, in the House neither unanimous consent nor a two-thirds vote was possible. Besides, the joint resolution was placed at the foot of the calendar. So the Committee on Rules brought in a special rule to take up the joint resolution, which was adopted

[1] Article i, 6, says: " No Senator or Representative shall, during the time for which he was elected, be appointed to any civil office under the authority of the United States, which shall have been created or the emoluments whereof shall have been increased during such time." However, questions have arisen under this paragraph on a few occasions. See Hinds, *op. cit.*, i, 506.

by a majority vote.[1]   The usefulness of this device in expediting legislation was stressed by Speaker Cannon, who asserted that, without the special rule, much of the progressive legislation recommended by President Roosevelt and demanded by the people could not have been considered, as these bills were so low on the calendar as to make it difficult to reach them during the life of a Congress.[2]

The Committee on Rules is also useful in dealing with obstructions of the minority.   Asher C. Hinds spoke of the system of special order as " a form of martial law " in meeting the rebellious members or a group of members of the House in their attempt to obstruct legislation.

Toward the end of the Fifty-seventh Congress Mr. Cannon, while chairman of the Committee on Appopriations, once asked unanimous consent to take from the Speaker's table a sundry civil appropriation bill with Senate amendments and asked for a conference.   Never before had the House refused to give its consent in such a case, but this time a member objected, palpably for the purpose of impeding legislation.   In accordance with the orderly procedure of the House this bill had to go to the Committee on Appropriations; and when reported back from the committee, a motion to go into the Committee of the Whole House on the state of the Union for the consideration of the bill would be in order.   Right here the minority could have ample opportunities to indulge in dilatory tactics: they could demand an aye-and-nay vote on the motion, possibly three such votes on the previous question and one on another motion.   While in the Committee of the Whole the usual call for tellers [3] and other dilatory proceedings might be re-

---

[1] *Cong. Record*, 60th Cong., 2nd Sess., p. 2408.

[2] Cannon, " The Power of the Speaker," *Century*, vol. lxxviii, p. 309.

[3] In the full House (that is 435 members) tellers are ordered by 44 members, and in the Committee of the Whole by 22 members.

sorted to. As the bill came back from the Committee of the Whole to the House, the minority could demand literally hundreds of roll-calls on the Senate amendments, on the adoption of the previous questions and on the adoption of the report of the Committee of the Whole, not to mention the possibility of making the point of order as to the lack of a quorum. Estimating at the rate of from thirty-five to forty-five minutes for every roll-call, one can easily conceive the length of time consumed by the filibustering minority. Mr. Cannon was, however, quick to meet such exigencies.[1] From the Committee on Rules he brought in a special order which provided that:

Immediately upon the adoption of this rule, and at any time thereafter during the remainder of this session, it shall be in order to take from the Speaker's table any general appropriation bill with Senate amendments, and such amendments having been read, the question shall be at once taken without debate or intervening motion on the following question: " Will the House disagree to said amendments en bloc and ask a conference with

---

[1] A special order was once resorted to by Mr. Cannon to elude a ruling made by the chairman of the Committee of the Whole. On February 11, 1903, a sundry civil appropriation bill was considered in the Committee of the Whole on the State of the Union. Mr. Cannon offered two amendments to the bill providing for the construction of an office building near the Capitol and also for the extension of the Capitol building. Both amendments were ruled out by the chairman of the committee as results of points of order made by a Democratic member. Immediately Mr. Cannon moved that the committee rise, and thereupon the Speaker took the chair. Two special orders from the Committee on Rules were brought into the House providing that it should be in order to consider, as amendments to the appropriation bill, provisions for the construction of an office building and for the extension and completion of the Capitol building. Both of these orders were agreed to by the House. Then the Committee of the whole resumed its sitting, and the amendments which had been previously ruled out, were again offered and agreed to, no point of order being possible. *Cong. Record,* 57th Cong., 2nd Sess., p. 2051.

the Senate?" And if this motion shall be decided in the affirmative, the Speaker shall at once appoint the conferees, without the intervening of any motion. If the House shall decide said motion in the negative, the effect of said vote shall be to agree to said amendments.

And further, For the remainder of this session the motion to take a recess shall be a privileged motion and take precedence of the motion to adjourn.[1]

" It must be recognized," says Mr. Dalzell in defending the Committee on Rules, " that the existence of such a body

[1] *Cong. Record*, 57th Cong., 2nd Sess., p. 2760. Ordinarily the motion to adjourn not only has the highest precedence when a question is under debate, but, with certain limitations, it has the highest privilege under all conditions. Because of this fact it is one of the most effective dilatory tactics for the minority. A motion to adjourn can not be amended, Jefferson's *Manual*, 1; it takes precedence of questions of privilege, Hinds, *op. cit.*, iii, 2521; also of the motion to reconsider, *ibid.*, v, 5605; of a conference report unless the report is before the House, *ibid.*, 6451-6453; it may be made after the yeas and nays are ordered and before the roll-call has begun, *ibid.*, 5366; before the reading of the *Journal*, *ibid.*, iv, 2757; or when the Speaker is absent and the Clerk is presiding, *ibid.*, i, 228. Party feeling ran very high during the Speakership of Mr. Cannon, and by way of counteracting the filibuster of the minority, the practice had been for the majority to make the legislative day continuous by a motion for recess instead of adjournment at the end of each calendar day, as the session of Congress was approaching its end. To illustrate how it was done, the following special order will suffice. The special order read: " *Resolved*, That on this day [April 8, Wednesday] and on Thursday of this week the House shall take a recess at 5 o'clock p. m. until 11:30 a. m. of the next calendar day; that on Friday, April 10, at 11:30 a. m., the Speaker shall declare the House in the Committee of the Whole on the state of the Union for the consideration of H. R. 20471, the naval appropriation bill; that at 5 o'clock p. m. on Friday, April 10, the chairman of the Committee of the Whole on the state of the Union shall declare the committee in recess until 11:30 on Saturday, April 11; that at 5 o'clock p. m. Saturday, April 11, the chairman of the Committee of the Whole on the state of the Union shall declare the committee in recess until 11:30 o'clock a. m. on Monday, April 13." *Cong. Record*, 60th Cong., 1st Sess., p. 4505.

is a necessity, and second that the only power it exercises is the power of the House." The Committee on Rules does not dictate legislation: it simply makes suggestions. A special order, so the argument goes, is of no consequence unless adopted by a majority of the House. The fact that special orders from the committee have been uniformly adopted [1] is evidence of the discretion of the committee in recognizing and making possible what the House wants to do. " The real temper of the House upon any question at any given time," Mr. Dalzell concluded, ". . . is better known by the Committee on Rules " which, far from being the master, is the servant of the House. [2] Mr. Hinds also dwells on the fact that " a majority of the members [of the House] could at any time reach any bill on the calendar by voting down the consideration of intervening bills, usually appropriation bills, until the desired bill was reached." [3] And even more outspoken was, perhaps, Mr. McCall who asserts that special

[1] But, twice in the Fifty-third Congress the Committee on Rules was beaten in the House. See Follett, *op. cit.*, p. 277. In the Sixty-second Congress the Committee on Rules reported a special order for the consideration of a bill on the Presidential term of the office, etc. Mr. Henry of Texas, chairman of the committee, demanded the previous question which was answered negatively by a vote of 69 against 143. In view of the negative vote, Mr. Henry withdrew the report. *Cong. Record*, 62nd Cong., 2nd Sess., p. 7476. However, the report was re-submitted. *Ibid.*, p. 7509. On July 2, 1926, the Committee on Rules reported a special order for the consideration of a bill to fix the salaries of the Federal judges. The previous question was voted down by the House by a division. Mr. Williams of Illinois then moved to postpone consideration of the bill till December 9, 1926, the following session of Congress. The motion was passed. *Cong. Record*, 69th Cong., 1st Sess., pp. 12770-12772.

[2] Dalzell, " Rules of the House of Representatives," *Independent*, vol. lxiv, p. 581.

[3] Gardner, " Rules of the House of Representatives," *North American Review*, vol. clxxxix, p. 237; also see *infra*, p. 231 relating to Mr. Gardner's statement.

orders " require the approval of the majority of the House, in order to become effective," and that, important as the powers of the committee are, they " are for use in emergencies. Sometimes for months in succession this committee has been entirely inactive." Mr. McCall, therefore, doubts " whether any juster system could be adopted for managing the business of a great body like the House." [1] It was not at all impossible, even though very improbable, for the members of the House, or a certain fraction of them, to secure, if so determined, the desired action from the committee. In the Sixtieth Congress the Payne tariff bill was referred, April 30, 1908, to the Committee on Rules for a special order for its immediate consideration. But for over two weeks the bill was not reported. It was charged that Speaker Cannon, chairman of the committee, being opposed to the bill, held up the resolution. On May 16, Mr. Payne, however, moved to suspend the rules and discharge the Committee on Rules from further consideration of the resolution on the bill. The motion was carried by a vote of 154 to 92.[2]

How far the time-honored principle of partisan rule had been observed by the members of the Committee on Rules

[1] McCall, *op. cit.*, p. 144. There is, however, the other side of the argument. Mr. Nelson of Wisconsin said: " It is true that the rule of the Committee [on Rules] must be approved by a majority of the Members. In theory this seems to be satisfactory; but in practice is there a man that takes any thought but that as a matter of fact the rule will be adopted, Why? Because this committee, with the Speaker as chairman, has in its power, in many ways, to induce Members to vote that way. It controls the appointment of committees. It controls their right of recognition. It controls the fate of measures upon which the legislative fortunes of Members largely depend. Naturally, under such circumstances, the committee is sustained as a matter of course, except, perhaps, in extraordinary times, when the people bring pressure to bear upon the Members." See *Cong. Record*, 60th Cong., 1st Sess., p. 1650.

[2] *Ibid.*, pp. 6430 *et seq.*

was almost impossible to ascertain, as meetings of the committee were held behind the veil of secrecy. Generally speaking, this principle had a firmer grip in the House before the European War. During the days of Reed and Cannon régime party partisanship was at its apogee. In the Fifty-first Congress the Committee on Rules consisted of Speaker Reed, McKinley of Ohio and Cannon of Illinois, from the Republican majority side, and McMillin of Tennessee and Blount of Georgia, Democrats. McMillin was once late for a committee meeting, and his tardiness brought forth adverse remarks from Speaker Reed. " Yes," retorted McMillin, " I am a little behind the time, but I hope I have not obstructed business." " Not at all," said the Speaker, " Joe and Mack and I went along by ourselves. And by the by "—handing out a paper—" we have just decided to commit the herein-mentioned outrage, and we thought you'd better glance over it so as to be able to tell your Democratic friends." [1] Miss Follett stated that " the minority members are not consulted on questions of state." [2] Yet, on the other hand, Speaker Cannon pointed out, not without pride, to the fact that partisanship among members of the committee melted before an emergency proposition. He cited a case in which the Committee on Rules " unanimously " authorized John S. Williams, a minority member of the committee, to report a special order for the immediate consideration of a bill " to further enlarge the powers and authority of the Public Health and Marine Hospital Service and impose further duties thereon." [3] This probably was the only case of

[1] Leupp, "Humors of Congress," *Century*, vol. lxv, p. 763; *cf.* Busbey, *Uncle Joe Cannon: The Story of a Pioneer American* (New York, 1927), p. 243.

[2] Follett, *op. cit.*, p. 273.

[3] *Cong. Record*, 59th Cong., 1st Sess., p. 4661; also see Cannon, *loc. cit.*, *Century*, vol. lxxviii, pp. 308, 309.

its kind in the history of the committee since 1896, and Speaker Cannon could find justification in his pride.

Thus far the weight of the argument has been on the side of the Committee on Rules. Granted, for the sake of argument, that no system could be " juster " than that of the Committee on Rules, the question would present itself: From whom has come complaint against the " tyranny " of the committee? The answer from Speaker Cannon was:

Those who complain against the Committee on Rules are the minority, who wish to prevent the majority from legislating, or those who desire to adopt this short-cut legislation and have the committee recommend special rules for their bills, each member naturally assuming that the legislation they desire by his constituents should be regarded as emergency legislation.[1]

And moreover

The complaint is not that some of the bills are promptly handled under special rules, but that other legislation demanded by a few or by a class of people was not also considered.[2]

Mr. Hinds was of the opinion that the power of the Speaker in his relation to the Committee on Rules was " much overestimated." " When a committee has once reported a bill," he said, " that bill is in the hands of the House. The Speaker and the Committee on Rules are alike powerless to prevent its consideration and passage." [3] Admittedly this is true, as far as Mr. Hinds goes. On the other hand, it must also be admitted that the Speaker together with his " two assistants " had the power, almost to the degree of absolutism, of selecting what bills were to

[1] Cannon, *loc. cit.*, vol. lxxviii, p. 308.

[2] *Ibid.*, p. 309.

[3] Hinds, " The Speaker of the House of Representatives," *American Political Science Review*, vol. iii, pp. 161, 162.

be reported before the House under a special order and of regulating the manner in which a reported bill was to be considered in the House. It is one thing to admit the great power of the committee in the conduct of business in the House, and it is quite another to seek the cause of the " strange submission " of the members to the dictatorship— for dictatorship it was—of the committee. John Nelson of Wisconsin gave us a partial explanation:

The Members of this House believe that we must have rules, and that any rules are better than no rules. We voted for the rules, because it had been found impractical to change the rules satisfactorily in a few hours' discussion at a caucus, or, for that matter, during the first thirty day of the opening of Congress, with committee appointments hanging over the heads of Members.[1]

The rules of the House are interdependent and inter-woven. To change a part of them would inevitably have effects upon the united whole, which would ultimately change the internal organization of the House. This the leaders of the House, developed under the then existing system, would not attempt to do. The American inventiveness and aggres-siveness in the spheres of mechanics and money-making, as Lord Bryce would say, give in to the conservatism of the leaders in matters of governmental affairs. Moreover, this was the system that " worked "—a fact very decisive to the pragmatic American people. The author can say with Lord Bryce that " the Americans surpass all other nations in their power of making the best of bad conditions." Furthermore, the hidden desire to follow the line of least resistance is a force that we must reckon with. Every member of the House has hopes and ambitions and private measures to advocate; and to fall in line with the leaders and to vote with

[1] *Cong. Record*, 60th Cong., 1st Sess., p. 1650.

and for them are really helping himself in promoting his own political career.

And, then, there was the personal influence of the members of the committee. The Speaker and the two majority members had been the leaders of the majority party before or at the time of their entrance to the Committee on Rules.[1] Mr. Luce admitted that " there is no necessity to ignore the advantageous position in which leaders [on the Committee on Rules] are placed, the weight that position gives their influence and the difficulties in the way of revolt." [2]   This personal influence was, however, by no means a secondary effect, as Mr. Luce seems to think, of the system that had succeeded in buttressing the members of the House: rather it was a primary cause for its existence. It was not position that gave influence; it was influence combined with position that made the committee invincible.

The commencement of the Sixty-first Congress was as dramatic as it was interesting. The customary resolution for the adoption of the rules of the previous Congress as the rules of this Congress was disagreed to by a vote of 193 to 189.[3] Champ Clark of Missouri, seizing upon the psychological moment, presented a resolution providing that the rules of the House of Representatives of the Sixtieth Con-

[1] Speaker Clark said: " It would be a strange and unfortunate thing if the Speaker of the House and the majority leader, after being here for going on twenty years, would not have some influence in the House. Why, once in a long while somebody will come along and say, ' How ought I to vote on this question?' And sometimes I know and sometimes I do not. If I know, I tell him what I think; and if I do not know, I tell him that I do not know, for I have not studied it ... "   *Cong. Record*, 63rd Cong., 2nd Sess., p. 4471.

[2] Luce, *op. cit.*, p. 481.

[3] On paper the Republican party claimed to have had 219 members, with 172 members to the credit of the Democratic party. Speaker Cannon voted " aye " on agreeing to the resolution. *Cong. Record*, 61st Cong., 1st Sess., pp. 19, 20.

gress be adopted as the rules of the first session of the Sixty-first Congress with the proviso that (1) the Speaker be authorized only to appoint the Committee on Ways and Means, on Printing, on Accounting, on Mileage, and on Enrolled Bills, and (2) that section I of Rule X relating to the Committee on Rules be amended to read thus: " On Rules to consist of 15 members who shall be elected by the Members of the House, said committee to elect its own chairman." [1]

The resolution was disagreed to by a vote of 203 to 180.[2] John J. Fitzgerald of New York, a Democrat, then rose and offered a resolution [3] which, as far as the Committee on Rules was concerned, provided that " the Committee on Rules shall not report any rule or order which will prevent the offering of a motion to recommit." [4]

[1] Clark proceeded to present a list of 15 members considered as elected and appointed members of the Committee on Rules "with all rights, powers, and privileges conferred upon the Committee on Rules by the Rules of the House." This said committee was also authorized to revise, amend, simplify, and codify the rules of the procedure of the House and report its conclusions to the House on the first Monday in December, 1909, which report should be of highest privilege, and remain so until disposed of by the House. *Cong. Record*, 61st Cong., 1st Sess., p. 21.

[2] Speaker Cannon voted "nay" on agreeing to the resolution.

[3] The other features of the resolution were (1) the creation of a unanimous consent calendar, for a discussion of which see *infra*, pp. 186 *et seq.*, (2) The requirement of a two-thirds vote, instead of a majority vote, to set aside the Calendar Wednesday, which will be treated in chapter vi and (3) matters on recognition. See chapter iv.

[4] Mr. Luce writes: "When the machinery for majority control of the House had become remarkably efficient under Speaker Cannon, one of the devices most criticized was the shaping of special rules by the Committee on Rules so that amendments could not be offered from the floor. This was far from a novelty in Congress, but now attracted wide attention for the first time through being seized upon as one of the pretexts for revolt. Indeed it embodied virtually the autocratic idea of Louis Napoleon —the take-it-or-leave-it-policy. As adapted here, this meant domination

The difference between the Fitzgerald and Clark resolutions, said Mr. Underwood of Alabama, of the Democratic party, lay in that the former " contemplates that the Speaker shall control the House of Representatives," while the latter " contemplates that the House of Representatives shall control the House." The importance of the difference between these two points of views as presented by Mr. Fitzgerald and Mr. Clark, should be noted. Mr. Fitzgerald aimed, in his amendment to the rules, to restrict the legal power of the Committee on Rules but without curtailing the power of the Speaker. It was apparent that what he had in view was the preservation of the then existing system, centralization of power in the hands of the Speaker. On the other hand, Mr. Clark—and the Republican insurgents—attempted to curtail the power of the Speaker by his removal from the membership of the Committee on Rules or by enlarging the membership of the committee, and left the legal power and privileges of the committee under the rules of the House unimpaired. Mr. Murdock of Kansas, one of the insurgent leaders, stated that what the insurgents proposed to do was:

(1) To make the Speaker ineligible to a place on the Committee on Rules; (2) to take away the power of the Speaker to refuse recognition when recognition is in order and there is no rival for the floor when a Member asks it; (3) to have the House itself select its own standing committees. There is no effort by the insurgents, and there has been none, to do away with any of the procedure which makes for expedition in public business. The power of closing debate is not to be touched. The Reed rules against dilatory motions and for counting a quorum are to be left undisturbed. The means to overcome the filibuster and proceed to a final vote on all measures will stand in all its efficacy.[1]

by the majority caucus, and was intolerable to members of the majority with independent minds, as it was to all of the minority." Luce, *op. cit.*, p. 230.

[1] See *Cong. Record*, 61st Cong., 2nd Sess., p. 6276.

The Fitzgerald amendment was agreed to by the House by a vote of 210 to 173.[1] So "Cannonism" was at least saved for the time being.

However, the force of the revolt manifested by the dauntless spirit of a small body of men, the "insurgents,"[2] as they were called, was irresistible. It was only a question of days as to when that force, invincible as it was, would turn loose, and the day at last arrived. On March 16, 1910, Edgar D. Crumpacker, chairman of the Committee on Census, called up for consideration a census bill. Being Calendar Wednesday, the bill, though privileged under the Constitution,[3] was declared by a decision of the House not in

---

[1] Speaker Cannon voted "aye" on agreeing to the amendment. *Cong. Record*, 61st Cong., 1st Sess., pp. 33, 34. Mr. Norris of Nebraska wrote that the Fitzgerald amendment was very conservative and only made a few changes in the rule. Every Tammany member of the House, save one, voted for the Fitzgerald amendment. "For value received" the Republican members of the Committee on Ways and Means, under the influence of the Speaker, put petroleum on the free list of the tariff bill, *Cong. Record*, 61st Cong., 2nd Sess., p. 6279; also see *Searchlight*, vol. i, no. 9, pp. 10, 12-17. Altogether twenty-three Democrats voted for the amendment.

[2] This insuragent movement against Cannonism, as an organized effort, took shape in the first session of the Sixtieth Congress. In December, 1908, there was a meeting held by the insurgents. As a result, a permanent organization was formed and a "small legislature" was organized, and committees were appointed. This small body of men met regularly about three times a week during the Sixtieth Congress, *Cong. Record*, 61st Cong., 2nd Sess., pp. 6274-5; also *cf*. Norris, "The Secret of his Power—A History of the Insurgent Movement in the House of Representatives," *La Follette Magazine*, vol. ii, pp. 7-8. The Democratic side of the history of the revolt was told by Mr. Clark of Missouri. See Clark, *op. cit.*, vol. ii, pp. 260, 283.

The movement was not without encouragement from President Roosevelt. For Roosevelt's friendly attitude toward the movement, see *Cong. Record*, 68th Cong., 1st Sess., pp. 962, 963. For how Roosevelt came to be interested in the movement, see *Cong. Record*, 61st Cong., 2nd Sess., p. 3413.

[3] A census bill under the rules of the House has no privileged status,

order.[1] On March 17, Mr. Crumpacker again called up the same bill. Thomas Butler of Pennsylvania made a point of order that the resolution had no privileged standing, being an amendment to a certain section of the Census Act. The point of order prompted a heated debate. And finally Speaker Cannon submitted to the House the question.[2] " Is the House resolution called up by the gentleman from Indiana in order now?" The House decided in the affirmative by a

but section 2 of article I of the Federal Constitution says that "the actual enumeration shall be made within three years after the first meeting of the Congress of the United States, and within every subsequent term of ten years, in such manner as they shall by law direct..." The second section of the Fourteenth Amendment to the Constitution also says that "Representatives shall be apportioned among the several States according to their respective numbers, counting the whole number of persons in each State, excluding Indians not taxed."

In 1882 a census bill was reported for consideration from the Committee on Census as a privileged bill. A point of order was made and was overruled by Speaker Keifer. Speaker Keifer held that he was "of the opinion that the rules of the House are subject to any constitutional provision that may be found. It may be true that under the rules, strictly speaking, this bill may not be in order. The Chair is, however, of the opinion that the consideration of an apportionment bill by this Congress, fixing the representation in the next Congress under the last census, is one of high constitutional privilege..." Hinds, *op. cit.*, i, 308; also *ibid.*, 307, 306.

[1] *Cong. Record*, 61st Cong., 2nd Sess., p. 2286. Mr. Underwood of Alabama said on the following day, March 17: "Yesterday we did not deny that under the precedents established, a long line of them, it had been held that a matter affected the census was privileged. Nobody denied the precedents that were cited by the Speaker, but the argument we made to this House was that this rule establishing Calendar Wednesday had been written subsequent to the making of these precedents, and that the purpose of the rule was to wipe out every precedent that interfered with the calling of the calendar and the consideration of bills under the Wednesday Calendar..." *Ibid.*, p. 3284.

[2] Speaker Cannon preferred not to give a ruling on the point of order "in view of the recent vote of the House and of the value of the vote of yesterday as a precedent and what this vote may be a precedent..." *Cong. Record*, 61st Cong., 2nd Sess., p. 3287.

vote of 210 to 72. In the wake of the convulsion George Norris of Nebraska, who had long been waiting for a chance of hearing, arose to seek recognition to " present a resolution made privileged by the Constitution." " If it is a resolution made privileged by the Constitution," Speaker Cannon retorted, " the gentleman will present it." The resolution was presented. It set the House aflame. It provided for a Committee on Rules of 15 members, 9 of whom should be members of the majority and 6 of whom should be members of the minority, to be selected as follows:

The States of the Union shall be divided by a committee of three, elected by the House for that purpose, into nine groups, each group containing, as near as may be, and equal number of Members belonging to the majority party. The States of the Union shall likewise be divided into six groups, each group containing, as near as may be, an equal number of Members belonged to the minority party.[1]

It was further provided that each of the groups should meet at 10 a. m. of the day following the adoption of the report of the committee for the selecting of the members for the Committee on Rules; that the Speaker should not be eligible to membership on the Committee on Rules (which was the cardinal point in the scheme); and that the committee should select its own chairman. "All rules or parts thereof inconsistent with the foregoing resolution are hereby repealed." As was expected, Mr. John Dalzell of Pennsylvania made the point of order against the resolution. A spirited debate ensued,[2] which kept the House in continuous

[1] Mr. Norris had introduced practically the same resolution in the second session of the Sixtieth Congress. *Cong. Record*, 60th Cong., 2nd Sess., p. 1056.

[2] Mr. Norris said: "If the action of the House just had makes a census bill privileged because of the Constitution, then any proposition to amend the rules must be privileged by virtue of the same instrument.

session until afternoon of the following day.[1]   A recess was then taken, followed by a postponement until noon of the day after.

At the fixed hour, March 19, the House assembled. " Planting himself upon the law made for the House by Mr. Speaker Randall,[2] appealing from the passion of this

It does not add to the privileged nature of the census bill that it is reported by a committee and that was practically admitted in the discussion that took place under [on] the floor of the House in the colloquy between myself and the gentleman from Pennsylvania [M. E. Olmstead]," *Cong. Record*, 61st Cong., 2nd Sess., p. 3292.   The Norris resolution had neither been introduced into the House nor had it been referred to the Committee on Rules.   Mr. Oscar Underwood of Alabama said : " . . . . The Speaker has repeatedly said to this House that he rules by the will of the majority.   The majority of this House today can make this a matter of privilege the question of amending the rules of the House by a majority vote," *ibid.*, p. 3293.   Champ Clark of Missouri, then leader of the minority party, defended the Norris resolution with great vigor : " . . . Now suppose that a majority of the Members of this House had made up their minds to change these rules, how are you going to do it?   If it is not a matter of privilege and you cannot get it up that way, how are you going to accomplish it? . . ." *ibid.*, p. 3294.   Precedents are, however, against the Norris resolution as privileged.   See Hinds, *op. cit.*, p. 1063.

[1] Four times the House refused to take a recess.   Two roll calls were made on account of the lack of a quorum, one of which was refused by a vote of the House.   From 2 a. m. until 2 p. m., March 18, the House was in session in the absence of a quorum.   Warrants of arrest were issued authorizing the Sergeant-at-Arms to bring in absent members.   With four automobiles, the search for the absentees, largely of the Republican party, began at 2 a. m., March 18, and by 4:15 five members were brought in, *Cong. Record*, 61st Cong., 2nd Sess., pp. 3394, 3395.

[2] Speaker Cannon cited the Rogers Q. Mills case of 1878 as precedent. The argument of Mills was that " it is the constitutional privilege of the House of Representatives to adopt rules at any time; it is a continuing power of which the House cannot divest itself."   James Garfield objected to Mills' line of reasoning and said that it was proposed " to carry the power of the House in this respect further than the Constitution justifies.   If the position of the gentleman were correct, a Member could at any time interrupt our proceedings by bringing in a proposition for the amendment of the rules."   See *Cong. Record*, 61st Cong., 2nd Sess., p. 3426.

day to the just reason of that day," Speaker Cannon sustained the point of order and held that the resolution was not in order.[1] " Loud and long continued applause on the Republican side " greeted the Speaker's much-delayed ruling. Promptly Mr. Norris appealed from the ruling, and Mr. Dalzell of Pennsylvania moved to lay the appeal on the table, which motion was refused by the House.[2] Then the question on the ruling was: " Shall the decision of the Chair stand as the judgment of the House?" The House answered in the negative,[3] and proceeded to consider the Norris amendment which Mr. Norris, after consulting with other insurgents, offered as a substitute, providing that:

There shall be a Committee of Rules, elected by the House, consisting of ten Members, six of whom shall be Members of the majority party and four of whom shall be Members of the minority party. The Speaker shall not be a member of the Committee and the Committee shall elect its own chairman from its own members.[4]

[1] *Cong. Record*, 61st Cong., 2nd Sess., p. 3426.

[2] Speaker Cannon voted " aye " on the motion to lay the appeal on the table.

[3] The vote stood—161 yeas, 182 nays. It is dangerous to prophesy, especially in the realm of politics. Speaker Reed said in 1892, " I have been fifteen years in Congress, and I never saw a Speaker's decision overruled, and you will never live to see it either," Luce, *op. cit.*, p. 442; also see *Cong. Record*, 52nd Cong., 1st Sess., p. 647. A year later, Jan. 9, 1911, however, the Fuller resolution, introduced in the same manner as the Norris resolution and seeking to amend the House rule as a privileged resolution under the Constitution, was declared out of order, the House thus confirming Speaker Cannon's ruling, *Cong. Record*, 61st Cong., 3rd Sess., pp. 679-86. It is still impossible to amend the House rules without resorting to revolutionary action.

[4] Two amendments were presented to the Norris substitute: (1) An amendment by Mr. Martin of South Dakota. This amendment was practically the same as the Norris substitute, with this difference: that it would not become effective until after March 3, 1911, *Cong. Record*, 61st Cong., 2nd Sess., p. 3430. (2) An amendment by Mr. Olmstead

As it was provided in the Norris substitute, the then existing Committee on Rules was to be dissolved upon the election of the proposed committee, which was to take place " within ten days." The substitute was agreed to by the House.[1] With it ended one of the most exciting chapters in the annals of the American Congress.

of Pennsylvania. It provided for a committee on revision of the rules, consisting of 15 members, to report its conclusion to the House on the first Monday of December next. *Cong. Record,* 61st Cong., 2nd Sess., p. 3434.

[1] The defeat of Speaker Cannon at the hands of the Members of the House left "two courses for the Speaker to pursue," declared Speaker Cannon, "One is to resign and permit the new combination of Democrats and the insurgents to choose a Speaker in harmony with its aims and purposes. The other is for that combination to declare a vacancy in the office of the Speaker and proceed to the election of a new Speaker. After consideration, at this stage of the session of the House, with much of the important legislation pending involving the pledges of the Republican platform and their crystallization into law, believing that his resignation might consume weeks of time in the re-organization of the House, the Speaker, being in harmony with the Republican policies and desirous of carrying them out, declines by his own motion to precipitate a contest that might greatly endanger the final passage of all legislation necessary to redeem Republican pledges and fulfill Republican promises ... ; and another reason is this: in the judgment of the present Speaker, a resignation is in and of itself a confession of weakness or mistake, or an apology for past action. The Speaker is not conscious of having done any political wrong. (Loud applause on the Republican side)." He then continued that he was, however, willing to entertain, in conformity with the highest constitutional privilege, a motion by any member to vacate the office of the Speakership. This declaration, too, was met by loud applause on the Republican side, and as he ended it by saying, " The Chair is now ready to entertain such a motion," the applause on the Republican side became louder. The drama of this political eruption now reached its climax, nay, its anti-climax. The House was thrown into wild confusion. Burleson of Texas was bold enough to present the resolution declaring the office of the Speakership vacant. The resolution was, however, not agreed to. The vote stood 155 yeas, 192 nays. *Cong. Record,* 61st Cong., 2nd Sess., p. 3437. The insurgents agreed at the beginning of the movement that no attempt would be made against the Speaker to defeat him for re-election. But as time progressed, the

A decade and more has elapsed since the "revolution." During this time each of the two parties has gained control of the House for a period of eight years, a reasonable length of time for students of government to examine the fruits of that much-heralded revolution. The new rule lessened the power of the Speaker in two ways. First, it removed him from the Committee on Rules. Secondly, it deprived him of his power to appoint the members of the committee, which was enlarged from five to ten.[1] If what the insurgents—and curiously enough they were seldom called "reformers," negligible as implication of the term has become—if what the insurgents aimed to do was to bring about the removal of the Speaker from the Committee on Rules and

sentiment changed. At a meeting of the insurgents, held on March 15, 1910, they expressed their willingness to vote against Speaker Cannon provided enough votes could be pledged to bring about his defeat. There were only seven insurgents present; it needed 14, or possibly 15, votes to carry out the *coup d'etat*. They therefore decided "not to undertake the proposed action". *Cong. Record*, 61st Cong., 2nd Sess., p. 6275.

On March 25, Mr. Currier of New Hampshire presented a resolution containing therein a list of ten members who were considered as "elected" members of the Committee on Rules under the new rule. They were: John Dalzell of Pennsylvania, Walter S. Smith of Iowa, Henry S. Boutell of Illinois, George P. Lawrence of Massachusetts, S. Sloat Fassett of New York, Sylvester S. Smith, of California, Champ Clark of Missouri, Oscar W. Underwood of Alabama, Lincoln Dixon of Indiana and John J. Fitzgerald of New York. The selection was made previously in the caucus meetings of the two parties. It is interesting to note that none of the insurgents was placed on the committee. As to the rank of the Democratic members of the committee, Mr. Clayton of Alabama, as chairman of the Democratic caucus, said that they had been ranked in the order on the list in accordance with the number of votes they received. However, Mr. Clayton did so "without any instructions by the Democratic caucus on that subject at all," and he was ready to assume "all responsibility for the rank given to the Democrats on the committee." *Cong. Record*, 61st Cong., 2nd Sess., p. 3759.

[1] The membership of the committee was increased to 11 in the Sixty-second Congress. During the Sixty-fifth Congress the number once reached 13. And since then the number has been 12.

the limitation on his power to control legislation, the revolution might be said to have accomplished its purpose. But the conditions which led to the need of some authority to select bills for passage were, nevertheless, not removed. These conditions will ever be present so long as the conditions under which the House works remain unchanged. In other words, the revolution has curtailed the power of the Speaker in his relation with the Committee on Rules, but the power of the committee remains unchanged. Or to put it differently, the House of Representatives, by removing the Speaker from the Committee on Rules, has not succeeded in gaining " control " over the committee.

The power formerly exercised by the Speaker as chairman of the Committee on Rules has only been transmitted from the Speaker to the Steering Committee,[1] of which the floor leader is chairman, and the chairman of the Committee on Rules. As Mr. Luce writes:

The reformers believed they had put an end to dictatorship. Yet that some few continue to guide is not to be questioned. What was really accomplished was to lessen the public knowledge of who those men were. Congressmen might know who should be rewarded or punished. Irresponsibility has been increased. . . . The Committee on Rules is no longer the organ of the Speaker. But the benefits of the change have not been conspicuous enough to impress anybody as important.[2]

The floor leader of the majority party and the chairman of the Committee on Rules have become powerful. During the last session of the Sixty-seventh Congress " a minority of two members practically controlled all legislation in the House." [3] The Woodruff resolution was a case in point.

[1] See *infra*, pp. 329 *et seq.* on a discussion of the Steering Committee.

[2] Luce, *op. cit.*, p. 483.

[3] *Cong. Record*, 68th Cong., 1st Sess., p. 1053.

On April 11, 1922, a resolution was introduced by Roy O. Woodruff, of Michigan, to investigate the Department of Justice. On May 3, Mr. Campbell, chairman of the Committee on Rules, was ordered by the committee to report the resolution to the House, which order he did not comply with. On May 26, Royal C. Johnson, of South Dakota, raised the question of privilege on the ground that " whenever a resolution is ordered reported by a committee, and that committee has spoken, the House is entitled to have the action of the committee." Mr. Johnson charged that the resolution was " quietly resting and reposing in the pocket " of Mr. Campbell. However, Mr. Walsh of Massachusetts raised a point of order which was sustained by Speaker Gillett:

The Committee on Rules has adopted within the last month a number of rules, including this, and one that is much older than this still is pending, and there are others which are a little older. . . . If we should adopt the doctrine when the Committee on Rules had adopted several rules any individual interested in one of these rules, as matter of the privilege of the House, has the right to raise and claim that the rule should immediately be reported, and that it was unreasonable for the chairman to withhold it, the business would be in confusion.[1]

The power of the chairman of the committee seems to have no limit. To the house, Mr. Campbell said in connection with the case of the Woodruff resolution that he was " answerable to his committee " and " to the majority of the House." [2] "Even though every member wants this resolution," Mr. Campbell declared with an air of complacency,

[1] An appeal was taken from the ruling but the motion was laid on the table by a vote of 149 to 114. *Cong. Record*, 67th Cong., 2nd Sess., pp. 7741-5.

[2] *Ibid.*, p. 7745.

" what will that avail you. I have the resolution in my pocket and shall keep it there." [1]   To the members of the Committee on Rules, Mr. Campbell was even more positive: " You can go to ——; it makes no difference what a majority of you decide; if it meets with my disapproval, it shall not be done; I am the committee; in me reposes absolute obstructive power." [2]   Later the Committee on Rules met to rescind its action ordering the resolution to be reported. So the resolution was never reported.

In the same Congress Mr. Campbell refused to report two bills of importance under special order. One was the national prohibition bill. Mr. Volstead, chairman of the Committee on Judiciary, having reported the bill to the House, applied to the Committee on Rules for a special order for its immediate consideration. Mr. Campbell refused to grant the request on the ground that there were " too many things in the bill." He made it plain, however, that he would report the bill under a special order only if the Committee on Judiciary accepted the several amendments which he proposed to it. The bill was finally considered under a motion to suspend the rules.[3] On June 28, 1921, Mr. Britten of Illinois, a stalwart Republican, complained:

. . . Now, three or four men control absolutely everything that comes before the House. That was illustrated yesterday in the case of the Volstead bill. The Committee on Rules says, " You must not bring in this bill," or " You must not bring that bill. We will substitute one of our own." The Committee

---

[1] *Searchlight*, vol. vi, no. 12, p. 5.

[2] *Ibid.*, p. 6; also see *ibid.*, vol. vii, no. 1, pp. 15-21. The confession of the futility of the revolution in 1910 by John Nelson, himself a leading insurgent, was interesting. He said that the " evils " after the March revolution were the pocket veto of the chairman of the Committee on Rules. *Cong. Record*, 68th Cong., 1st Sess., p. 962.

[3] *Cong. Record*, 67th Cong., 1st Sess., p. 3095.

on Rules dominated the situation entirely, and said that the House would get its amended Volstead bill or none.[1]

Then the Muscle Shoals bill. It went to the Committee on Rules for a special order, but was pocketed by Mr. Campbell. At one of the meetings of the committee a minority member made a motion that the bill be reported under a special order for immediate action by the House. Whereupon a motion to adjourn was made and the committee voted to adjourn. On the floor of the House Mr. Garner of Texas asked Mr. Campbell why the rule was not reported. In reply Mr. Campbell stated: " I have only five minutes. Laughter. I will state to the gentleman from Texas, that one of the purposes was to give the gentleman from Texas an opportunity to read the bill and the report." [2]

Moreover, the Committee on Rules reported bills which had never been referred for its consideration. And more than once the committee brought in a special order for a bill which had not even been introduced to the House. As to the latter, the Ship Purchase Bill is a case in point. The bill was presented to and " passed " by the Democratic caucus on the evening of February 15, 1915, and the following morning the Committee on Rules reported a special order for immediate consideration. Before the adjournment of the day the bill was passed by the House.[3]

In the Sixty-second Congress, not far from the time of

[1] *Cong. Record*, 67th Cong., 1st Sess., p. 3170.

[2] *Ibid.*, 2nd Sess., p. 9125.

[3] Haines, *Your Congress* (Washington, D. C., 1915), p. 95. *Cf. Cong. Record*, 63rd Cong., 3rd Sess., pp. 3875-3923. On January 18, 1924, the House passed an amendment to the rule with the proviso that the Committee on Rules can not call up a report for consideraion on the same day it is presented unless otherwise decided by a two-thirds vote. This amendment shall not apply during the last three days of a session of Congress. Rule xi, 56.

the March revolution, the Committee on Rules reported a special order for the consideration of an appropriation bill.[1] The bill was never considered before—and much less was it referred to—the committee. In reply to interrogations from members of the House on the floor, Mr. Henry of Texas, chairman of the committee, said: "I saw nearly every member of the Committee on Rules, I think nine out of eleven on yesterday, and the majority agreed to report the resolution. It is a fact that the committee did not actually assemble in the committee room but they were on the floor of the House."[2]

However, in view of the "highly technical" objection, Mr. Henry withdrew the resolution. Later in the Sixty-seventh Congress Bertrand H. Snell of New York, the ranking majority member on the Committee on Rules, brought in a privileged report for an "immediate" consideration of a bill to continue certain land offices. Louis C. Crampton of Michigan raised the point of order that the committee had no jurisdiction over the bill, as it was neither introduced to the House nor was it referred to the Committee on Rules for action. What was the most important thing was the decision of Speaker Gillett in overruling the point of order:

> The Committee on Rules is an executive organ of the majority of the House. If it were held that it could not act until the subject had been referred to it, then it would be impossible for it in the morning before a session to make a decision and bring in a rule which is often necessary and desirable at the first meeting of the House.[3]

By custom the chairman of the committee is the sole person authorized to call up a resolution. In the Sixty-

[1] *Cong. Record*, 62nd Cong., 2nd Sess., p. 5889.

[2] *Ibid.*, p. 6889.

[3] *Cong. Record*, 67th Cong., 2nd Sess., pp. 5976-7.

second Congress, on a Calendar Wednesday, the call fell on the Committee on Rules. Mr. Henry, chairman of the committee, asked unanimous consent to pass the committee without prejudice. There were then two " propositions " reported from the committee, and James Mann, of Illinois, inquired if Mr. Henry ever intended to call up one of the " propositions." " Well," replied Mr. Henry, " I may and I may not. I had not made up my mind that I shall call it up." [1] And in the Sixty-seventh Congress Finis Garrett, of Tennessee, asserted that " the Committee on Rules never within my experience upon it, has passed a resolution authorizing or directing any particular member of that committee to call up a resolution reported by the committee." [2] It was not until the Sixty-eighth Congress that the House passed an amendment to the rule which provided that any member *designated* by the Committee on Rules may after a lapse of nine days call up for consideration a rule or order reported from the committee.[3]

The difficulty in securing a quorum in the Committee on Rules presents itself when the membership becomes large.[4] Mr. Campbell found consolation in the fact that the difficulty "did not begin in either the Sixty-sixth or the Sixty-seventh Congresses " when he was chairman of the committee, but it was "quite as manifest in the Sixty-fourth and Sixty-fifth Congresses " when the Democratic party was at the helm in the House. No one would be so prejudiced as to think that in matters of maladministration the Republican party is behind the Democratic party, or vice versa. In point of fact,

---

[1] *Cong. Record*, 62nd Cong., 3rd Sess., pp. 1586-7.

[2] *Cong. Record*, 67th Cong., 2nd Sess., p. 8924.

[3] Rule xi, 56.

[4] "A majority of the committee constitutes a quorum for business." Jefferson's *Manual*, xxvi, 402. However, there is no quorum rule in the House for the committees.

the choice is like that "between the devil and deep sea." As to the reason for the difficulty in getting a quorum, Mr. Campbell explained that, in a majority of cases, meetings are called all of a sudden, that members of the committee were either "in the departments" or "attending to other duties," and that "in some instances they [members of the committee] do not get notice of the meeting." [1]

The difference between the system prior to 1910 and the one since that time is then apparent. Prior to 1910 the Speaker was chairman of the Committee on Rules, but he had himself never appeared on the floor to report a special order from the committee. Nor had he ever called up a report from the committee for consideration during the

[1] The occasion upon which Mr. Campbell made this statement was when he reported, May 3, 1921, a special order for the consideration of the budget bill. The bill was reported without the action of a quorum of the committee. Mr. Campbell said: "Under strict construction of the rules of the House this bill could not be brought in here today, because there was not a majority of the Committee on Rules present to report it, but we will waive that, because this side of the House is in favor of the legislation. *Cong. Record*, 67th Cong., 1st Sess., pp. 976, 974, 979. Mr. Crampton of Michigan also brought to light the fact that the bill to continue certain land offices referred to was reported under a special order from the Committee on Rules in the absence of a quorum. The committee then consisted of twelve members. Six of them were not in the Capitol and another was reported to have been absent. Mr. Campbell did not deny "the question about the fact. There was not a quorum of the committee present. That is a fact... The presumption, however, has been when any committee of this House has transacted business and the question of quorum not being raised, that it had the right to transact business that was ransacted, just as the House passed bills every week when a quorum is not present." Referring to the Committee on Rules during the administration of the Democratic party, Mr. Campbell said: "During the period of war, as a member of the Committee on Rules, I met with the gentleman from North Carolina (Mr. Pou) and one or two others. Much of the most important legislation of this Republic... was brought on the floor of the House... when sometimes there were not to exceed three members of the committee." *Ibid.*, 2nd Sess., pp. 8925-8929.

morning hour. The functions were usually performed by the ranking majority member of the committee and were only occasionally done by the other majority member.[1] No case has ever come to the surface where a " pocket veto " was exercised by the two majority members of the committee in halting a bill from being reported for consideration under a special rule. On the other hand, it was very improbable that a bill could be reported for " immediate " consideration from the committee without the consent of the Speaker, as chairman of the committee, even though the two majority members were in favor of its being reported. The fact that these two majority members were appointed by the Speaker was important. As Mr. Bailey had asserted, " the Committee on Rules is considered the Speaker's official family, and no gentleman of the Speaker's party would serve upon it unless he could support the Speaker's policy." [2] Moreover, with his " two assistants," the two majority members on the committee, who were always present on the floor of the House, the Speaker could call a meeting of the committee whenever exigency demanded, and the minority members on the committee were not usually needed even to make a quorum.[3]

Since 1910 the power to control the action of the House is divided between the Steering Committee and the Committee on Rules with power in the chairman to pocket-veto their decision. In the words of Mr. Campbell, chairman of the Committee on Rules from the Sixty-sixth to Sixty-seventh Congresses, " the Committee on Rules takes into account the bills that the steering committee has sifted into a place for privileged consideration. Then the Committee

[1] As to the role of the minority members on the committee, see *supra*, p. 133.

[2] *Cong. Record*, 56th Cong., 1st Sess., p. 7.

[3] See *supra*, p. 133.

on Rules provides the machinery whereby the bill may be considered." [1] Finally, the chairman of the committee may report or may not report a bill thus decided upon by the Steering Committee and the Committee on Rules, and when there is more than one bill, he may report any one when he sees fit. Under this system the Speaker has no power over the Committee on Rules, except whatever outside pressure he, as a party leader, can exert. Nor can the Speaker refuse recognition to the chairman of the committee [2] when he rises to report a bill for immediate consideration, even though the Speaker may object to the bill in question. In other words, the revolution in 1910 developed power in an independent and " elected " chairman of the Committee on Rules and the rise of the caucus during the Democratic administration and of the Steering Committee during the Republican administration in the House.

Since the March revolution special orders have become more numerous. During the Speakership of Mr. Cannon [1] the number reached fifty-eight. From the Sixty-second to Sixty-fifth Congresses that number was exactly doubled— reaching one hundred and sixteen, and during the three succeeding Congresses the figure increased to one hundred and forty. The largest number of special orders ever reported in one session by the committee during the stewardship of " Czar " Cannon was only sixteen, whereas in the Sixty-seventh Congress thirty orders were reported in one session. The fact becomes all the more interesting as one compares the number of special orders reported in the Sixty-first and Sixty-seventh Congress with the number of bills introduced during these two Congresses. [3] Still more interesting is the

[1] *Cong. Record*, 67th Cong., 2nd Sess., p. 8052.

[2] See Rule xi, 56.

[3] The Fifty-eighth, Fifty-ninth, Sixtieth and Sixty-first Congresses.

[4] In the Sixty-first Congress 33,015 bills were introduced, out of which

fact that about half of the bills and resolutions reported for consideration under special order failed of passage either in the House or in the Senate, while a few of them were pocketed or vetoed by the President and still fewer died in conference committee.[1] For instance: out of the fifty-eight

2,302 were reported, while in the Sixty-seventh Congress the total number of bills introduced was 14,475, out of which 1,763 were reported. For the special orders reported during these two Congresses and also other Congresses since the Fifty-eighth in which Mr. Cannon was elected Speaker, see the following table.

Special orders from the Committee on Rules since the Fifty-eighth Congress (*cf. supra*, p. 115, footnote 3):

Congress	Number of special orders reported				
	1st Session	2nd Session	3rd Session	4th Session	Total
58............	1	11	1	..	13
59............	16	3	..	.	19
60............	6	3	..	..	9
61............	5	6	6	..	17
62............	8	11	4	..	23
63............	6	15	5	..	26
64............	17	13	..	..	30
65............	3	24	10	..	37
66............	22	12	9	..	43
67 *...........	26	30	1	12	69
68............	19	9	..	..	28
69............	27	14	..	..	41

* The Sixty-seventh Congress met under "abnormal" conditions due to the World War, and the business in the House during that Congress was enormous. It was but natural that the number of the special orders reported by the Committee on Rules was greater than what was reported either before or after the Sixty-seventh one.

[1] Bills and resolutions enacted by way of special order are indicated as follows:

special orders [1] during the Speakership of Mr. Cannon only twenty-eight bills and two resolutions succeeded in finding their places on the statute book.[2]   And this number is cer-

	Congresses											
	58	59	60	61	62	63	64	65	66	67	68	69
Total of bills & resolutions reported	13	17	9	16	32	33	31	36	39	77	28	37
Failing of passage in House	..	..	1	2	4	8	7	3	..	11	8	9
Failing of passage in Senate	5	3	..	3	9	7	5	7	10	9	6	12
Died in conference committee	..	..	..	..	..	1	1	..	1			
Vetoed or pocketed by President	..	..	..	..	4	.	..	2	5	1	..	1
Resolutions on order of business or suspension of rules passed	..	2	3	2	1	..	..	1	..	2	1	
Resolutions on investigations passed	..	..	..	2	6	..	1	1	..	2		
Bills or resolutions unclassified	1	..	..	1	1							
Bills & resolutions enacted into laws or agreed to	7	12	5	6	7	17	17	22	23	52	13	15

It must be noted that the number of special orders, as was shown on page 155, is not corresponding with the number of bills and resolutions reported for consideration.   The reasons are: (1) sometimes several bills were reported for consideration under one special order; (2) sometimes a bill was twice reported under a special order; and (3) at other times a special order was reported for the consideration of the conference report on a bill which had been previously considered in the same manner.

It must be noted, moreover, that too much stress ought not to be placed on the contrast of these figures, for, as a matter of fact, there has been a steady tendency to have all the important bills reach the House through the Committee on Rules.

[1] These fifty-eight special orders consisted of forty-four reports for the consideration of bills (three of them were reports on conference reports), while the rest were reports for the consideration of joint resolutions, order of business, of bills on the Private Calendar and of the suspension of rules.

[2] Those bills and resolutions which were enacted by way of special orders, were as follows: The Celebration at Portland, Oregon, of the one hundredth anniversary of the Exploration of the Oregon country (Public no. 111), 33 *Statutes at Large*, p. 175; regulating shipping in trade between ports of the U. S. A. and those in the Philippine Islands (Public no. 114), 33 *Stat. L.*, p. 181; employment of vessels of the country for public purposes (Public no. 198), 33 *Stat. L.*, p. 518; creating a commission to consider and to recommend legislation for the develop-

tainly small in contrast with the 12,375 laws and resolutions enacted during the same period. This fact shows that a bill or resolution brought before the House for consideration under the special order cannot be sure of its passage through the legislative mills of Congress. Moreover, it shows that the Speaker—and in this case it was Mr. Cannon—had not, as it was commonly supposed, " the absolute control through the Committee on Rules " in steering the course of a bill to the road of enactment.

ment of merchant marine (Public no. 245), 33 *Stat. L.*, p. 561; providing for the manufacture, distribution and supply of electric power and light on the island of Oahau, Territory of Hawaii (Public no. 128), 33 *Stat. L.*, p. 227; for the maintenance and supply of fuel and illuminating gas and its by-products in Honolulu (Public no. 129), 33 *Stat. L.*, p. 231; appropriations for the Post-Office Department (Public no. 191), 33 *Stat. L.*, p. 429; the statehood bill on the admission of Arizona and New Mexico (Public no. 234), 34 *Stat. L.*, p. 267; the pure food bill (Public no. 384), 34 *Stat. L.*, p. 768; on hazing at Naval Academy (Public no. 87), 34 *Stat. L.*, p. 104; the immigration bill (Public no. 96), 34 *Stat. L.*, p. 898; extending the time limit for the completion of the Alaska central railway (Public no. 390), 34 *Stat. L.*, p. 798; amending the anti-trust act of 1887 (Public no. 337), 34 *Stat. L.*, p. 584; appropriations for legislative, executive and judicial expenses of the Government (Public no. 267), 34 *Stat. L.*, p. 389; appropriations for the Post-Office Department (Public no. 297), 34 *Stat. L.*, p. 467; increasing the limit of cost of certain public buildings (Public no. 385), 34 *Stat. L.*, p. 772; appropriations for Post-Office Department (Public no. 172), 34 *Stat. L.*, p. 1205; the sixteen-hour law for railway employees (Public no. 274), 34 *Stat. L.*, p. 1415; appropriations for the Government of the District of Columbia (Public no. 139), 35 *Stat. L.*, p. 274; an army appropriation bill (Public no. 112), 35 *Stat. L.*, p. 106; a naval appropriation bill (Public no. 115), 35 *Stat. L.*, p. 127; the Brownsville Affray bill (Public no. 318), 35 *Stat. L.*, p. 836; reducing the salary of the Secretary of the State (Public no. 235), 35 *Stat. L.*, p. 626; amendment relating to premiums of bonding companies (Public no. 6), 36 *Stat. L.*, p. 118; the thirteenth census bill (Public no. 2), 36 *Stat. L.*, p. 1; the Payne tariff bill (Public no. 5), 35 *Stat. L.*, p. 11; authorizing advance to the " Reclamation Fund " (Public no. 289), 36 *Stat. L.*, p. 835; establishing postal savings depositories (Public no. 9078), 36 *Stat. L.*, p. 814.

The resolutions were: the Senate Joint resolution for the purchase of material and equipment for the use in the construction of Panama Canal

As will be shown,[1] a wide range of bills since the Fifty-

(Public Res. no. 35), 34 *Stat. L.*, p. 835; Senate Joint Resolution to re-affirm the boundary lines between Texas and New Mexico (Public Res. no. 57), 36 *Stat. L.*, p. 1454.

The table showing the classes of bills and resolutions reported under special order since the Fifty-eighth Congress:

Class of Bills and Resolutions	Congresses											
	58	59	60	61	62	63	64	65	66	67	68	69
Agriculture	..	..	..	2	2	..	3	2	2	3	4	5
Appropriations	..	..	2	..	2	3	3	2	2	5	..	1
Banking & Currency	..	..	..	..	1	2	1	2	2	8	1	1
Budget	..	..	..	..	..	..	..	..	..	1	1	
Census	..	..	..	1								
Claims	..	..	..	..	..	..	..	..	..	..	..	1
Civil Service	..	..	..	..	..	..	..	..	..	2	1	
District of Columbia	..	..	..	..	..	..	1	..	..	1	1	
Education	..	..	.	..	..	..	..	..	3	..	1	1
Election	..	..	1	..	1	1						
Expenditures in Executive Departments	..	..	..	..	..	..	..	..	2			
Foreign Affairs	..	..	..	..	..	..	2	2	3	1	4	2
Immigration	..	1	..	..	1	1	1	2	3	2	1	1
Indian Affairs	1	..	..	..	..	2						
Industrial Arts	1	..	..	1	..	..	..	..	..	1		
Insular Affairs	1	..	..	..	..	..	1	..	..	3		
Interstate & Foreign Commerce	1	4	..	1	2	4	4	5	2	9	3	2
Investigations	..	..	..	2	6	..	..	..	..	..	..	1
Irrigation	..	..	..	..	..	..	..	..	1	..	1	1
Judiciary	..	1	..	1	4	2	3	2	5	4	4	6
Merchant Marine	3	1	..	..	6	..	1	..	1	1	..	1
Military Affairs	..	..	1	..	..	1	3	3	4	8	2	3
Militia	..	..	..	1								
Mines & Mining	..	..	..	..	..	..	1	..	2	1		
Naval Affairs	..	1	1	..	..	2	2	1	2	3	1	4
Patents	..	..	..	..	..	..	..	..	1	1		
Pensions	..	..	..	..	3	..	..	2				
Post Offices	1	2	..	1	1	2	1	1				
Printing	..	..	..	..	..	..	..	..	..	..	1	
Public Buildings	..	2	..	..	..	..	1	4	2	2	1	
Public Lands	..	..	..	..	..	3	..	..	1	2		
Revision of Laws	..	..	1									
Revenue	1	1	..	3	1	3	1	1	1	9	1	2
Rivers & Harbors	..	..	..	..	..	..	..	..	..	1	1	1
Roads	..	..	..	..	..	1	1	..	..	..	..	2
Territories	3	2	..	..	..	1	..	..	2	1		
War Claims	..	..	..	..	..	..	..	..	..	..	..	1
Weights & Measures	..	..	..	..	..	..	..	..	..	3		
Woman Suffrage	..	..	..	..	..	1	..	1				
Order of Business	..	2	2	..	1	..	..	..	1	..	1	
Suspension of Rules	..	..	1	2	..	..	..	..	..	1	1	
Resolutions of various nature	1	..	..	1	1	..	3	1	..	2	1	3
Total	13	17	9	16	32	33	31	36	39	77	28	37

eighth Congress has been brought in by special orders for consideration in the House. A bill is under special order for immediate consideration partly because of the importance of the bill itself but largely in response to the demand of political exigencies. It is interesting to note that even appropriation and revenue bills which have privileged status under the rules of the House,[1] have at times traveled the same road. A special order from the Committee on Rules can do two things for an appropriation or a revenue bill— prescribe the conditions under which debate on such bill is to be held and amendments be made or, when the bill is returned from the Senate with amendments, provide for nonconcurrence *in gross* and ask for the appointment of a conference committee.[2] Consequently the special order has been resorted to since 1896 to speed the passage of tariff bills. The three great tariff bills, the Payne tariff bill of 1909, the Underwood tariff bill of 1913 and the Fordney tariff bill of 1921 were considered and passed under special orders. In the debate under the five-minute rule [3] in the Committee

---

[1] See Rule xi, 56.

[2] A recent case occurred in the first session of the Sixty-ninth Congress. It was the independent offices appropriation bill from the Committee on Appropriations. After the bill was returned from the Senate with amendments, the Committee on Rules brought in a special order providing that it be taken from the Speaker's table and that a conference committee be appointed by the Speaker. The managers of the conference committee "be given authority, as provided by clause 2 of Rule xx, to agree to the amendment of the Senate No. 19, with or without amendment." Mr. Burton of Ohio, the ranking majority member of the Committee on Rules, presented the rule and said: "The ordinary request was made that the House disagree to the Senate amendments and ask for a conference. That request for unanimous consent was refused. The basis of the refusal is a difference of opinion in regard to two amendments by the Senate." After much debate and several roll calls the special order was passed by a majority vote of the House, thereby depriving the House of the right to consider the amendments. *Cong. Record*, 69th Cong., 1st Sess., pp. 6252-6261.

[3] The Payne tariff bill had about two weeks of general debate—from

of the Whole House on the state of the Union on the Payne and Fordney tariff bills the restrictions of the special orders were almost identical in words: both of them provided that "committee amendments to any part of the bill shall be in order at any time" and preference "shall be given to amendments to paragraphs" as prescribed; that "said specified amendments shall take precedence of committee amendments" to other paragraphs; that "consideration of the bill for amendment shall continue" till a certain hour of day, "at which time the said bill, with all amendments that shall have been adopted by the Committee of the Whole on the state of the Union, shall be reported to the House;" and that "the previous question shall then be considered as ordered on said amendments and said bill to its engrossment, third reading, and final passage." [1] The Underwood tariff bill was not considered in this wise. However, on one point the provisions of special orders for all the three tariff bills agreed: they all provided for nonconcurrence *in gross* in the

March 22 to April 5, 1909. See *Cong. Record*, 61st Cong., 1st Sess., pp. 139, 1112. The Underwood tariff bill had five days of general debate with night sessions. See *Cong. Record*, 63rd Cong., 1st Sess., pp. 316-318. But general debate is usually not confined to the pending bill. "General debate," Mr. Underwood said on April 5, 1909, "is no consideration of the bill." "When," Mr. Underwood continued, "you come to consider a great appropriation bill or a great revenue bill the only way the House can express the sentiments of the country and the Members can express the sentiments of their constituencies, is to consider the items contained in the bill item by item." *Cong. Record*, 61st Cong., 1st Sess., p. 1113. The Fordney tariff bill was considered under general debate from July 7 to July 14, 1921, but it was provided in the special order that the "general debate shall be confined to the bill." *Cong. Record*, 67th Cong., 1st Sess., pp. 3453, 3607.

[1] Other provisions in the rule for the consideration of the Fordney tariff bill were that "clause 3 of Rule xxi shall not apply to committee amendments," and that this bill "shall be the continuing order until its consideration is concluded, subject only to conference reports, privileged matters on the Speaker's table, and the reports from the Committee on Rules." *Ibid.*, pp. 3607, 3608.

Senate amendments to these bills, and without intervening motion for the appointment of conference committee by the Speaker.[1]

The passage of the bill H. R. 12812 to reduce duties on the manufacture of cotton and the Senate amendments thereto under a special order in the first session of the Sixty-second Congress was but one more proof that the removal of the Speaker from the Committee on Rules did not loose the grip of the committee upon the House. In the special order it was provided that " there shall be four hours of general debate on the Senate amendments, at the end of which time the previous question shall be considered as ordered on the bill and amendments to its final passage, and that the vote shall be taken on one motion to concur in all the Senate amendments without consideration in the Committee of the Whole House on the state of the Union, and without other intervening motions, except one motion to recommit shall be in order." [2] Mr. Madison of Kansas, in opposing the special order, declared:

. . . The chairman of the committee [on rules] said that he would give me all the time, because he feels secure in the fact that anything that is offered by the Democratic Committee on Rules will be taken without question by the gentleman on the other side. . . . It makes no difference to this country from whence the tyranny proceeds, whether from the one man in the chair or by the several seated around the table in the room of the Committee on Rules.[3]

[1] For special order for the Payne tariff bill see *Cong. Record*, 61st Cong., 1st Sess., p. 4364; for the Underwood tariff bill see *Cong. Record*, 63rd Cong., 1st Sess., p. 4713; for Fordney tariff bill see *Cong. Record*, 67th Cong., 2nd Sess., p. 11652. The Payne tariff bill had 801 Senate amendments and the Underwood tariff bill 676 Senate amendments. The Fordney tariff bill was voted to recommit to the conference committee with instructions. See *ibid.*, p. 12531.

[2] *Cong. Record*, 62nd Cong., 1st Sess., p. 4312.

[3] *Ibid.*, p. 4312.

The reconstruction of the Committee on Rules in 1910 resulted in the shortening of the duration of membership on the committee. From 1890 to 1910 only nine Republicans and eleven Democrats were members of the committee. Of these members the maximum length of service in the House was eighteen terms and the minimum was five terms, with an average length of nine terms for each of them. Without exception, all of those who had served on the committee were leaders of their respective parties, whose names were known throughout the length and breadth of the country. Examination shows, furthermore, that they had served on an average more than five and a half terms on other committees before their entrance to the Committee on Rules. Since 1910 there have been fifteen Democrats and nineteen Republicans, with two members listed at one time with the Democrats and at another with the Republicans.[1] The length of their services ranges from one to thirteen terms. The average duration of membership on the committee during this period was less than four and a half terms. Few, if any, had been much known to their fellow Congressmen— and much less to the general public—before their advance to the committee. The more recent custom prohibiting a member from serving on more than one of the ten or twelve " exclusive " committees [2] has had a decided effect upon the personal distinction of the committee. Since 1910 the great committees of Ways and Means, Appropriations and Judiciary are no longer, as they had been before, the stepping-stones to the committee. Whether this lowering of personal distinction is a gain to the House of Representatives still remains to be seen.

" The function of the Committee on Rules," wrote Mr.

[1] The " Progressives " are counted as Republicans.

[2] See *supra*, p. 69 (footnote).

Hinds, " is remedial." [1]   Unimportant in the early days of the House, the committee has, with the growth both in volume and diversity of the business in the House, gradually but steadily risen to a place of unusual importance, as a means of expediting desired legislation.   Usually it reports, by way of a special order, bills introduced to the House, referred to appropriate committees for consideration, reported therefrom and placed on calendars in accordance with the nature of business.   In fact " most of the bills which it assists might be passed in another way."   Mr. Hinds continued, " to use a commonplace illustration; the Committee on Rules, by the special order, takes a bill up on the elevator instead of requiring it to be carried up by the stairs." [2] Prior to March, 1910, the Speaker appointed the committee with himself as its chairman.   It had power and influence unequaled by any other committee in the House.   In the small size of the membership of the committee and the presence of the Speaker as the guiding-hand lay the secret of the power wielded by the committee.   As a legislative organ, it was efficient, smooth-running, though, to be sure, at the expense of the " rights " and " privileges " of the individual members of the House.

However, in March, 1910, the structure of the committee was torn asunder by the revolutionary storm surging in the House.   Since then it has been an " elective " committee without the presence of the Speaker.   The membership of the committee has also been increased.   With these changes, also, responsibility was divided.   As has been shown, there have been, since March, 1910, more abuses committed by the chairman of the committee—abuses at which even the Czar Cannon would look with disfavor.   The immensity of the business in the House meanwhile has made the committee

[1] *Cong. Record*, 60th Cong., 2nd Sess., p. 588.
[2] *Ibid.*, p. 588.

more and more indispensable to the wheels of legislation. To quote Mr. Campbell:

The business now coming to the Committee on Rules practically covers the business of the House.   Even the Committee on Ways and Means, the Committee on Appropriations, committees that report privileged business, now come to the Committee on Rules for rules governing the consideration of matters that they have reported out.   Practically every resolution, every bill from every committee of the House, is referred to the Committee on Rules and a special rule asked for its consideration.[1]

[1] *Cong. Record*, 67th Cong., 2nd Sess., p. 8051.

CHAPTER IV

Power Through Recognition

WE have thus far seen both the rise and " fall " of the power of the Speaker in his relation to the Standing Committees of the House in general and the Committee on Rules in particular. We have also seen the introduction in the Sixty-first and the subsequent Congresses of the reforms which aimed at the " destruction " of that power. It now remains for us to see another aspect of the power of the Speaker, that is, the power through recognition.

The House of Representatives adopted as early as 1789 the rule that " when two or more members rise at once the Speaker shall name the member who is first to speak." [1] This was the first rule set up by the House with reference to recognition. But in actual practice, as the business of the House during its early stages of growth proceeded on the presentation by individual members, the Speaker recognized the member who rose first, and in case of doubt, an appeal might be made, as it has actually been made, from his recognition. [2] The rules provided, moreover, that " when a Member desires to speak or deliver any matter to the House, he

---

[1] Hinds, *op. cit.*, v, 4978. The rule of the Continental Congress provided that "when two persons rise together, the President shall name the person to speak." *Ibid.*, v, 4978; also see Rule xiv, 2.

[2] Hinds, *op. cit.*, ii, 1429-1434. According to the old Parliamentary Law it was provided that " If two or more rise to speak nearly together, the Speaker determines who was first up, and calls by name, whereupon he proceeds, unless he voluntarily sits down and gives way to the other. But sometimes the House does not acquiesce in the Speaker's decision, in which case the question is put, ' Which member was first up? ' " Jefferson's *Manual*, xvii.

shall rise and respectfully address himself to ' Mr. Speaker,' and on being recognized, may address the House from any place on the floor, or from the Clerk's desk." [1]   Relying on this rule, Speaker Grow held that a member, in addressing the House, must also address the Chair.   On one occasion he even refused to recognize a member who spoke for several minutes with his back to the Chair.[2]   Again in the Fifty-fifth Congress, when the House was about to consider a postal bill, the question pertaining to the division of time for debate was raised.   Whereupon Speaker Reed ruled:

Under the rules of the House, unless the House unanimously agrees to the contrary, the Speaker recognizes the members who address the House, and it has usually been understood that the Speaker will endeavour to see that the debate is fairly conducted. This is a part of the duties of his office.[3]

The general and broad statement of the rule governing recognition soon gave rise to the interpretation that to " name the Member who shall be first to speak " is a matter of discretion with the Speaker.   Thus in the Thirty-second Congress when a point of order was once raised that a certain member, not having risen at the time he addressed the Chair, was not entitled to the floor, the Speaker *pro tempore* (Mr. Stuart of Michigan) held that " The rules confer authority upon the Speaker to name who is entitled to the floor."   An appeal was taken from the ruling, but the House sustained the Speaker's decision.[4]   In the same Congress Speaker Blaine gave the following ruling:

The rules provide that the Member first addressing the Chair

---

[1] Rule xiv, 1.
[2] Hinds, *op. cit.*, v, 4980.
[3] *Cong. Record*, 55th Cong., 2nd Sess., p. 2328.
[4] Hinds, *op. cit.*, ii, 1422.

shall be recognized; but when fifteen or twenty address him at the same moment, some other mode of assigning the floor must of necessity be resorted to; and there is none so fair as to award precedence according to the relative importance of the motions.[1]

The principal causes conducive to the broad interpretation of the rule of recognition were, however, due to the increase of membership as well as that of the business of the House. As has been shown, in the early history of the House, when the business of the House was done upon presentation by individual members, the Speaker recognized the member who rose first. But, as the membership of the House was enlarged with the corresponding increase of its business, recognition could no longer depend on the quickness of an individual member in catching the Speaker's eye, but must be used to assure orderly consideration of business under the rules. That the Speaker was not obliged to heed the claims of members as individuals, was plainly stated in 1879 in a report by Mr. Garfield, of Ohio, from the Committee on Rules, which declared that " in the nature of the case discretion must be lodged with the presiding officer." [2] In the following year Speaker Randall ruled that " the right of recognition is with the Chair under the rules and under the practice " of the House.[3]

The power of recognition was further augmented in 1881 when Speaker Randall of Pennsylvania declined in that year an appeal on the question of recognition and ruled:

There is really no power in the House itself to appeal from a recognition of the Chair. The right of recognition is just as absolute in the Chair as the judgment of the Supreme Court

[1] Hinds, *op. cit.*, ii, 1422.

[2] *Ibid.*, ii, 1424.

[3] Follett, *op. cit.*, p. 250.

of the United States is absolute as to the interpretation of the law.[1]

Speaker Keifer presided over the House from 1881 to 1883, and made one more decision to strengthen the power of recognition. In ruling out an appeal by Mr. Cannon who twenty years later, as Speaker, ruled the House with an iron hand, for not having been recognized, Speaker Keifer said that "the question of recognition does not admit of an appeal. . . . No appeal of that kind has ever been entertained by any Speaker."[2]

When Speaker Reed came to the chair, the principle that the power of recognition is not subject to any appeal was already well established. In the Fifty-first Congress Mr. Reed, in declining to entertain an appeal by Mr. Springer of Illinois, held that "the Chair does not think there can be any appeal from a decision upon a question of recognition. That is very well known."[3]   With the election of Mr. Car-

[1] Hinds, *op. cit.*, ii, 1425. Under the earlier practice of the House appeals were made from the decisions of the Speaker on questions of recognition. See *ibid.*, ii, 1429-1434. Speaker White once ruled, however, that the right of recognition was with the House, and that "the Speaker merely decided conflicting claims to the floor in the first instance, but that if he transcended justice, appeal might at any time be taken from his decision." Follett, *op. cit.*, p. 258.

[2] Hinds, *op. cit.*, ii, 1426. Speaker Keifer was, however, historically in error. See footnote above.

[3] Hinds, *op. cit.*, ii, 1427. In the same Congress when a naval appropriation bill was under consideration in the Committee of the Whole House on the state of the Union. Mr. Vandiver, of Missouri, offered an amendment to the bill. Mr. Dayton, of West Virginia, made the point of order against the amendment, whereupon Mr. Underwood, of Alabama, asked recognition to speak on the point of order. The chairman (Mr. Payne of New York) of the committee recognized Mr. Underwood for ten minutes, but the latter protested that he could not be thus limited:

"The Chairman. The Chair declines to recognize the gentleman otherwise than as he has already recognized him.

"Mr. Underwood. I wish to appeal from the authority of the Chair to limit the time on this..."

Mr. Payne declined to entertain the appeal. *Ibid.*, v, 6946.

lisle of Kentucky to the Speakership, this principle was, however, broadened in its uses. For hitherto Speakers had used the power of recognition with the distinct view of carrying out the party wishes, but Speaker Carlisle thought it should be exercised " in accordance with the Speaker's individual judgment." [1] The Blair Educational Bill was a case in point. This bill was pending during the whole of Speaker Carlisle's administration, although it passed the Senate three times. [2] But the most important case was perhaps a bill to repeal the internal revenue tax on tobacco, over which a bitter controversy raged, as was evidenced by the exchange of correspondence between Speaker Carlisle and his fellow Democratic members of the House. [3]

The custom which required members to seek previously the Speaker's permission in order to address the House, was initiated by Speaker Carlisle, [4] who was, by the way, a Democrat. The Republican Speakers who succeeded him were never slow to use this practice to the advantage of themselves and their party. Thus on May 7, 1900, when William Sulzer of New York claimed recognition, Speaker Henderson ruled that " the gentleman was not recognized, and the Chair may as well state that the Chair will recognize no gentleman unless he has some knowledge of what is going to be called up."

Mr. Sulzer. I would like to have the resolution read.
The Speaker. The gentleman has not been recognized.
A little later Mr. Sulzer rose again.
Mr. Sulzer. Mr. Speaker—
The Speaker. For what purpose does the gentleman rise?

[1] Follett, *op. cit.*, p. 262.
[2] *Ibid.*, p. 262.
[3] *Ibid.*, pp. 262-265.
[4] McClellan, " Leadership in Congress," *Scribner's*, vol. xlvix, p. 596.

Mr. Sulzer.   I rise for the purpose of moving a suspension of the rules, this being suspension day, for the purpose of passing a resolution sympathizing with the patriotic Boers in their struggle to maintain their freedom and independence.

The Speaker.   The Chair declines to recognize the gentleman from New York at this time.

Mr. Sulzer.   Does the Chair refuse to recognize me, because—

The Speaker.   The gentleman from New York is out of order.

Mr. Sulzer.   Mr. Speaker, I rise to make a parliamentary inquiry.

The Speaker.   The gentleman will state it.

Mr. Sulzer.   My parliamentary inquiry is, Have I no rights on the floor of this house, as a member, to move the suspension of the rules on suspension day?

The Speaker.   The gentleman is not making a parliamentary inquiry.   The Chair must exercise his duty to this House and recognize members upon matters which the Chair thinks should be considered.[1]

Later in the Fifty-seventh Congress Mr. Shafroth of Colorado threw more light on the Speaker's arbitrary power of recognition in connection with a Senate bill for a National Sanitarium at Hot Springs, South Dakota.   Mr. Shafroth secured the floor from Mr. Richardson of Tennessee who yielded it to the former, and said on the floor:

[1] *Cong. Record,* 56th Cong., 1st Sess., p. 5227.   In the Fifty-fourth Congress Mr. Reed was reelected to the Speakership.   In protesting against his arbitrary exercise of the power of recognition, Mr. Bell of Colorado, of the Populist party, said on the floor: " We have stood here during the last four weeks and pleaded with the Speaker and with the members leading this House for the majority, and not one member of the Populist party has been permitted by them during this session the privilege of addressing the House in his own time.   The few moments I obtained heretofore were from Judge Crisp and taken out of his time. We represent a constituency that casts 1,600,000 votes."   *Cong. Record,* 54th Cong., 1st Sess., p. 577.

The Committee on Military Affairs reported my bill [on the same subject] in the Fifty-sixth Congress and again reported it in this Congress. I hope, Mr. Speaker, to continue to press my pressure until I do get recognition in behalf of the same [bill which recommended the sanitarium to be built at Denver].

The following colloquy then occurred:

Mr. Maddox. Why is it you can not get recognition for your bill?

Mr. Shafroth. I do not know.

Mr. Maddox. Have your asked for it?

Mr. Shafroth. I think we have as favorable a place for a Soldier's Home as any place in the United States.

Mr. Maddox. But, I say, have you asked for it.

Mr. Shafroth. I have.

Mr. Sulzer. How many times? (Laughter.)

Mr. Shafroth. The Speaker treated me very frankly. He said he would consider the matter. (Laughter.) He wanted information as to the number of Homes.

Mr. Clayton. He said you were a good boy. (Laughter.)

Mr. Shafroth. He has not said he would not recognise me, and I am in hopes he will recognize me yet. (Laughter and Applause.)[1]

Speaker Cannon's manner of exercising the power of recognition can be, to a great extent, characterized by the following instance. In the Fifty-eighth Congress Mr. Lucking, of Michigan, attempted to recommit the Yakima Indian Reservation Bill with instructions and was not recognized for that purpose. But immediately Speaker Cannon recognized Mr. Grosvenor, of Ohio, when the latter rose to move to recommit the same bill. A point of order was made against Mr. Grosvenor's motion. Speaker Cannon, however, ruled that:

[1] *Cong. Record,* 57th Cong., 1st Sess., p. 5658.

The present occupant of the Chair, the Speaker of the House, follows the usual rule that has been obtained ever since he has been a member of the House, that the Chair chooses whom he will recognize. That is the universal rule, according to parliamentary usages. In a body of 386 men it would be impossible to proceed in a practical way and do otherwise, and the Chair will go further and say to the gentleman, to be exactly fair to him, that other things being even or anything near even, if there be a question, under present conditions, in the closing hours, the Chair has a perfect right . . . to prefer some one with whom, perchance, the Chair is in sympathy, or upon the Chair's side of the House.[1]

The House in session is but the House in public exhibition. Nearly everything is prearranged and predetermined. The Speaker and the party leaders know what measure or measures will come before the House for consideration; who will debate for or against the measure; and usually the point of order to be raised on the floor of the House. The whole proceeding is really what is called a dress rehearsal at which members of the House recite their respective parts to the constituents in Buncombe. This condition is possible only through the Speaker's control of recognition. The Speaker knows in advance those members who are to speak, and for his own convenience he has a list of the names of these members.[2] As early as 1879 opposition to the keeping of

[1] *Cong. Record*, 58th Cong., 2nd Sess., p. 5801.

[2] Follett, *op. cit.*, p. 251. In the English House of Commons the question of the "Whip's Lists" was raised on February 20, 1911, as an objection to the election of Mr. Lowther as Speaker for the fourth term. The debate on this question disclosed the methods by which "full dress debates" in the House of Commons are organized. The objection was made on the ground that such methods were detrimental to right of free discussion in the Commons. Speaker Lowther made on this occasion a statement of extreme importance and weight:

"Perhaps the House will allow me to say a word or two. I need hardly say that I do not propose to defend myself against a charge of impartiality (Hear, Hear), but the House may like to know exactly

the list by the Speaker had made itself felt in the House. A motion was introduced in the House that the Speaker " should not consider himself absolutely controlled by the list." [1] But whether the list was imperative on the Speaker

how the matter stands with regard to what has been the system termed handing in the lists of members. When a big debate takes place it is extremely convenient for the Speaker—and this also includes the Chairman of Committees—to know what Members on either side of the House are prepared with speeches with regard to the particular motion under discussion. Our time is generally limited, and the Chair is anxious to discover the most representative men in order to call them, so that the different views of different sections of the House may be before it. In 1906 when I was confronted by a very large number of new faces that I did not know, I asked the whips, continuing a former custom, to supply me with the names of the Members desiring to take part in debate. That custom was continued. It is only applicable to what the House calls full-dress debates. I do not—and I am sure the Chairman of Committees does not—consider myself bound in any way to limit my discretion to the number of names which appear on the list... One hon. Member has been kind enough to inform me—a matter of which I am not aware— that although his name never appeared on my official list handed in either to myself or to the Chairman of Committees, during one session he was called upon no fewer than twenty times. I think that this is a sufficient refutation of the suggestion that the Chairman of Committees and myself are in any way limited to list of names..." However, Mr. Martin, of the Liberal party, wrote, February 21, 1911, to the London *Times* with regard to the Speaker's power of recognition in the Commons: " On one occasion, in order to put himself right with his constituents (Laughter), he wanted to say a very few words indeed upon a question then before the House. He tried three days (Laughter)—yes—he got up every time the Member speaking sat down, but presently he began to notice that the hon. Member who was to call upon had not been in the House at all a few moments before, but rose with calm confidence and was called upon. On a subsequent occasion, noticing the same thing again, an hon. Member said to him: "You have not taken the right way. You should go to the Chairman of Committees and tell him you want to speak.' Being a new Member he acted upon the advice. The Chairman said: "What do you want to say?" He should be here a long time before he should think it possible to explain to the Chairman of Committees what he was going to say (Laughter and cheers)." MacDonagh, *The Speaker of the House* (London, 1914), pp. 373-375.

[1] Follett, *op. cit.*, p. 251.

or was merely in the nature of suggestion was a question for the Speaker only to answer. One of the distinguished members of the House told the author that the list is a " potential " rather than an " actual " thing. Speaker Randall stated that:

> He himself liked the practice of keeping a list because it relieved him from a great many personal controversies between members as to who shall be first recognized by the Chair. If the Chair has a list he has something to go by, and in addition he has also an exact knowledge of who desires to speak. The Chair thinks that no real hardship has ever resulted from the practice of keeping a list.[1]

Speaker Randall's opinion was upheld by Mr. Garfield in a report from the Committee on Rules:

> . . . The practice of making a list of those who desire to speak on measures before the House or Committee of the Whole is a proper one to enable the presiding officer to know and remember the wishes of members. As to order of recognition, he should not be bound to follow the list, but should be free to exercise a wise and just discretion in the interest of full and fair debate.[2]

On the other hand, undue importance seems to have been attached to the ability on the part of the members to catch the Speaker's eye for recognition. It was stated that a Democratic member once inquired of Speaker Cannon if a certain bill, in which he was interested, could pass the House. In reply the Speaker said: " Oh, this House could pass an elephant if the gentleman in charge of it could catch the Speaker's eye." The Speaker was reported to have then closed both of his eyes and proceeded to call for the next

[1] Follett, *op. cit.*, p. 252. For further discussion of the Speaker's list, see *infra*, pp. 215-6.

[2] Hinds, *op. cit.*, ii, 1224.

order of business.[1]   To say that what did really matter was due to the elusiveness of the Speaker's eye was not true, however, under the rules and practices of the House.   In the first place, the Speaker's eye, important as it was, was almost always steering at a course either previously decided upon or under the guidance of a list.   As a matter of fact, no member would ever think of the possibility of being recognized merely by catching the presiding officer's eye.

It must also be pointed out that for nearly three-fourths of the legislative days the House is in the Committee of the Whole House on the state of the Union [2] over which a member of the House appointed by the Speaker, but not the Speaker himself, presides.   In other words, no more than one-fourth of the time when the House is in session does the Speaker sit in the Speaker's chair, and consequently the opportunity for the Speaker to exercise the power of recognition is not as ubiquitous as is generally supposed.

"Although there is no appeal from the Speaker's recognition, he is not a free agent in determining who is to have the floor.   The practice of the House establishes rules from which he may not depart.   When the order of business brings before the House a certain bill he must first recognize, for motions of its disposition, the Member who represents the committee which has reported.   This is not necessarily the chairman of the committee, for a chairman who, in committee, has opposed the bill, must yield the prior recognition to a member of his committee who has favored the bill. Usually, however, the chairman has charge of the bill and is entitled at all stages to prior recognition for allowable motions intended to expedite it.   This principle does not, how-

---

[1] *Independent*, "The Big Four of the House of Representatives," vol. lxiv, p. 1187.

[2] See *supra*, pp. 92-3 for a discussion of the Committee of the Whole House on the state of the Union.

ever, apply to the Chairman of the Committee of the Whole. The Member who originally introduces the bill which a committee reports has no claim to recognition as opposed to the claims of the members of the committee, but in cases where a proposition is brought directly before the House by a Member the mover is entitled to prior recognition for motion and debate. Thus, the Member on whose motion the enacting clause of a bill is stricken out in the Committee of the Whole is entitled to prior recognition when the bill is reported to the House, and in a case where a Member had raised an objection in the joint meeting to count the electoral vote the Speaker recognized him first when the House had separated to consider the objection. But a Member may not, by offering a debatable motion of higher privilege than the pending motion, deprive the Member in charge of the bill of possession of the floor for debate. . . ." [1]

Moreover, under the practice of the House the Speaker is bound to recognize the chairman of the Committee on Ways and Means, who, prior to 1919, usually was the majority floor leader, and also the minority leader in preference to any other member upon the minority side of the House. [2] In debate—the general debate—members of the committee reporting the pending bill are given priority of recognition unless the committee is unanimously in favor of the bill, in which case members of the House opposing it are recognized, alternating with members of the committee who are in favor of it. [3]

[1] *House Manual*, section 738, 69th Congress; also see *Cong. Record*, 60th Cong., 2nd Sess., pp. 583, 584. House Rule xiv, 3, reads: " The Member reporting the measure under consideration from a committee may open and close, where general debate has been had thereon; and if it shall extend beyond one day, he shall be entitled to one hour to close, notwithstanding he may have used an hour in opening."

[2] *Cong. Record*, 60th Cong., 2nd Sess., pp. 583, 584.

[3] Hinds, *op. cit.*, ii, 1438-1445, 1448; also see *Cong. Record*, 60th Cong., 2nd Sess., pp. 583, 584.

Furthermore, the time for general debate is usually agreed upon by unanimous consent or through a special order from the Committee on Rules, and is equally controlled by two members representing the two contending sides on a bill. In this case these two members, usually the chairman and the minority ranking member of the committee, and not the Speaker, have the control of the floor. In this case, too, a member having been recognized to speak on the measure, say, for ten or twenty minutes, can yield the floor to another member to make a speech out of his own time, in which case the presiding officer has no choice but to accord recognition to the latter. Thus in 1898 a Senate concurrent resolution was brought before the House through a special order. After an unsuccessful attempt to divide the time between Mr. Dingley of Maine and Mr. Bailey of Texas, both of whom, as floor leaders of their respective parties, were leading members on the Committee on Ways and Means which reported the resolution, Speaker Reed was, under the practice of the House, given the right to control recognition. The Speaker first recognized Mr. Dingley, chairman of the committee, and then Mr. Bailey, the minority ranking member of the committee. Under the rules both Mr. Dingley and Mr. Bailey were entitled to speak for an hour.[1] The Speaker, then, proceeded to recognize other members of the committee who, under the rules, could also speak for an hour, but as members of the House were pressing for time to be heard, all of them used much less time than they were entitled to. Mr. Dingley spoke thirty minutes and yielded the rest of his time to his Republican associates. Mr. Bailey spoke even less time than Mr. Dingley did and also yielded the remaining minutes. Likewise did the members of the committee, so that more time might thereby be saved to

[1] See Rule xiv, 2. For rulings on the hour rule see Hinds, *op. cit.*, 5004, 5005; also *Cong. Record*, 67th Cong., 3rd Sess., p. 143.

accommodate eager members of the House who wanted to make themselves heard.[1] As a rule, members of the House recognized in this wise proceed to speak, under previous agreement, for five or ten minutes.

Furthermore, the Speaker has to accord recognition to the mover of a measure to offer a motion to reconsider.[2] The member who is in charge of a bill and secures the floor should also be recognized to demand the previous question,[3] although another member may make a motion of higher privilege.[4] As to motions to recommit, the Speaker gives preference " in recognition . . . to a member who is opposed to the bill or joint resolution." [5] Such preference is almost always given to a member of the committee rather than a Congressman who is not on the committee.[6] However, there may be exceptions to this rule. For example, in the Fifty-eighth Congress when a general deficiency appropriation bill was being read before the House for a third time, John A. Moon of Tennessee rose to move to recommit the bill to the Committee on Appropriations with instructions. Speaker Cannon denied recognition to Mr. Moon " for that purpose." But no sooner had Mr. Moon taken his seat than Speaker Cannon recognized Mr. Payne of New York, who rose to move to recommit the bill, and on that motion demand the previous question. It was intimated that Speaker Cannon recognized Mr. Payne because of a previous request made by the latter.[7] Be that as it may, there seemed to be another reason for Speaker Cannon's action, and that

[1] *Cong. Record*, 55th Cong., 2nd Sess., p. 1260.

[2] Hinds, *op. cit.*, ii, 1454.

[3] *Ibid.*, v, 5480.

[4] *Ibid.*, v, 5480.

[5] Rule xvi, 4.

[6] *Cong. Record*, 65th Cong., 2nd Sess., p. 10051.

[7] *Cong. Record*, 58th Cong., 2nd Sess., p. 5050.

was, that Mr. Payne was the floor leader of the majority party, although not a member of the Committee on Appropriations.

" There is no more apathetic body in the world than Congress when a question of political science is under consideration," wrote Mr. Nelson, " but there is no more alert body when a question touches the pockets of the constituencies, or the wealth-producing powers of the country." [1] That this indictment, severe as it was, was true, could be readily seen from the bitterness of the fight waged by the members of the House against the Speaker's power of recognition for unanimous consent. Historically the request for unanimous consent was first resorted to as early as 1832 when the House, under the pressure of business, felt the necessity of adhering to a fixed order.[2] In practice a request for unanimous consent by a member is a motion to suspend temporarily the order of business in the House for the consideration of a bill [3] which is generally of private or local nature, and which " touches the pockets of the constituencies or the wealth-producing powers of the country." Being a request for unanimous consent, any member, and the Speaker is included, may therefore object and demand " regular order," [4] which is another way of making objection.

The methods of control over unanimous consent differed from Speaker to Speaker. For instance, William L. Terry of Arkansas was once assured of recognition by Speaker Reed to call up a bill to compensate a church in his district for damages caused by Union soldiers. But at the same time the Speaker sent for John Dalzell of Pennsylvania, who

[1] Nelson, " Making Laws at Washington," *Century*, lxiv, p. 178.

[2] Hinds, *op. cit.*, iv, 3155-3159.

[3] *Ibid.*, iv, 3058, 3059.

[4] *Ibid.*, iv, 3058.

immediately appeared upon the floor. "John," the Speaker said as Mr. Dalzell passed him, " I have told Terry that I would recognize him to call up his church bill. I want you to be in your seat, and when he calls up his bill you must object to its consideration." The Speaker's order to Mr. Dalzell was overheard by Mr. Terry, who, however, thought of it as a mere jest. But as soon as the session started, Mr. Terry went to Mr. Dalzell and jokingly remarked:

" So you are going to object to my bill."

" I most certainly will," answered Dalzell.

" But that will kill it," Terry returned.

" Of course."

Whereupon Terry started to leave the chamber of the House. As he passed the Speaker's chair, Speaker Reed called to him:

" You are not going to quit now, Terry, as I am about to recognize you to call up your church bill ?"

" There is no use of calling up my bill, Mr. Speaker," replied Terry, " when you had already arranged with Dalzell to object to its consideration."

" Why," the Speaker exclaimed, with a twinkle of his eye, " I thought you would like to call the bill up anyhow, so as to convince your folks at home that you are doing the best you can." [1]

In the Sixty-first Congress Mr. Heflin of Alabama requested unanimous consent to call up a bill to prevent cotton speculation in New York. The bill had been unanimously reported from the Committee on Agriculture, of which Mr. Heflin was a member, but was objected to by Mr. Payne of New York. Consequently Mr. Heflin presented to Speaker Cannon a petition which bore the signatures of one hundred

---

[1] Leupp, "Humors of Congress," *Century,* lxv, p. 763. *Cf. Cong. Record,* 54th Cong., 1st Sess., p. 575 where Mr. Hepburn of Iowa referred to a somewhat similar case.

members and requested the Speaker to recognize Mr. Heflin or any other member among the one hundred to call up the bill and to put it on its passage. Several days after the presentation of the petition Mr. Heflin rose from the floor, thinking that the Speaker would recognize him. But as soon as Mr. Heflin was on his feet, Speaker Cannon said, " The Chair has reason to suppose there would be objection," and " the Chair, to be entirely frank with the gentleman, at this time at least, can not recognize the gentleman to move to suspend the rules." [1] Thus ended the matter. The "reason" was, however, that Speaker Cannon had privately promised Mr. Payne not to let the bill be called up during the latter's absence. [2]

Some Speakers, both Democrats and Republicans, have granted unanimous consent as a favor and at the same time let the majority floor leader or some other members of his party voice the objection. [3] To this end, a Speaker might have done it either by way of a messenger, by directing his eyes, by tapping his pencil in such a way as was previously agreed upon, or by some other methods prearranged with his lieutenants. When Mr. Henderson was in the Chair, Mr. Payne, the majority floor leader, made a gentleman's agreement with him that he would raise objection to private bills which were called up every morning by unanimous consent request. " Well," said Speaker Henderson to Mr. Payne, " that being the case, I might as well tell the gentlemen [of the House] that there is no use of their being recognized for unanimous consent on private bills, because objection will be made." [4] And " so far as private bills are concerned," Mr. Payne admitted, " as a member of the House, I am more to

---

[1] *Cong. Record*, 61st Cong., 2nd Sess., p. 1083.

[2] *Ibid.*, p. 1093.

[3] Cannon, " The Power of the Speaker," *Century*, lxxviii, p. 311.

[4] *Cong. Record*, 60th Cong., 2nd Sess., p. 585.

blame than the Speaker is for their not being recognized for unanimous consent." [1]   Mr. Payne effectively played the same role during Speaker Cannon's administration.   However, this does not mean that Speaker Cannon had nothing to do directly with the requests for unanimous consent.   Indeed, he thought that:

The better way and more manly and fair way was to exercise his right as a member to object to a request for unanimous consent.   Therefore the practice has grown up that gentlemen [of the House] see the Speaker, and if he has objections then he invariably says that it is useless to recognize the member for unanimous consent, because if nobody else objects, the Speaker in his capacity as a member of the House would object. [2]

The practice of requiring members to go to the Speaker's private room to seek previous permission for requests for unanimous consent had caused much personal humiliation to members of the House.   Thus Mr. Cooper of Wisconsin narrated of his experience with a Speaker in connection with one of his requests for unanimous consent:

. . . A former Speaker of this House compelled me to go to his room at one time.   I went there to present a bill which provided simply for the changing of the material which was to go into a public building and which had been recommended to him in a letter from the officer of the Supervising Architect.   I did not know that that letter had been written to him; I did not ask that it should be written him. . . . I went to the Speaker's

[1] *Cong. Record*, 60th Cong., 2nd Sess., p. 585.

[2] *Ibid.*, 1st Sess., p. 8.   Speaker Cannon told of his basis upon which he granted recognition for unanimous consent: "...His [Mr. Cannon] only restriction has been that the bills for which unanimous consent was requested should be such that no serious objection could be presented to them, such as bridge bills and other more or less *pro forma* legislation recommended by the executive department and unanimously reported from the committees..."   Cannon, *loc. cit., Century*, lxxviii, p. 311.

chamber. I had refused on a former occasion to do his bidding. When I went to his room he said, " I will see about that, come in again." I went in again. He did not ask me to sit down. He said, " I do not think I can do that; I do not want to do that; I can not allow that to come up." Not only that, but he compelled me to stand there, and when a perfect stranger came in, he sat him down in his seat and turned his back upon me. (Laughter.)

But soon Mr. Cooper took revenge upon the Speaker:

A very important rule had previously come before the House of Representatives. That same Speaker had stopped me at the entrance there and put his hand upon my breast and said, " Mr. Cooper, will you oblige me very much by not opposing this rule." That rule related to the Pacific Railroad Funding Bill. I did oppose it. . . . For the first time in thirty years the Pacific Railroad people lost their bill.[1]

The line of defence upon which the upholders of the Speaker's veto power over unanimous consent had so judiciously played, was that any member of the House could, if he desired, exercise that power on the floor in just as effective a way as the Speaker did in the Chair. " Why should the complaint be made if the Speaker exercises his right of objection by refusing . . . an applicant for recognition in any particular case?" so Mr. Dalzell of Pennsylvania argued, " Because he is a Speaker he is no less a member of the House; no less a representative of his congressional district." [2] " The embarrassment in this procedure," Speaker Cannon added, " was to the Speaker, for he was compelled

---

[1] *Cong. Record*, 60th Cong., 1st Sess., p. 6.

[2] " If he were on the floor he could interpose an objection to any request for unanimous consent. Should he be less able to interpose that objection because he is in the Chair? Certainly not..." Dalzell, *loc. cit.*, *Independent*, vol. lxiv, p. 580; also *cf. Cong. Record*, 60th Cong., 1st Sess., p. 3537.

to read all such bills and the reports on them to determine in his own mind whether he would give his consent as a member." [1]

Members of the House had at times made objection to requests for unanimous consent as a means of attaining certain ends which would be otherwise unobtainable. Thus William E. Mason of Illinois, who had been repeatedly denied recognition by Speaker Reed, finally came to know that the Speaker was interested in a certain bill which was bound to come up through unanimous consent. When the bill was called up, Mr. Mason objected, and repeated his objection each time when request for unanimous consent for its consideration was made. At last Speaker Reed was obliged to send a friend of his to inquire for the ground of Mr. Mason's objection. " I am a member of Congress," Mr. Mason informed the Speaker's representative, " but the Speaker seems to think me otherwise. He treats me as if he did not know me by sight." The same day Speaker Reed encountered Mr. Mason. Informally the Speaker advanced and held out his hand with this remark:

" Mr. Mason, I believe that if you were to rise and address the Chair tomorrow, the Chair would know who you are."

" Mr. Speaker," retorted Mr. Mason, " I have been giving greater attention to a bill in which I hear you are interested, and I have come to the conclusion that it ought to pass."

---

[1] Cannon, *loc. cit., Century,* lxviii, p. 311. At another place Speaker Cannon argued. "When a member asks for unanimous consent and a member on the floor objects, we hear nothing of it; when a Speaker objects, exercising his right simply as a member, it affords a text for ' the autocratic Speaker.'... It isn't undignified for them to ask other members not to object, as they are constantly doing, and there is no more reason why they should have any delicacy about approaching the Speaker than in trying to induce other members to give their consent." *Cong. Record,* 61st Cong., 1st Sess. (Appendix), p. 108.

So the bill was passed the following day without objection. And as soon as it was passed, Mr. Mason rose:

" Mr. Speaker," said Mr. Mason.

" The gentleman from Illinois," responded the Speaker. So Mr. Mason was recognized.[1]

Mr. Dalzell also cited a case to show that every member of the House has as much power over request for unanimous consent as the Speaker. During the Speakership of Mr. Reed, Mr. Kem of Nebraska once declared that he would object to the consideration of all bills by unanimous consent. On the following day when a member was recognized to make request for unanimous consent, Mr. Kem objected. For two days he persisted, and on the third day the eager members who had formerly crowded the Speaker's room, surrounded Mr. Kem's desk.[2]

Such tactics to counteract the Speaker's power were not, however, always successful. For example, during the closing days of the Fifty-sixth Congress Mr. Moon of Tennessee announced that he would henceforth object to any request for unanimous consent unless the Committee on Rules reported out a bill which he introduced. The threat of Mr. Moon prompted a reply from Speaker Henderson, who unyieldingly declared: " There will be no more unanimous consent until he [Mr. Moon] gives way entirely. As long as I am the Speaker of this House, I propose to be the Speaker." [3]

Whatever justification the Speaker might have for his objection to a member's request for unanimous consent, the fact was that the proceedings conducted in the Speaker's private room had caused much suspicion and magnified the

---

[1] Leupp, *loc. cit., Century*, lxv, p. 764.

[2] Dalzell, *loc. cit., Independent*, lxiv, p. 580.

[3] Richard, " The Passing of Speaker Henderson," *Independent*, lv, p. 653.

Speaker's power. A change in the procedure was therefore demanded by the insurgent members. And this change was brought about on the opening day of the Sixty-first Congress on which the tidal wave for the reform of the rules was sweeping the House of Representatives. The broad aspects of the history of this reform movement have been already dwelt on in connection with other manifestations of the Speaker's power. Suffice it to say that on March 15, 1909, when the demand for previous question on the motion for the adoption of the Rules was rejected, Mr. Fitzgerald of New York moved, among other things, to amend the motion with the following proviso:

> After a bill which has been favorably reported shall have been upon either the House or the Union Calendar for three days any Member may file with the Clerk a notice that he desires such a bill placed upon a special calendar to be known as the " Calendar for Unanimous Consent." On days when it shall be in order to move to suspend the rules the Speaker shall, immediately after the approval of the *Journal,* direct the Clerk to call the bills upon the " Calendar for Unanimous Consent." Should objection be made to the consideration of any bill so-called it shall immediately be stricken from the Calendar for Unanimous Consent, and it shall not thereafter be placed thereon.[1]

This amendment, together with several others, was agreed to by the House by a vote of 211 to 173. Commenting on the innovation, Speaker Cannon writes:

> He welcomes the Fitzgerald amendment as a relief from much drudgery in reading hundreds of bills and also from the sham autocracy of his position in having the other members ask his consent to the passage of such bills. More particularly does he welcome the amendment because it disposes of the old, threadbare excuses of members who wrote to their constituents: " I have tried to get your bill passed, but the Speaker would not

recognize me." The members who have been writing such letters for years will now have to change the phraseology of their excuses and write: " I am willing to pass your bill, but I am only one. There are 390 other members [under the twelfth census in 1900 the full membership of the House was 391], and they would not give me unanimous consent to act for the whole House. In other words, the Fitzgerald amendments will compel the members to tell the truth to their constituents or to invent other fiction to take the place of that regarding the autocratic objection of the Speaker which has done service for so many years.[1]

As is provided in the rule, this calendar is in order for two days (the first and third Mondays) in each month and during the last six days in each session of Congress. On such days the Speaker " shall, immediately after the approval of the *Journal,* direct the Clerk to call the bills " upon the Calendar for Unanimous Consent. In case objection be made to the consideration of any such bill, it will go off this calendar to the original calendar from which it came. Herein lies one of the chief disadvantages of the rule. For under the old system a bill, when once objected to by a member for consideration under unanimous consent, might be called up for the second and third times, and indeed *ad infinitum,* until its sponsor could get recognition from the Speaker, whereas under this rule a bill has only one chance to be called up. It is true that under this rule members of the House no longer make their pilgrimage to the Speaker's private room to supplicate the Speaker's permission. But, on the other hand, the tyranny of one-man power still persists, for both under the old practice and the new rule, one member—and the Speaker is included [2]—can object to the

---

[1] Cannon, *loc. cit., Century,* vol. lxxviii, p. 312.

[2] When the Fitzgerald amendment was before the House, Mr. Randall of Texas asked Mr. Fitzgerald: " If unanimous consent is necessary

consideration of a bill, thereby blocking the passage of a worthy bill. And, furthermore, according to the purpose of the framers of the rule, private bills cannot be called up for consideration through the Calendar for Unanimous Consent.[1]

Since its adoption several changes have been made in this rule. In the Sixty-eighth Congress the name of the Calendar for Unanimous Consent was changed into " Consent Calendar." Bills on this Consent Calendar are to be called up only after those on the Calendar of Motions to Discharge Committee are disposed of. If a bill, after being called up from the Consent Calendar, is objected to by a member, it will be immediately stricken from this calendar, but it can be restored to the calendar at the instance of its sponsor. If again objected to by three or more members, it will not thereafter be placed upon the calendar. It was also provided that the same bill shall not be called twice on the same legislative day.[2] With the commencement of the Sixty-ninth Congress this procedure again underwent slight modifica-

under the rule you propose, would not the Speaker, being a member of the House, have the same right to object to the bill that he now has to refuse recognition for it?

" Mr. Garner of Texas. Yes.

" Mr. Fitzgerald. He could object when the Clerk calls the bill; but the complaint that has been made has been this: under the present practice, the Speaker objects in the private and not in the open like other members; but this [rule] put him on the same with other members. If he wishes to object, he must object when the bill is called up by the Clerk." *Cong. Record*, 61st Cong., 1st Sess., pp. 22, 23.

[1] In the Sixty-third Congress a private bill was once called up from the Committee on Military Affairs, and was given unanimous consent after much debate. Mr. Mann of Illinois, who was one of the framers of the rule, said that private bills were not intended to be called up from the Calendar for Unanimous Consent. Mr. Underwood said, however, that the bill under consideration was an " emergency " matter. *Cong. Record*, 63rd Cong., 2nd Sess., p. 4883.

[2] *Cong. Record*, 68th Cong., 1st Sess., p. 95.

tions. It is now provided that bills, after three days upon the Consent Calendar, are in order for consideration on the first Monday of each month "immediately after the approval of the *Journal*" and on the third Monday of each "immediately after the disposition of motions to instruct committees." [1]

It has been pointed out that the decided advantage in the establishment of the Calendar for Unanimous Consent, or the Consent Calendar as it is now called, is that members of the House are now not obliged to go to the Speaker's private room to beg permission to make a request for unanimous consent. Moreover, there has also been a certain definiteness introduced in the procedure. On the first and third Mondays of each month when business on this calendar is in order, the Speaker will say: "The order of today is the Consent Calendar. The Clerk will report the first bill on the calendar." He then goes on to name the bill and ask: " Is there objection to the present consideration of the bill?" Bills on the Consent Calendar are thus considered in the order in which they appear thereon. Under such procedure the Speaker cannot but accord recognition to a member who rises to object, to ask a question or to speak on the bill. The rule provides, furthermore, that "the Speaker shall direct the Clerk to call the bills which have been for three days upon the ' Consent Calendar '." Both Mr. Mann of Illinois and Mr. Fitzgerald of New York, " father " of the Consent Calendar, declared that this provision is the " real " *raison d'être* of the rule [2] as against the haphazard procedure under

---

[1] Rule xiii, 3.

[2] Mr. Mann said: "...I take it that the real reason of this rule is that the Members may be informed when unanimous consent is to be asked of the House on bills, so that any Member who was interested in the investigation of any bill might know from the calendar when he would need to be in his seat to object. That was the real reason for the rule." *Cong. Record*, 61st Cong., 2nd Sess., p. 1549.

the old system. In the second session of the Sixty-first Congress objection was made to the consideration of a bill which had been less than three days upon the Consent Calendar. In making the objection Mr. Fitzgerald of New York said: ". . . The object of the rule is to give Members an opportunity to ascertain what the bills for which unanimous consent was to be asked purported to do." If bills are reported late on Friday and placed on the Unanimous Consent Calendar on the following Monday, "with possibly no opportunity to obtain copies of the bill and report on Saturday, the object of the rule will be destroyed." Speaker Cannon sustained Mr. Fitzgerald's point of order.[1]

The definiteness in the procedure of the rule has, however, no bearing upon the frequency of the call of the calendar by the House. During the first session of the Sixty-first Congress the Unanimous Consent Calendar was never once called by the House, mainly because the House committees, except those on the Ways and Means, on Rules, on Mileages and on Accounts, were not appointed until the last day of the session.[2] It was not in fact until December 20, 1909, the second session of the Sixty-first Congress, that the calendar was for the first time called by the House. In this session not a single Unanimous Consent Calendar day was dispensed with. In the Sixty-second Congress the House used twenty-three out of the total thirty-one Unanimous Consent Calendar days to consider bills on that calendar. Since then statistics show that more than half of the Unanimous Consent Calendar days have been used for the purpose for which the rule is established. Take one of the

---

[1] It was a bill reported from the Committee on Rivers and Harbors. The bill was reported on December 17, 1909, and was called up from the Unanimous Consent Calendar on December 20, the third Monday of the month. Sunday, being December 19, is *dies non*. *Ibid.*, pp. 263-265.

[2] See *Cong. Record*, 61st Cong., 1st Sess., pp. 57, 5091, 5092.

recent Congresses, for instance. In the Sixty-eighth Congress nine out of the eighteen Unanimous Consent Calendar days were used for the consideration of bills on this calendar.

The rule relating to the Consent Calendar does not stand by itself; it is linked together both with the Suspension Rule and the rule pertaining to the Calendar on Motions to Discharge Committees, which is now called the Calendar on Motions to Instruct a Committee. In order to see the power of the Speaker in his relation to the operation of the Consent Calendar, it is therefore necessary to see it in his relation to the working of the other two rules.

However, let there be no confusion as to the difference between the Consent Calendar, upon which a bill automatically comes before the House for consideration on certain prescribed days in a month, and requests for unanimous consent,[1] to suspend temporarily the order of business of the day and to consider a bill which would otherwise not be in order, made on days other than those under the Consent Calendar. Over the latter requests, most of which are made in the closing days of a session of Congress, the Speaker has discretionary power of recognition. It is interesting to note here that in the Sixty-first Congress Speaker Cannon refused to recognize any member for a unanimous consent request for the consideration of a bill not in accordance with the rule for the Consent Calendar.[2] Mr. Clark was the first

---

[1] Request for unanimous consent are also necessary for the following purposes: (1) withdrawal of papers, Hinds, *op. cit.*, v, 7259; (2) swearing in a Member without certificate, *ibid.*, i, 162-168; (3) to change the text of a conference to which both Houses have agreed, *ibid.*, v, 6433-6436; (4) a recount of a vote by tellers after result is announced, *ibid.*, v, 5993, 5994; (5) correction of reference of public bills, Rule xxii, 3; (6) private claims to be referred to certain committees, Rule xxi, 3. For other purposes see Hinds, *op. cit.*, v, 5640; iii, 1951.

[2] See *Cong. Record*, 61st Cong., 2nd Sess., p. 378. Mr. Fitzgerald quoted Speaker Cannon as saying that the Speaker "would not recognize any one for unanimous consent for a bill which could be placed upon this [Consent] calendar," *ibid.*, p. 1545.

Speaker who established the precedent of according recognition for unanimous consent requests to consider a bill on days other than those under the Consent Calendar. Mr. Clark did it out of his " good judgment " when " there was a matter of pressing emergency, to which there could be no reasonable amount of objection." [1] In other words, Speaker Clark could recognize, or refuse to recognize, a member at his own discretion under such circumstances. Here is a case in point. In the Sixty-sixth Congress Mr. Igoe of Missouri attempted in vain to secure recognition for a request for unanimous consent to consider a resolution which directed the Federal Trade Commission to investigate and to report the high prices of shoes. Finally Mr. Clark of Missouri, then the minority leader, took the matter into his own hands, and on August 2, 1919, rose to ask unanimous consent for the consideration of the Igoe resolution. Upon his request Speaker Gillett put the question: " Is there objection?" After a pause, no objection was heard. Then, and not until then, Speaker Gillett said: "The Chair declines to recognize the gentleman (Mr. Clark) for the present." The following colloquy then occurred:

[1] Toward the end of the second session of the Sixty-second Congress Speaker Clark recognized on one Saturday several members for unanimous consent to consider certain bills, one of which was to authorize the Secretary of War to convey by deed to a certain land company a strip of land in Tennessee. Mr. Cooper of Wisconsin made an parliamentary inquiry that such action would revert to the "evils of former system." In reply Speaker Clark said that he "has no desire to break down that [unanimous consent] rule . . . but there were four or five matters in which the Government of the United States is interesed, and if certain bills or resolutions did not go through it would stop Government work." *Cong. Record*, 62nd Cong., 2nd Sess., p. 10702. On June 28, 1913, he said: " It was the intention of the House to confine unanimous consent to that calendar, and the Chair has adhered to that except there was a matter of pressing emergency..." *Cong. Record*, 63rd Cong., 1st Sess., p. 2280; also see p. 2445.

Mr. Blanton. Mr. Speaker, regular order.

The Speaker. The Gentleman from Texas demands regular order.

Mr. Clark of Missouri. The regular order is putting my request.

The Speaker. But the Chair did not recognize the gentleman.

Mr. Clark of Missouri. Mr. Speaker, a parliamentary inquiry.

The Speaker. The gentleman will state it.

Mr. Clark of Missouri. What went with my request I made that "the gentleman from Missouri" could call up this resolution?

The Speaker. The Chair is not obliged to state it unless he desires.

Mr. Clark of Missouri. I understand that.

The Speaker. The Chair did not recognize the gentleman to present a request.

Mr. Clark of Missouri. Did the Chair recognize me or not?

Mr. Speaker. The Chair did recognize the gentleman.

Mr. Clark of Missouri. And I made the request.

The Speaker. The Chair is not obliged to recognize the gentleman to prefer a request.

Mr. Clark of Missouri. Well, my understanding was—

The Speaker. The gentleman from Michigan (Mr. Fordney) is recognized.[1]

Usually the Speaker voices his objection to unanimous consent request by declining to recognize the member who seeks it, for the Speaker never says " I object." But the " outrage," as Mr. Clark put it, in this case was that Speaker Gillett had recognized Mr. Clark and had also put the question to the House, and, having proceeded thus far, then de-

---

[1] *Cong. Record*, 66th Cong., 1st Sess., p. 3586. It was said that the shoe manufacturers in Speaker Gillett's district had brought pressure to bear upon the Speaker not to allow members to call up the resolution in question. *Searchlight*, vol. iv, no. 5, p. 9.

prived Mr. Clark of recognition. Two days later the case was debated on the floor. In the course of the debate the whole question of recognition was once more brought to the front. In the first place, it was admitted that the practice for the Speaker to ask of a member when he rises, " For what purpose does the gentleman rise," is a desirable one. Speaker Cannon was carped at for having resorted to it. When Mr. Clark was elected to the Chair, he abandoned that practice. But after two or three weeks he was " compelled " to adopt it " out of self-defence and for the good of the House." [1] Speaker Gillett " often " resorted to the practice, but " when the leader of the minority [Mr. Clark] rises, the Chair generally recognizes him, because he knows the leader of the minority has a sense of responsibility and is familiar with the rule." [2] Then, the Speaker went on to admit his discretionary power over motions made out of the regular order: " Most Members on both sides of the House who wish to make a motion out of order consult the Speaker in advance and then it is arranged whether and when they be recognized so as least to interfere with regular order of the House." [3]

Members of the House who intended to ask unanimous consent for the consideration of a bill out of its regular order, had to " inform " in advance the Speaker and the floor leaders both of the majority and minority sides.[4] If,

---

[1] *Cong. Record*, 66th Cong., 1st Sess., p. 3664. It was stated that there might be said to have been two recognitions. First, when a member rises from his seat and addresses the Chair who says " the Gentleman from ——." And having been thus recognized, the member proceeds to state his purpose for which he rises, and the Chair then decides whether to recognize or refuse to recognize him for the purpose which the latter stated. *Ibid.*, p. 3664.

[2] *Ibid.*, p. 3664.

[3] *Ibid.*, p. 3664.

[4] *Cong. Record*, 65th Cong., 3rd Sess., pp. 4350, 4351.

however, unanimous consent is asked of a bill which is under the jurisdiction of the Committee on Judiciary or any such important committee, the member asking for it should also consult the chairman of that particular committee and the minority ranking member.[1] Even during the days of Cannonism the minority leader was always kept informed of the bills to be called up by unanimous consent.[2] And with the overthrow of Cannonism that practice remained for a time unchanged. On June 11, 1919, Mr. McKinley of Illinois asked unanimous consent to change the reference of a bill from the Committee on Public Lands to the Committee on Military Affairs. When the request was made, Mr. Clark of Missouri, the minority leader, rose to inquire: "What is it about, Mr. Speaker?" Whereupon Mr. Mondell of Wyoming, the majority leader, explained:

. . . In this connection may I again suggest to the gentlemen [of the House] that when they have requests of this kind to make they refer the matter, before making the requests, to the gentleman from Missouri (Mr. Clark), who ought to be informed with regard to them before they are presented to the House. I was under the impression that the gentleman from Missouri had been informed with regard to this.[3]

On the same occasion Speaker Gillett also said that in the future he would not recognize any member to ask unanimous consent "unless he knows in advance the subject for which unanimous consent is asked."[4] A little later when Mr. Campbell of Kansas rose to make a request for unanimous consent, Speaker Gillett inquired if he had conferred both with Mr. Mondell of Wyoming and Mr. Clark of Missouri.

[1] *Cong. Record*, 69th Cong., 1st Sess., p. 3027.
[2] Cannon, *loc. cit., Century*, vol. lxxviii, p. 311.
[3] *Cong. Record*, 66th Cong., 1st Sess., pp. 971, 972.
[4] *Ibid.*, p. 972.

" He certainly has not conferred with the Chair." [1]   Mr. Campbell was not recognized.   However, since 1919, while both the Speaker and the majority floor leader are kept informed of unanimous consent requests by members of the House, it is difficult to ascertain the extent to which the practice of informing the minority floor leader in advance has been observed.

[1] *Cong. Record*, 66th Cong., 1st Sess., p. 972.

CHAPTER V

POWER OVER SUSPENSION OF RULES

CLOSELY related to the unanimous consent request is the motion for suspension of rules. As early as 1794 a rule was adopted which provided that " no standing rule or order of the House shall be rescinded without one day's notice being given of the motion therefor." [1] In 1811 the words " or changed " were added after " rescinded." [2] And in 1822 the House added to it a provision: " nor shall any rule be suspended, except by a vote of at least two-thirds of the Members present." [3] This was the beginning of the suspension rule. The purpose of adopting this additional clause is to provide for a method whereby the House can get at a particular bill for consideration which otherwise is not in order under the rules. But at the same time the rule was so worded so as to ward off the House from wasting its time in voting unnecessary, nay undesirable, motions. [4]

Speaker Colfax held, in 1868, that it is possible, on one motion and by one vote, both to suspend the rules and pass a bill or resolution. [5] On the same occasion, it was decided that, after a motion to suspend the rules, the Speaker should entertain only one motion, that to adjourn, and no other dilatory motions. [6]

[1] Hinds, *op. cit.*, v, 6790.

[2] *Ibid.*, v, 6790.

[3] *Ibid.*, v, 6790.

[4] See *ibid.*, v, 6790, 6797.

[5] *Ibid.*, v, 6846, 6847.

[6] *Ibid.*, v, 6846.

A motion to suspend the rules must, before being submitted to the House, be seconded upon demand by a majority by tellers. Failure to secure a majority in seconding means the refusal of the House to consider the motion. But if a majority votes to second it, the House will proceed to a debate under the forty-minute rule.[1] Bills and resolutions brought up under suspension of rules are not subject to any amendment by members of the House and cannot be voted on separately, paragraph by paragraph. In the third session of the Sixty-second Congress when the Federal employees' compensation bill came before the House under the suspension of rules, Mr. Roddenberg, of Illinois, put the following questions to the Speaker:

Mr. Roddenberg. Mr. Speaker, a parliamentary inquiry.
The Speaker. The gentleman will state it.
Mr. Roddenberg. Can a vote be had on any particular paragraph of this bill?
The Speaker. It will not be.
Mr. Roddenberg. At any time will it be in order to offer an amendment to the bill?
The Speaker. It will not be.[2]

Since 1874 motions to suspend the rules are in order during the last six days of a session, and since 1880 they are also in order on the first and third Mondays of each month.[3] On the first Monday of the month preference has been given to individual members to offer such motions, and on the third Monday to committees.[4] Speaker Henderson held that " the Chair is of the opinion that the motion to suspend

---

[1] Rule xxvii, 2, 3.

[2] *Cong. Record*, 62nd Cong., 3rd Sess., p. 4476.

[3] Such motions are originally in order on any day. Hinds, *op. cit.*, v, 6790; also see Rule xxvii, 1.

[4] Rule xxvii, 21.

the rules on committee suspension day must be specifically authorized by the committee. On individual suspension day, of course, it is different, because then it is an individual privilege." [1]

The necessity for limiting the frequency of motions to suspend the rules was plainly set forth by Mr. Hinds:

Formerly the Speaker was compelled to recognize any Member who first got his attention on the motion to suspend the rules. The result was that the motion was greatly abused. Men would prepare resolutions on subjects of no practical standing in the House, sometimes so artfully worded as to be politically traps, condemning many Members to political danger in their districts, whether they voted for or against them. Members therefore did not naturally like to run the risk of such pitfalls or to be put on record upon questions not of practical moment to the United States or which might involve local prejudice in their homes, and thus destroy their usefulness without any compensating good. So it happened that frequently the House on suspension day adjourned in order to escape this snare, and in 1880 the number of suspension days were reduced to two a month so as to make the dangers of the day as little as possible. [2]

So much for the history of this rule—which is indeed a sort of gag rule. The restrictive manner in which it is operated has strengthened the power of the Speaker, who has repeatedly declared that recognition over motions to suspend the rules is at the discretion of the occupant of the Speaker's chair. As early as 1881 Speaker Randall held that it was not compulsory on the Speaker to recognize for the motion to suspend the rules. [3] Six years later, in 1887, Speaker Carlisle, through the exercise of the power of recognition

---

[1] *Cong. Record*, 56th Cong., 1st Sess., p. 5821.

[2] *Cong. Record*, 60th Cong., 2nd Sess., p. 589.

[3] Hinds, *op. cit.*, v, 6791.

for motions to suspend the rules, prevented a bill for the repeal of the internal revenue taxes on tobacco from being brought before the House. It " would have been possible to pass it by a combination of Republicans and a part of the Democratic majority," Miss Follett writes, " if it could have reached a vote." She noted in full the letter sent, February 5, 1887, to Speaker Carlisle by three " prominent " Democrats who " appeal . . . most earnestly to recognize, on Monday next, some Democrat who will move to suspend the rules for the purpose of giving the House an opportunity of considering the question of the total repeal of the internal revenue taxes on tobacco." [1]

In 1893 Speaker Crisp stated in the course of a discussion on a point of order:

The Chair fully appreciates the fact that according to the practice which has always prevailed the motion to suspend the rules has been one depending on recognition; that is, it can not be made unless the Member is recognized to make it. The Chair, in speaking of this motion as one of the highest privilege, did not mean to convey the idea that necessarily when the day comes for motions to suspend the rules the Chair must recognize a gentleman to make such motion.[2]

Again, in 1894, Mr. J. W. Bailey, the Speaker *pro tempore,* held that the rule relating to suspension merely permitted, but did not require, the Speaker to entertain such motions on the first and third Mondays of a month.[3] In 1900 Speaker Henderson " refused " to recognize Mr. J. J. Lentz and stated, in addition, that " the Chair under the laws [precedents] has that discretion." [4]

[1] Follett, *op. cit.,* pp. 262-265.
[2] Hinds, *op. cit.,* v, 6794.
[3] *Ibid.,* v, 6791.
[4] *Cong. Record,* 56th Cong., 1st Sess., p. 6890.

Under the rules there are only two motions which the Speaker cannot entertain for the suspension of rules, namely, the one which admits a person not named in the rules to the privileges of the floor,[1] and the other is to let the Hall of the House of Representatives to a person for purposes other than the business of the House.[2]

The Speaker can recognize a member to move to suspend the rules and pass a bill even by a unanimous consent request on days other than suspension days. On February 23, 1906, Mr. William Richardson, of Alabama, made a unanimous consent request to suspend the rules and agree to a concurrent resolution providing for certain amendments to an enrolled bill which authorized the construction of dams and power stations on the Tennessee River at Muscle Shoals, Alabama. The request instantly brought Mr. Dalzell, of Pennsylvania, to his feet to make a point of order that, it not being a suspension day, it would be " a bad precedent " to entertain such a request. Mr. Dalzell then went on:

. . . It seems to me that it was the intention of the rule to place limitation upon the power of the House by placing a limitation on the power of the Speaker. It [the rule] says that he shall not entertain a motion to suspend the rules except on the first and third Mondays of each month. It is very much like the case of the rule that prohibits the Speaker from entertaining a motion to permit parties not permitted by the rule to come upon the floor of the House.[3]

Speaker Cannon overruled the point of order and said:

But the rule [Mr. Dalzell last referred to],[4] the gentleman will

[1] Rule xxxiii.
[2] Rule xxxii.
[3] *Cong. Record*, 59th Cong., 1st Sess., p. 2889.
[4] Rule xxxiii.

recollect, prohibits the Speaker from submitting a request for unanimous consent. This [suspension] rule does not. The Chair could not and would not entertain a motion on any except the two Mondays specified, but this comes by a request for unanimous consent that the Speaker shall entertain a motion to suspend the rules under the terms of Rule XXVII. It seems to the Chair that the House may under the rule, if it sees proper to do so, give unanimous consent.[1]

The adoption of the Calendar for Unanimous Consent, March 15, 1909, brought forth a change in the order of procedure for motions for the suspension of rules. Under this new rule, it was provided that " on days when it shall be in order to move to suspend the rules the Speaker shall, immediately after the approval of the *Journal,* direct the Clerk to call the bills upon the Calendar for Unanimous Consent." [2]   In other words, motions on the Calendar for Unanimous Consent took precedence of those for the suspension of rules.   Then, on June 17, 1910, came the Calendar of Motions to Discharge Committees,[3] which again took precedence of the suspension rule.   The order of business under this procedure ran as follows: (1) Calendar for Unanimous Consent; (2) Calendar of Motions to Discharge Committee; and (3) motion to suspend the rules.[4]

Under this rule, motions to suspend the rules were placed at a disadvantage.   On suspension days, that is, on the first and third Mondays of each month,[5] motions to suspend the

---

[1] *Cong. Record,* 59th Cong., 1st Sess., p. 2891.

[2] *Cong. Record,* 61st Cong., 1st Sess., p. 22.

[3] See *infra,* pp. 259 *et seq.*

[4] This order underwent further changes. See *Cong. Record,* 62nd Cong., 1st Sess., p. 58; *ibid.,* 2nd Sess., p. 1686.

[5] Motions on the Unanimous Consent Calendar and the Calendar to Discharge Committee are usually not called up during the last six days of a session.

rules would not be in order until after the disposal of the bills or resolutions both on the Discharge and Unanimous Consent Calendars. The consequence was that it opened the way to obstructions. Under the rule, members of the House could file a hundred or more motions on each of these two calendars and keep on calling them up, thereby depriving the House of any possible chance to reach the motions to suspend the rules. Cases of this nature actually occurred in the House. "During the entire last session of Congress," Mr. Mann of Illinois declared, "I sat here with motions on the Calendar to Discharge Committee ready at any time to call up the preferential motion to discharge a committee if the Speaker would give recognition to any one to move to suspend the rules."[1] Mr. Mann admitted that he did it in order to "demonstrate its [the rule in question] utter absurdity."[2]

Attempts to modify this rule were therefore made. On January 11, 1911, Mr. Fuller of Illinois offered a resolution which provided that motions on the Unanimous Consent Calendar "shall not have precedence over motions to suspend the rules."[3] In presenting the resolution Mr. Fuller claimed that it was a question of constitutional privilege. Mr. Mann made a point of order. Mr. Fuller argued:

Mr. Speaker, so far as the point of order is concerned, that question was settled by this House on the 19th day of last March, by a vote of the House itself, and that is the law of this House until repealed. It was then decided that under the Constitution of the United States a motion of this kind is in order at any time. . . .[4]

Referring to the question at issue, he further argued:

[1] *Cong. Record*, 62nd Cong., 3rd Sess., p. 4451.
[2] *Cong. Record*, 61st Cong., 3rd Sess., p. 680.
[3] *Ibid.*, p. 679.
[4] *Ibid.*, p. 679.

That little clause there which provided that motions [on the Unanimous Consent Calendar] shall have precedence over motions to suspend the rules makes it absolutely impossible for a motion to suspend the rules at any time for any purpose, if any gentleman sees it fit to obstruct; . . . if one astute and industrious Member, like the gentleman from the second district of Illinois [Mr. Mann] is opposed thereto.   Mr. Speaker, on last suspension day, which was the 19th of December last—and we can have only two suspension days in a month—the gentleman from Illinois called up, under clause 4 of Rule XXVIII, a bill that consumed the entire day, and would consume the entire next suspension day if this rule remains unchanged.   Fearing, then, that there might, after that motion was disposed of, be some time on a suspension day when the Members of this House could be heard upon an important bill that same gentleman [Mr. Mann] has caused to be placed upon this calendar 107 other like motions, so that if the rule stands at it is and Congress were to remain in session day and night for the next two years we can not reach the order of suspension of the rules.   The only way that the majority of this House can exercise its will is by wiping out this provision of the rule.[1]

As the debate progressed, it soon developed that the real question was not whether motions for the suspension of the rules should have precedence over those on the Calendar for Unanimous Consent, but whether the resolution as presented was in order as a matter of highest privilege under the Constitution.   In other words, it was a test case either to affirm or to reverse the decision of the House on March 19, 1910, on the Norris resolution.[2]   In arguing against the privileged character of the resolution Mr. Mann said:

Mr. Speaker, it is true that at the last session of Congress a motion to revise the rules was held of high privilege as a con-

[1] *Cong. Record*, 61st Cong., 3rd Sess., p. 680.
[2] *Cf supra*, pp. 141 *et seq.*

stitutional privilege. It was also true that that was decided in such manner that no one in the House ought to consider it as binding in the future. I am glad that my colleague has raised the question, in the hope that the Speaker and the House will now determine in the interest of the future that such a motion is not a matter of high privilege to be presented at any time. If it should be held now that the motion of my colleague to amend the rule is in order as a matter of high privilege, no matter what rules the House might adopt, I could rise, or any other Member of the House could rise, with a hundred motions upon his desk, presenting one after another, and obtaining the floor with the right to an hour when obtaining the floor on each occasion, and keep the House forever from transacting business. Such a situation may arise sometime when the two parties in the House are fighting bitterly and when one party desires to filibuster.[1]

Mr. Underwood also pointed out:

. . . We recognized that the Norris resolution was not in order under the rules of this House, but that the time had come for a legislative revolution in order that we might write in the rules of this House the will of the American people. That was the course of our vote for the Norris resolution, to make it in order, notwithstanding the decision of the Speaker. . . .[2]

By an overwhelming vote the House decided that the Fuller resolution was not in order as matter of high privilege under the Constitution. It is important to note that during the entire course of debate the merit of the resolution was scarcely touched upon.

In the third session of the Sixty-second Congress the question as to whether motions to suspend the rules should take precedence over the business on the Calendar for Unanimous Consent again came before the House. On February

---

[1] *Cong. Record*, 61st Cong., 3rd Sess., p. 680.

[2] *Ibid.*, p. 680.

28, 1913, Mr. Small moved to suspend the rules and pass a Senate bill for the compilation of revolutionary records, with committee amendments. Mr. Hardwick of Georgia raised a point of order and made reference to clause 3 of Rule XIII which provided that:

After a bill which has been favorably reported shall be upon either the House or the Union Calendar any Member may file with the Clerk a notice that he desires such a bill placed upon a special calendar to be known as the Calendar for Unanimous Consent. On days when it shall be in order to move to suspend the rules the Speaker shall immediately after the reading of the *Journal*, direct the Clerk to call the bills which have been for three days upon the Calendar for Unanimous Consent.[1]

Mr. Hardwick argued that "under the rules, the Calendar for Unanimous Consent has preference over motions to suspend the rules and pass a bill." Speaker Clark sustained the point of order and added:

It is in order to move to suspend the rules, and while the Chair does not think that the men who drafted this clause of Rule XIII ever intended that it should apply to the last six days, yet if it is literally construed, it does apply. The Clerk will call the Calendar for Unanimous Consent.[2]

On the same day, but a little later, Mr. Clayton of Alabama moved to suspend the rules and pass S. 5382 " to provide an exclusive remedy and compensation for accidental injuries, resulting in disability or death, to employees of common carriers by railroads engaged in interstate or foreign commerce, or in the District of Columbia." [3] Mr. Hardwick again raised a point of order, which was sustained by Speaker Clark.

[1] *Cong. Record*, 62nd Cong., 3rd Sess., p. 4329.

[2] *Ibid.*, p. 4329.

[3] *Ibid.*, p. 4357.

That Speaker Clark had little intention of asserting power of recognition for the suspension of rules was evidenced by his decisions in relation to the aforementioned cases. He made a literal interpretation of the rules, as far as the rules for the Calendar for Unanimous Consent and the suspension were concerned.

Although Speaker Clark was " inclined " to adhere to the literal construction of the rules, the House, the very next day, decided, by a vote, to reverse his rulings. On March 1, 1913, one of the last six suspension days, Mr. Underwood brought forth a resolution providing that " during the remainder of this session it shall be in order for the Speaker to entertain motions to suspend the rules without calling the Calendar for Unanimous Consent." [1] Once more the watchful Hardwick made a point of order, which prompted a lengthy debate on the floor of the House. During the debate Mr. Underwood admitted that he offered the resolution " for the purpose of bringing the matter before the House and of letting the House decide." Several members argued eloquently either for or against the pending resolution, but Mr. Mann's speech was by far the most forceful one in its bearing upon the power of the Speaker over the suspension:

Mr. Mann. This is the situation: The old rule provides for a suspension on suspension days, of which this is one. Then came along the rule providing for the Unanimous Consent to be called immediately after the approval of the *Journal*. I remember very distinctly that when the rule was put in operation and the Unanimous Consent Calendar was called among the first bills which were reached on the calendar was one to which objection was made. Thereupon the gentleman in charge of the bill sought to receive recognition to move to suspend the rules and pass the bill, and that was done. It was done on more than one occasion, and it was always considered during the last Congress

[1] *Cong. Record*, 62nd Cong., 3rd Sess., p. 4449.

that the right of the Speaker to recognize for suspension of the rules was a right of recognition at any time, and if the motion prevailed it set aside the rule for the Unanimous Consent Calendar in the same way that it set aside the old rules.

I think the difficulty has arisen in the minds of gentlemen because of the change of the rules at the beginning of this Congress. We had a rule for unanimous consent and a rule for suspension and a rule for discharge of committees. The rule for the committee discharge expressly provided that the motion to discharge a committee should take precedence over a motion to suspend the rules. So that during the entire last session of Congress I sat here with motions on the calendar to discharge committees ready at any time to call up preferential motion to discharge a committee if the Speaker would give recognition to anyone to suspend the rules.

We were in the position that the Unanimous Consent Calendar was being called with the right of the Speaker to recognize for the suspension of the rules, but the prior right for a motion to discharge a committee was entered, that cut off the suspension and you could not make a motion to discharge a committee until the Unanimous Consent must be called before you could be recognized for the suspension. . . .

But the rule was abrogated or changed by the House some time ago, and suspensions were given priority over motions to discharge committees.

While the Speaker, it appears, has ruled otherwise, I am very clear in my own mind that all the time the right of the Speaker to recognize for a suspension was the [a] right which, if made and the motion prevailed, set aside the Unanimous Consent Calendar just as much as it did any other portion of the rules. But since the rules have been changed so that suspension is ahead of a motion to discharge a committee, I think the motion to suspend is in order at any time.

The Speaker. The gentleman does not mean to make that broad statement?

Mr. Mann. I mean on suspension days.

The Speaker. That is a qualification.

Mr. Mann. At any time during the last six days. The Unanimous Consent Calendar is never called except on suspension days, so that my statement is literally correct.

The Speaker. The question the Chair asks is this: Does the gentleman contend that on the first and third Mondays, leaving this particular difficulty out of consideration for the moment, when somebody objects to a bill that is called the Chair ought to recognize the Member then to suspend the rules?

Mr. Mann. I do not contend that the Chair ought to recognize the Member. Quite the contrary. I do contend that the Chair has the right to recognize him.

And Mr. Mann continued:

. . . Of course, it is not intended by the Unanimous Consent Calendar to allow bills to be placed on the calendar which, when objected to, gives the right to a motion to suspend the rules, because *the right to recognize for suspension has always been considered arbitrary in the Speaker, and, I take it, is necessary so. . . .*[1]

Speaker Clark submitted the resolution before the House, which, by a vote of 189 to 23,[2] held it to be in order, not because of the reason as presented in the resolution but rather on the ground that a motion to suspend the rules is in order on suspension days, regardless of whether the Calendar for Unanimous Consent has been called.

Another case occurred on October 5, 1914, which was suspension day. The special order of the House on that day was to consider, in the Committee of the Whole House on the state of the Union, a bill on the Philippines. But in its stead, Mr. Adamson of Georgia moved to suspend the rules and pass a Senate bill for the increase of cost for lighthouse

[1] *Cong. Record*, 62nd Cong., 3rd Sess., p. 4451.

[2] *Ibid.*, p. 4453.

tenders. Whereupon Mr. Henry of Texas raised a parliamentary inquiry whether in abandoning the special order of the day the Speaker should call up first the Calendar for Unanimous Consent before giving recognition to move to suspend the rules. This time Speaker Clark, however, asserted himself. In reply to the question, he ruled:

> . . . The more the Chair studies this subject of a motion to suspend the rules the more certain he is that the men who made the rule gave the Speaker authority to recognize Members on the first and third Mondays and the six last days of the session to move to suspend the rules in order that the Speaker by entertaining the motion might help the House out of a hole when it gets into one.[1]

He then stated in conclusion that the right of the Speaker to recognize members for suspension on a suspension day is an " unquestionable " one.[2]

Again on January 17, 1919, came a case which revealed, but in a much more striking manner, the range of discretion which the Speaker has on suspension days. This time the Speaker *pro tempore* (Mr. Crisp of Georgia), having entertained motions for the suspension of the rules " immediately " after the approval of the *Journal,* caused the Calendar for Unanimous Consent to be called. Mr. Stafford of Wisconsin inquired if it was in order to call the calendar under such crcumstances. In response, the Speaker *pro tempore* held: " The fact that there had been some motions to suspend the rules entertained previously in no wise vitiated the right that the Unanimous Consent Calendar should be called if the House should remain in session." [3] But much

---

[1] *Cong. Record,* 63rd Cong., 2nd Sess., p. 16182.

[2] *Ibid.,* p. 16182. For a similar case see *Cong. Record,* 66th Cong., 1st Sess., p. 4870.

[3] *Cong. Record,* 65th Cong., 3rd Sess., p. 1120.

more vigorous and pointed were Mr. Mann's words on this occasion:

> . . . It is the duty of the Speaker to have the Unanimous Consent Calendar called today under the rule. It is the privilege of the Speaker to recognize some one to ask unanimous consent to do something, and it is within the power of the Speaker to recognize any Member of the House today to move to suspend the rules, but meanwhile when those things are out of the way, then the Unanimous Consent Calendar automatically is called under the rules. . . .[1]

Several cases have occurred which give evidence of the control of the present Speaker, Mr. Longworth, over motions for the suspension of the rules. On April 5, 1926, Mr. Robsion of Kentucky was recognized to move to suspend the rules and pass a pension bill for Spanish war veterans. "I wish to take this opportunity to thank the distinguished Speaker of the House," said Mr. Robsion, "and our distinguished floor leader, Colonel Tilson, for giving us the opportunity to bring this bill before the House and afford the Members of the House an opportunity to express themselves."[2] On February 7, 1927, Speaker Longworth, in according recognition to Mr. Drane of Florida, a Democratic member, to move to suspend the rules and pass H. R. 16622 for survey of Coloosahatchee River drainage in Florida, made this statement:

> . . . The Chair desires to state in the interest of order that the Chair recognizes the gentleman from Florida because he has satisfied the Chair that his matter is a matter of urgency. Otherwise the Chair would not have recognized him to move to suspend the rules and pass the bill. The gentleman from Florida is recognized.[3]

[1] *Cong. Record*, 65th Cong., 3rd Sess., p. 1119.
[2] *Cong. Record*, 69th Cong., 1st Sess., p. 6910.
[3] *Ibid.*, 2nd Sess., p. 3217.

The passage of the longshoremen's bill toward the end of the second session of the Sixty-ninth Congress was another case. The bill had been before the House for several years. In the second session of the Sixty-ninth Congress Mr. Graham, chairman of the Committee on Judiciary, applied for a rule from the Committee on Rules which, after consideration for more than three weeks, refused to grant it, owing to the inclusion of seamen in the bill. Mr. Graham went back to his committee and obtained authorization to eliminate the seamen clause from the bill. As he said, on March 2, 1927, on the floor of the House:

> The bill then received the rule, which came up on Saturday of last week, but owing to the lateness of the hour and the uncertainties attending it, we did not start it on that day. Now, under a motion to suspend the rules, graciously granted by the Speaker, the measure is before you for consideration.[1]

That the power of recognition for the suspension of the rules is discretionary with the Speaker is a *fait accompli*. Whether the Speaker will take the majority floor leader into his confidence or will let the minority floor leader know in advance of the suspension motions is a matter for the Speaker to determine. Thus, on August 28, 1922, Mr. Mondell, the majority floor leader, asked unanimous consent to set a Wednesday for the consideration of business on the Unanimous Consent Calendar, but, as he had not discussed the matter with the Speaker,[2] he inquired if the latter " had any special legislation on suspension." In reply the Speaker, " who has control over suspension," stated " that he has no program as to suspension, and is willing to agree, if it will facilitate the agreement, that he will recognize no motions for suspension without the consent of the gentleman from

[1] *Cong. Record*, 69th Cong., 2nd Sess., p. 5319.
[2] Mr. Frederick H. Gillett was the Speaker.

Tennessee [Mr. Garrett],"[1] who was the minority floor leader.

On March 1, 1926, Mr. Garrett, of Tennessee, put the question to the Speaker: " This is Consent Calendar day. Many Members wish to know about any suspensions that may be coming on. Will there be any suspension today?" The Speaker replied that he had " agreed to recognize the gentleman from Maryland [Mr. Hill] to move to suspend the rules and pass a bill authorizing the War Department to sell certain lands. It is the intention of the Chair to proceed with the Consent Calendar until about 4 o'clock and then recognize the gentleman from Maryland."[2]

The question as to the role which the majority floor leader plays with regard to motions to suspend the rules was further answered by the following case. On December 21, 1926, Mr. Moore of Virginia complained of the uncertainty of the course of business in the House and inquired of Mr. Tilson, the majority floor leader, if he would consider it desirable to " enlarge " his " statement so as to indicate tentatively the business that will be taken up on the following day. . . . . For instance . . . . Monday is suspension day . . . . we have no means of forecasting what suspension will be asked for in the House on that day. It is conceivable that the gentleman from Connecticut might ascertain from the Speaker a little in advance as to who will be recognized and on what bills, to move to suspension."[3] Mr. Tilson rejoined:

So far as suspensions are concerned, as the House knows, the matter of recognition for suspension is one entirely within the control of the Speaker of the House. It is a prerogative that is

[1] *Cong. Record*, 67th Cong., 2nd Sess., pp. 11877-8.
[2] *Cong. Record*, 69th Cong., 1st Sess., p. 4784.
[3] *Ibid.*, 2nd Sess., p. 875.

his absolutely. I do not know that it would be proper for me to try to inform the House in advance as to a matter entirely within the Speaker's discretion, or that it would be possible for me, should the Speaker deem it proper, to tell in advance with certainty what motions to suspend he will eventually entertain.[1]

Moreover

It is not quite true that the Speaker or the floor leader always knows just what is coming up, as Members of the House will readily realize. So far as the Speaker granting recognition for suspension is concerned, he might be willing to entertain certain motions to suspend in case the Consent Calendar, for instance, had advanced to a certain stage, and he might be unwilling to do so unless it had advanced to that stage; so that the Speaker might not be able to state in advance what motions to suspend he would entertain.[2]

It has been the practice of the Speaker that on suspension days he will not recognize members for motions to suspend the rules unless the House has proceeded with the business on the Consent Calendar " to a certain stage," as Mr. Tilson put it. " Three or four times this last session," Speaker Clark declared in the second session of the Sixty-third Congress, " the Chair, recognizing the exigencies of the situation, has begun about 4 o'clock, or half-past 4, on the first and third Mondays to recognize Members to suspend the rules; and that has been his practice now for something like six weeks or two months." [3] Mr. Clark initiated the four o'clock " plan " because " he did not want to break up the Unanimous Consent Calendar, and did not want everybody to rush in with motions to suspend the rules every first and third Mondays." But if there are bills of importance, " the

---

[1] *Cong. Record*, 69th Cong., 2nd Sess., p. 875.

[2] *Ibid.*, p. 875.

[3] *Cong. Record*, 63rd Cong., 2nd Sess., p. 16182.

Speaker would be justified in interrupting the Unanimous Consent Calendar to entertain motions to suspend the rules." [1]

Speaker Gillett never made known his practice in respect to allowing motions for the suspension of rules on suspension days [not including the last six days of a session]. However, after examining the *Congressional Record* of the first and third Mondays during his administration we can fairly state that he generally followed the practice of his immediate predecessor. The same is true with Speaker Longworth, the present incumbent of the Speaker's chair. On February 21, 1927, Speaker Longworth announced that " about 3 o'clock he will begin to recognize motions for suspension. There is quite an important bill among them, and the Chair hopes that there will be a quorum present at that time." [2] The bill the Speaker referred to was the Porter resolution which urged the President of the United States to open negotiation with China to make a reciprocal treaty or treaties. That was the only utterance by the Speaker on this score, and it may be taken to indicate the general direction from which the wind blows on suspension days.

Mention has already been made of the Speaker's list,[3] in the exercise of his power over recognition. On suspension days the Speaker has a list of names of the members asking for recognition to suspend the rules. On March 3, 1913, Mr. Baker of California moved to suspend the rules and pass a bill for exchange of land for school sections in California. The bill not having a two-thirds vote in its favor, failed of passage. But " to show the fairness with which the Speaker has treated me," Mr. Baker gratefully

---

[1] *Cong. Record*, 63rd Cong., 2nd Sess., p. 16183.

[2] *Cong. Record*, 69th Cong., 2nd Sess., p. 4322.

[3] See *supra*, pp. 172-4.

stated, " I want to say that a month before this House adjourned at the second session I was placed six on the list.
The Speaker has continued to treat me fairly." However,
Mr. Baker yielded his place to members who had " matters
of importance," and was thus " further down the list." [1]   In
the same connection, Speaker Clark said:

. . . The Chair does not know whether he has adopted the
right or the wrong plan. This matter of suspension of the
rules is entirely within the discretion of the Speaker. The Chair
did not know any other way to do it, although he may study out
and find a better plan, but he took them in the order in which
they came, and the gentleman from California (Mr. Baker)
. . . stood six on the list to begin with, and he did let in gentlemen who had matters of pressing importance. The Chair
thought it was his duty to recognize him, and started in to try
and adhere to this list.[2]

There is no ironclad rule as to what bill the Speaker should
permit, or not permit, to come up under the suspension rule
for consideration. Sentiment of the members of the House
plays a part. " If," Speaker Clark tells us, " there is a pro-
nounced sentiment in the House amounting to a majority
or anywhere approximating two-thirds, in favor of the consideration of a particular bill, whether it be a big or a little
bill, I believe it is the business of the Speaker to recognize
some gentlemen, under the suspension of rules, to call that
bill up." [3]

No measure has a chance to be called up under the suspension of rules unless its sponsor can convince the Speaker
of its merit. A careful examination of the bills coming up
before the House under the suspension of rules in the Sixty-

[1] *Cong. Record,* 62nd Cong., 3rd Sess., p. 4822.

[2] *Ibid.,* p. 4822.

[3] *Cong. Record,* 63rd Cong., 2nd Sess., p. 1796.

ninth Congress discloses the fact that they were of various natures, as will be seen in the following table:

Bills Brought up under the Suspension of Rules in the Sixty-ninth Congress

Nature of Bills [1]	Number of Bills
Agriculture	4
Appropriations	1
Census	1
Civil Service	2
Flood Control	1
Foreign Affairs	2
Immigration	3
Interstate and Foreign Commerce	1
Irrigation	1
Judiciary	5
Library	1
Military Affairs	3
Mines and Mining	1
Naval Affairs	2
Patents	2
Pensions	4
Post-Office and Post-Roads	2
Public Buildings and Grounds	5
Revision of Laws	1
Ways and Means	3
World War Veterans	2
Total	47

Measures, such as appropriations, public buildings and rivers and harbors, are brought up under the suspension of rules with the distinct purpose of shutting off amendments or unnecessary " riders," while others, such as private bills relating to pensions and claims, are passed under this rule for the reason that it affords a short-cut to enactment. Occasionally a member of the minority party succeeds in

---

[1] Bills and resolutions are classified according to the character of the committees to which both bills and resolutions were referred under the rules of the House.

getting the Speaker to recognize him to move to pass a bill. During the last Congress, the Sixty-ninth, Speaker Longworth twice accorded recognition to Democratic members on suspension days: on February 7, 1927, he recognized Mr. Drane of Florida to move to pass a bill authorizing the Director of the Veteran's Bureau to make loans to veterans upon security of adjusted-service certificates,[1] and on February 28, 1927, he recognized Mr. Vinson of Georgia, the ranking minority member of the Committee on Naval Affairs, to move to pass a bill to authorize the Secretary of the Navy to proceed with the construction of certain public works.[2]

The Speaker may also recognize a member to move to suspend the rules and pass a bill in order to give members of the House an opportunity to put themselves on record on this particular measure, although he is aware of its impossibility of being passed by the House. The bill for the reapportionment of Representatives in Congress is a case in point. It came up, March 2, 1927, under the suspension rule, but lacking a two-thirds vote, failed of passage.[3] Members of the House, even proponents of the measure, knew that it would be defeated when brought up for consideration, but wished to vote on it as a matter of record.

As has been shown, only 47 bills and resolutions have been acted on under the suspension rule in the Sixty-ninth Congress, and of these 41 passed the House. With regard to the other six bills which failed of passage in the House, three lacked the necessary two-thirds vote and two were withdrawn after being called up.[4] One bill, H. R. 4475, providing for steel cars in the railway post-office service,

[1] *Cong. Record*, 69th Cong., 2nd Sess., p. 3217.
[2] *Ibid.*, p. 5112.
[3] *Ibid.*, p. 5323.
[4] *Ibid.*, 1st Sess., p. 13037.

failed to be seconded,[1] which means that the bill in question lacked the support of a majority vote of the House for its consideration under the suspension rule.

The small number of bills brought up under the suspension rule during the Sixty-ninth Congress shows that the Speaker has sparingly made use of his power of recognition under this rule.

Moreover, not all of the suspension days during the life of a Congress are used for the purpose for which they are set up, and therefore the occasions upon which the Speaker exercises his power of recognition are not as numerous as is generally supposed. Out of the nineteen suspension days [excluding the last six days of each session of Congress] during the Sixty-ninth Congress, only eleven were used by the Speaker for motions to suspend the rules.

Sometimes a special suspension day is set for the purpose of giving members of the House a chance to be recognized under this rule. "There are a number of bills," Mr. Underwood said on June 23, 1914, " [for] which applications have been made to suspend the rules and pass them. I ask unanimous consent that motions to suspend the rules and pass bills may be in order next Monday,"[2] the fifth Monday of the month. To quote the *Congressional Record* further:

Mr. Murdock. Reserving the right to object, have we had suspension days this season?

Mr. Underwood. There have been [a] good many suspension days, but no suspensions.

Mr. Murdock. What are these bills?

Mr. Underwood. The Speaker has the power of recognition for suspension of rules, and I am not proposing anybody's bill. I am merely proposing an opportunity for gentlemen who de-

---

[1] *Cong. Record*, 69th Cong., 2nd Sess., p. 5442.

[2] *Cong. Record*, 63rd Cong., 2nd Sess., p. 10973.

sire to be recognized for suspension of the rules to get a chance to get those bills up.

Mr. Murdock.   How does recognition come on suspension day?

Mr. Underwood.   That is entirely in the hands of the Speaker.

Mr. Murdock.   Members who have bills on the calendar and who desire to move to suspend the rules to pass those bills must see the Speaker and arrange for recognition?

Mr. Underwood.   That has always been the custom.[1]

A special suspension day may be also provided for the House to pass a certain bill or bills.   Thus, on February 10, 1925, Mr. Snell, of New York, called up a privileged resolution from the Committee on Rules which provided that " it shall be in order on Tuesday, February 10, 1925, after the adoption of this resolution, to move to suspend the rules under the provisions of Rule XXVII of the House of Representatives."

The real meaning of this resolution was set forth in a speech by Mr. Garrett of Tennessee:

. . . This special rule; that is, this rule to make this a special suspension day, is wholly for the purpose of the postal bill.   The other bills mentioned by the gentleman from Ohio [Mr. Longworth, who was then the majority floor leader] this morning I dare say had they been the only propositions involved, this rule would never have been brought in to consider them, when there is at least one more Monday and the last six days of the session set aside for suspension. . . . It is brought in for this postal bill, and it is brought in for the purpose of placing the membership of this House in the situation where they do not have an opportunity of correcting by amendment the inequalities of the revenue part of this bill.   (Applause.)   It places gentlemen in a position whichever way they vote they must vote for some injustice.[2]

[1] *Cong. Record*, 63rd Cong., 2nd Sess., p. 10973.
[2] *Cong. Record*, 68th Cong., 2nd Sess., p. 2414.

However, the resolution was passed by a vote of 245 to 97. Immediately thereafter the postal bill was brought up and passed under the suspension rule.[1]

The passage of the bonus bill in the Sixty-sixth Congress was brought about in a similar manner. On May 29, 1920, Mr. Campbell, of Kansas, offered a resolution from the Committee on Rules which provided that " it shall be in order for six legislative days, beginning May 29, 1920, for the Speaker to entertain motions of members of committees to suspend the rules under the provisions provided by the general rules of the House."

Before discussing the ulterior purpose of this resolution, we may at this juncture state the parliamentary interpretation with reference to the " last six days " of a session. Speaker Clark held, in answer to a question by Mr. Campbell of Kansas in the second session of the Sixty-second Congress, that " there are no ' last six days ' unless the two houses fix the last six days "[2] — that is, unless the two Houses have agreed to the date of final adjournment of that session. Commenting on the resolution of May 29, 1920, Mr. Clark said:

Now, about the adjournment. Of course, the short session has six days before the 4th of March, so that there is a definite time fixed for the beginning of the six days before adjournment in the short session in which to suspend the rules; but if the gentleman from Kansas (Mr. Campbell) brought in a rule here providing for adjournment in six days from now you could not pass it.[3]

Mr. Mann, of Illinois, a leader of the Republican party,

[1] *Cong. Record*, 68th Cong., 2nd Sess., p. 3431.

[2] *Cong. Record*, 62nd Cong., 2nd Sess., p. 11610.

[3] *Cong. Record*, 66th Cong., 2nd Sess., p. 7928.

criticized this resolution, which was sponsored by his own party:

Mr. Speaker, it has not been the practice of Congress to pass a resolution of this character at the long session. It has not been the practice to provide for suspensions being in order in the closing days of the long session. It has . . . never been done, with one exception, and that was when the Democrats were filibustering in a former Congress, and when we made suspensions in order by a majority vote.[1]

The general effect of the resolution was predicated by Mr. Clark:

I will tell the Speaker something he does not know, which he can learn only by experience; if they pass this rule [for suspension] he will be nearly insane by the time the six days are up. Every member here who has got a job on hand will be after him to get a chance to pass it under suspension rules.[2]

He continued:

I hope everybody understands what the situation is. I will state it again. In the first place, this rule is dangerous. Every kind of job can be put through under it. They [members of the House] will form an association—the suspension rules fellows—and you can not beat them when they form that association. I have seen it done.

If you beat this rule, the gentleman from Kansas (Mr. Campbell) will bring in a rule on the bonus bill that will not allow any amendment to it. If it does not go through, the public opinion of this House will drive him into bringing in a rule here to take up that bill under the general rules of the House.[3]

By a vote of 220 to 165 the resolution was passed. Im-

[1] *Cong. Record*, 66th Cong., 2nd Sess., p. 7927.
[2] *Ibid.*, p. 7928.
[3] *Ibid.*, p. 7928.

mediately Mr. Fordney of Michigan moved to suspend the rules and pass the bonus bill. By a vote of 289 to 92,[1] the Houses suspended the rules and passed the bill after forty minutes of perfunctory debate and without opportunity of offering amendments.

The Speaker is called upon to exercise the power of recognition over motions to suspend the rules during the last six days of the session — practically the short session — of a Congress more frequently than on the first and third Mondays of a month. Thus, out of the thirty-eight bills and resolutions brought up under the suspension of rules during the third session—the short session—of the Sixty-second Congress thirty-four were brought up during the last six days of the session. The first session of the Sixty-second Congress was a special session during which six bills were permitted by the Speaker to be called up under the suspension of rules and all of them were considered during the last two days of the session.[2] During the second session of this Congress—the long session—no member was recognized to present a matter before the House under the suspension rule during the last six days of the session.

Again, take the last Congress, the Sixty-ninth, for instance. Twenty-three bills and resolutions came up under the suspension of rules during the first session of this Congress which adjourned on July 3, 1926. Of these bills and resolutions only two were considered within the meaning of " the last six days' " clause of the rule. This was brought about by a unanimous consent request of June 30, 1926, made by Mr. Tilson. Mr. Tilson requested that " it may be in order at any time during the remainder of the present

[1] *Cong. Record*, 66th Cong., 2nd Sess., p. 7944.

[2] That session of Congress commenced on April 4, 1911, and closed on August 22, 1911. The bills were considered under the suspension of rules on August 21 and 22.

session to move to suspend the rules and pass . . . . the Green bill for the relief of World War veterans; and . . . . the Civil War pension bill passed by the Senate." [1]   On July 1, these two bills were thus passed.   During the second— the short—session twenty-three bills and resolutions were also considered under the suspension of rules, and twelve of them were brought up during the last six days of the session.

Two forms of dilatory tactics may be used to counteract the Speaker's power of recognition over motions to suspend the rules or as a means to defeat measures to which members of the House object.   A member may raise a point of no quorum after a bill is brought up under the suspension of rules.   Except the times when an important bill is under consideration, the House is usually working without a quorum.   Members of the House may be away "doing the chores " [2] for their constituents at the several departments, or may attend committee meetings or may remain in their offices attending to their voluminous correspondence both to and from his " folks at home."   Whenever a demand of no quorum is made, "unless the House shall adjourn, there shall be a call of the House," [3] which lasts for more than half an hour.   Mr. Mann of Illinois made use of this dilatory weapon to advantage.   " I will say," Mr. Linthicum of Maryland complained, " that I was eighth on the [Speaker's] list, and the gentleman from Illinois persistently raised the point of no quorum against me, and yet he let other bills of the very same nature . . . be passed without raising the point of no quorum." [4]

When the House is approaching the end of a session and when it is pressed for time to transact business, the Speaker

---

[1] *Cong. Record*, 69th Cong., 1st Sess., p. 12444.

[2] See *supra*, p. 151.

[3] Rule xv, 4.

[4] *Cong. Record*, 62nd Cong., 3rd Sess., p. 4832.

takes precautions to ward off from the House the attack of time-consuming, obstructive tactics. On March 3, 1913, the House was in continuous session until three o'clock in the morning of the following day—the day on which Congress adjourned. The House was then in " bad " temper and without a quorum. Speaker Clark therefore announced, when Mr. Baker of California rose to move to suspend the rules and pass a bill, that he would " not agree to recognize anybody to suspend the rules unless the gentleman is willing to withdraw it if it runs to a point where there is going to be a question of no quorum raised." [1] Mr. Baker agreed to the condition. " If," he said, " the point of no quorum is made I will have to withdraw it. I state that to the Speaker, and I will do it." [2]

Motion of adjournment is the other dilatory weapon for defeating a motion to suspend the rules over which the Speaker has control. The motion of adjournment is a preferential one, and when offered, takes precedence over that of the suspension of rules. Several times members of the House have resorted to this preferential motion to prevent the House from considering a bill which has received the permission of the Speaker to come up under the suspension of rules. The following case, occurring on January 20, 1913, may be cited as an illustration :

Mr. Hobson. Mr. Speaker—

Mr. Fitzgerald. Mr. Speaker, I move that the House do now adjourn.

The Speaker. The gentleman from New York moves that the House do now adjourn.

Mr. Clark. Mr. Speaker, a parliamentary inquiry.

The Speaker. The gentleman will state it.

[1] *Cong. Record*, 62nd Cong., 3rd Sess., p. 4821.

[2] *Ibid.*, p. 4821.

Mr. Clark of Florida.   The gentleman from Alabama (Mr. Hobson) addressed the Chair and was recognized.   Now, can the gentleman from New York take the gentleman off his feet by a motion?

The Speaker.   The gentleman from New York can do a thing which is equivalent to that.   The gentleman from Alabama had a right to make his motion, but the gentleman from New York had a right to make a preferential motion to adjourn, so the Chair shortened it a little—

Mr. Hobson.   I will make my motion, Mr. Speaker.

Mr. Fitzgerald.   I move to adjourn.

Mr Hobson.   I have the floor, Mr. Speaker.

The Speaker.   The Chair will recognize the gentleman—

Mr. Fitzgerald.   But I object to any consent being given to make any motion.

Mr. Garner.   Mr. Speaker.

The Speaker.   But the gentleman from Alabama was trying to make a motion before the gentleman from New York got up.

Mr. Fitzgerald.   I have already made the motion to adjourn, which is a preferential motion.

Mr. Hobson.   Mr. Speaker, I move to suspend the rules and take up for consideration the bill H. R. 1309 [providing for a Council of National Defense.]

The Speaker.   The gentleman from New York moves to adjourn.

Mr. Hobson.   Mr. Speaker, I have the floor.

The Speaker.   The gentleman from New York made a preferential motion.

Mr. Hobson.   How does he know it has the highest preference?

The Speaker.   The Chair knows it, even if the gentleman from New York does not.   (Laughter.)   A motion to adjourn is the highest motion that can be made in the House.

Mr. Hobson.   But it can not interrupt a sentence that is being spoken.

The Speaker.   The gentleman has finished his sentence.   He had moved to suspend the rules, and the gentleman from New York made a motion to adjourn.

Mr. Hobson. And pass the bill. That is all I desire to see in the *Record,* Mr. Speaker.

Mr. Fitzgerald. I have no desire to stand in the way of the gentleman doing that.

Mr. Hobson. I move that the House suspend the rules and pass the bill H. R. 1309.

The Speaker. That is the motion the gentleman made a short time ago, and the Chair recognized him for that purpose, and then the Chair recognized the gentleman from New York to move to adjourn.[1]

And the House accordingly adjourned.

On February 17, 1913, Mr. Small of North Carolina was recognized to move to suspend the rules and pass a bill authorizing the collection of the military and naval records of the Revolutionary War with a view to their publication. The Clerk having read the title to the bill, Mr. Clayton of Alabama rose to move that the House adjourn.[2] The motion was carried.

To summarize: The power of the Speaker over motions for the suspension of rules is discretionary. On suspension days the Speaker may recognize a member to move to suspend the rules and pass a bill whenever he sees fit or he may refuse to recognize any member to call up any bill under this rule. Great as the power is, the Speaker has sparingly exercised it. And great as the power is, a member of the House can obstruct its exercise by making a motion of no quorum or a motion of adjournment.

[1] *Cong. Record,* 62nd Cong., 3rd Sess., p. 1811.

[2] *Cong. Record,* 62nd Cong., 3rd Sess., p. 3304. *Cf. ibid.,* p. 4255 where Speaker Clark stated that "the gentleman from North Carolina has had a matter up for about 18 months, waiting to get a chance to suspend the rules ..."

CHAPTER VI

CALENDAR WEDNESDAY

THE adoption of Calendar Wednesday, March 1, 1909, marked another advance in the direction of parceling out the Speaker's power of control over the order of business in the House. Prior to its adoption the rules provided that after the unfinished business of the House has been disposed of, the Speaker " shall call each standing committee in regular order, and then select committees, and each committee when named may call up for consideration any bill reported by it on a previous day on the House Calendar." [1] This is what is called the " morning hour," [2] which occupies the sixth place in the order of business.[3] Largely due to the pressure of the business of the House but partly also due to the de-

---

[1] Rule xxiv, 4. There are three Calendars in the House: (1) The Union Calendar; (2) the House Calendar; and (3) the Private Calendar. To the House Calendar are referred "all bills of a public nature not raising revenue nor directly or indirectly appropriating money or property." See Rule xiii, 1.

[2] " The ' morning hour ' is one of the oldest devices of the rules for devoting an early portion of the session to a specific class of business. Until 1885 the hour was set for the reception of reports from committees. In 1890 it was provided that reports should be filed with the Clerk, and the ' morning hour ' was by this rule devoted to a call of committees for the consideration of bills on the House Calendar." *House Manual,* section 866, 69th Congress.

[3] The daily order of business of the House is as follows: (1) prayer by the Chaplain; (2) reading and approval of the *Journal;* (3) correction of reference of public bills; (4) disposal of business on the Speaker's table; (5) unfinished business; (6) the morning hour for the consideration of bills called up by committees; (7) motions to go into the Committee of the Whole House on the state of the Union; and (8) orders of the day. Rule xxiv, 1.

228

mand of political exigencies, the House never arrives at the sixth order. Almost always there are some privileged matters injected into the daily routine of the House before the arrival of the sixth order. Sometimes it may be a report from one of the committees which is privileged to " report at any time." [1] Or it may be a revenue or appropriation bill which is in order " at any time after the reading of the *Journal*." [2] Or still at other times it may be a report from a committee of conference, which is "always in order, except when the *Journal* is being read, while the roll is being called, or the House is dividing on any proposition." [3] On Fridays private business is in order for consideration " after the disposal of such business on the Speaker's table as requires reference only." [4] Very often the House spends days and even weeks in considering a single bill, to the exclusion of matters below the fifth order of business.

" For two years," Mr. Hepburn of Iowa said, ". . . that rule of ours, that order of business of ours, that sixth item of procedure in the order of business lay in disuse." [5] And " until this session," Mr. Gardner of Massachusetts declared on one occasion, " I have never except once known that seventh [sixth] order to be reached. On that single occasion a certain agricultural bill, brought in by Mr. Adams of Wisconsin, was considered and passed, but the time for debate was occupied with the discussion of an entirely different subject." [6] Mr. Gardner held that the impossibility—or the difficulty — for the House in reaching the sixth order of

[1] Rule xi, 56. Also see above chapter iii relating to the use of special orders from the Committee on Rules.

[2] Rule xvi, 9.

[3] Rule xxviii.

[4] Rule xxiv, 6.

[5] *Cong. Record*, 60th Cong., 2nd Sess., p. 2655.

[6] *Ibid.*, p. 601.

business was due to the control of the Speaker over the order of business of the House. As chairman of the Committee on Rules, the Speaker could cause a special order to be reported from that committee for the immediate consideration of a bill. And as chairmen of all other House committees were but members of his "cabinet,"[1] he could persuade those with privileged status under the rules of the House to bring in privileged matters to interrupt the daily order of business.[2] Moreover, the Speaker has certain discretion in laying before the House the business on the Speaker's table,[3] the fourth order. And as soon as the latter is disposed of the House arrives at the fifth order of unfinished business.[4] Frequently the House adjourns even before it is through with the business on this order. Furthermore, there was the power of recognition of the Speaker: the Speaker might recognize or refuse to recognize a member for the purpose for which he rises.[5] As a rule, with the exception of a few majority leaders, members of the House are ignorant of the course of business in the legislative mill. Mr. Moore of Virginia complained that it was almost impossible for a member to know in advance of the business in the House unless he was in the confidence of the Committee on Rules or of the leaders of the majority,[6] among whom the Speaker is the "dean."[7]

[1] See *Cong. Record*, 60th Cong., 2nd Sess., p. 2654.

[2] For the relation of the Speaker to the chairmen of the House committees with regard to legislation, see *supra*, p. 90.

[3] See *Cong. Record*, 66th Cong., 1st Sess., pp. 3954, 3955; also *cf.* Hinds, *op. cit.*, iv, 3107, 3111.

[4] See Rule xxiv, 1.

[5] See above chapter iv on the power through recognition.

[6] *Cong. Record*, 66th Cong., 2nd Sess., p. 6878. Mr. Clark of Missouri suggested a bulletin board, which practice was adopted by Mr. Mondell and Mr. Longworth when floor leaders of the Republican majority. For the practice of Floor Leader Tilson, see *supra*, pp. 213-4.

[7] *Cong. Record*, 62nd Cong., 2nd Sess., p. 11840.

Privileged matters, let it be noted, may interrupt the order of business " only with the consent of a majority of the House, expressed as to appropriation bills by a vote on going into the Committee of the Whole to consider such bill, and as to matters like conference reports, question of privilege, etc., by raising and voting on the question of consideration." [1] Argument was therefore advanced, in defense of the Speaker, that a majority of the House, if so determined, " could at any time reach any bill on the calendar by voting down the consideration of intervening bills . . . . until the desired bill was reached." [2] In theory this argument was sound, but in practice it was not so. And to prove the unsoundness of the argument, Mr. Gardner of Massachusetts stated at length:

. . . Mr. Hinds claims that when a majority of the House really wishes to reach any measure on the calendar, no matter how much privileged business intervenes, all that is required is to vote down the consideration of the intervening matters. He even pointed out, what is perfectly true, that this very step has been sucessfully taken in the past. The last time that the attempt was successful, so far as I can find, was in 1898, a decade ago. The bill reached under this process of elimination was the Hawaii bill, to which Mr. Speaker Reed was certainly opposed. It is perfectly true that in its earliest stages he used all the means in his power to prevent its consideration.

However, it is evident, upon consulting the *Record,* that as soon as Mr. Reed and his personal representatives, the Committee on Rules, saw that the House in all probability had made up its mind to reach the Hawaii bill, they no longer interposed for purposes of delay the various parliamentary devices at their disposal.

Since that time, so far as I know, there has been no success-

[1] *House Manual,* section 857, 69th Congress.
[2] See *supra,* p. 131.

ful attempt to repeat the mode of procedure then adopted. I may, of course, be mistaken, but if I am right it must be admitted that a precedent 10 years old goes to prove the rule. If the process of reaching unprivilegd bills by elimination has not succeeded more than once in a decade, it certainly is not a very practical method.

Let us confront the situation as we usually find it, and we shall quickly see the narrowness of the opportunity which Mr. Hinds suggests. Suppose that it is desired to reach a highly contentious but important bill on the Union Calendar, and that there are plenty of intervening bills more favorably placed. Some Member of the House thinks that a majority wishes to consider this bill. He would like the House to vote down the motion to go into Committee of the Whole to consider some appropriation bill; but he has no opportunity to explain his purpose, because that motion is not debatable. Generally the House does not understand what he is driving at.

But suppose that he has a chance to explain his plans before the motion is made, and suppose that the House sees their full bearing. Even so, Members will think a long time before voting down the consideration of one of the great supply bills of this Government, especially when they are told, as they will be told, and as they were told the only time I ever saw elimination attempted, that there would be plenty of time later on to reach the desired measure.

Not only is it true that Members will hesitate to vote down the consideration of a general approriation bill, but, even if they should do so, it takes a long time for a yea and nay vote. Then comes the call of the calendar. That exhausts an hour more, but at last the chance comes to reach the Union Calendar. All committees at this stage have equal right of recognition. Suppose that committee after committee is recognized and that one intervening bill after another is brought up. To each of them in turn consideration must be refused by a yea and nay vote, if demanded. How often under these circumstances would the House be persuaded to vote down adjournment? In other words, it might be necessary to take recess for several days before a majority, no matter how determined, could reach the desired bill? Meanwhile many a bill will have intervened against whose consideration Members will not care to vote. Members will say to themselves: " If I vote down the consideration of that bill, after I go home I shall be obliged to spend all my time in explaining why I did so." [1]

Such being the conditions, bills—and literally there are hundreds of them—on the House Calendar which have no privileged status and cannot get unanimous consent requests and for which special orders cannot be obtained from the Committee on Rules,—these bills practically have no chance to get a hearing before the House. [2] It is really little wonder that the House Calendar has earned the title of " legislative graveyard." To ameliorate these conditions was therefore one of the early attempts of the parliamentary reformers. As Mr. Gardner has well said:

I believe that some definite time should be set apart when nothing is in order except matters which are not at present privileged under the rules. I think the most imperative reform which presses is the provision of a day when unprivileged measures only shall be in order so long as any bill that a committee wishes to call up remain [s] on the calendar. . . . [3]

To this end, several suggestions were made. Mr. Gardner thought that the privilege to call up these measures should rest with a committee, or with a responsible group, or with a majority of members on petition rather than with individuals. He termed it " Calendar Tuesday." [4] Mr. Williams of Missouri, the Democratic floor leader, while agreeing in principle with Mr. Gardner, was, however, in favor of set-

---

[1] *Cong. Record*, 60th Cong., 2nd Sess., pp. 601, 602.

[2] See *supra*, p. 115 (footnote) relating to the number of bills and resolutions reported from the committees and are thus placed on the calendars.

[3] *Cong. Record*, 60th Cong., 2nd Sess., p. 603.

[4] *Ibid.*, pp. 603 *et seq.*

tling upon the majority of the House as the number required to render the petition valid, whereas Mr. Cockran of New York suggested that one-fifth of the membership of the House should be sufficient to demand consideration of any such bill, and in addition, he suggested that the minority leader should have the same privilege to demand that a bill be placed on its passage on a roll-call.[1]

Whatever suggestions members of the House might have advanced, the general trend of thought was, nevertheless, very much in the same direction, that is, to provide ways and means whereby unprivileged bills on the House Calendar might have a chance to be called up for action. Its importance lies in the fact that it was one of the many attempts on the part of the members to make the rules of the House more definite, more secure and less susceptible to the manipulations of the Speaker in conjunction with a few of the majority leaders.

Finally, on March 1, 1909, Mr. Dalzell of Pennsylvania reported from the Committee on Rules the following resolution for adoption:

On Wednesday of each week no business shall be in order, except as provided by paragraph 4 of Rule XXIV, unless the House by *majority* vote on a motion to dispense therewith shall otherwise determine. On such a motion there may be debate not to exceed five minutes for or against.

On a call of committees under this rule bills may be called up from either the House or Union Calendar, except bills which are privileged under the rules; but bills called up from the Union Calendar shall be considered in the Committee of the Whole House on the state of the Union.

This rule shall not apply during the last two weeks of the session.[2]

[1] *Cong. Record*, 60th Cong., 2nd Sess., pp. 611-614.
[2] *Cong. Record*, 60th Cong., 2nd Sess., p. 3567. Mr. Williams of

In other words, this resolution sought to achieve three things. First, there should be once a week, except during the last two weeks of the session, a call of committees. Secondly, Calendar Wednesday should not be dispensed with, except on a direct motion by a majority vote, for the consideration of any other privileged measure such as revenue or appropriation bills. This is an important point. As was shown, prior to the adoption of this rule, the tactics of the Speaker together with his party leaders, to do away with the " morning hour " call, was usually to call up a privileged bill, and the members of the House who intended to preserve the call of committees had no other choice but to take upon themselves the responsibility either of voting for or against the consideration of any such bill. But, with the adoption of this calendar, privileged bills are not in order on Wednesdays except on a direct motion by a majority vote. Thirdly, bills can under this rule be called, on Wednesdays, either from the House or Union Calendar. " From the Speaker's standpoint," said Mr. Dalzell in support of the new rule, " it will relieve him largely from requests for unanimous consent, and from the member's standpoint it will relieve him largely of the necessity of going to the Speaker and asking for unanimous consent." [1]

Missouri offered the following amendment to the resolution: "On Tuesdays of each week no business shall be in order except an alphabetical call of the membership of the House. Upon the call of each member's name he shall be permitted to offer for the consideration of the House one public bill to be selected from either the House or the Union Calendar. The bill called up from the Union Calendar shall be considered in Committee on the Whole House on the state of the Union; and there shall be given to general debate twenty minutes to the side, and the consideration of the bill under five-minute rule, for amendment, such time as shall be agreed upon or such time as shall, upon motion without debate, be voted by the House." *Ibid.*, p. 3568.

[1] *Ibid.*, p. 3568.

The " insurgent " members of the House were, however, opposed to the adoption of the rule. " It is in my judgment," declared Mr. Norris of Nebraska, " the most comical parliamentary joke that ever came down the legislative pike. In its application it is a homeopathic dose of nothingness." [1] Mr. Norris was concerned with the immediate effectiveness of the rule. As Congress was about to expire March 4, only three days from the introduction of the resolution, the House could not, so Mr. Norris argued, pass a rule that would live beyond the life of the Congress in which it was adopted. Moreover, by the very nature of its provision that the rule " shall not apply during the last two weeks of the session," there remained no opportunity for the House in that session to put the rule into operation. " We are therefore in the foolish and ridiculous position of adopting a rule," Mr. Norris continued, " that by its own terms and by its own stipulation can never have any legal effect, in life or in vitality." [2] Mr. Murdock of Kansas, later a Roosevelt Republican, also voiced his dissatisfaction. " The real danger of the adoption of this proposed amendment is that," Mr. Murdock reasoned, " it may defeat for a long time [the] real reform in the rules." [3]

The rule was adopted by a close vote of 158 to 163. It was not put into operation in the Sixtieth Congress which expired only three days after it passed the House. When the Sixty-first Congress convened on March 15, 1909, the rule for Calendar Wednesday was again adopted with, however, an important innovation in that this calendar could not be dispensed with except by a two-thirds vote, and, in addition, it shall not be in order for the Speaker to entertain a motion for a recess on any Wednesday except during the

[1] *Cong. Record*, 60th Cong., 2nd Sess., p. 3570.

[2] *Ibid.*, p. 3570.

[3] *Ibid.*, p. 3570.

last two weeks of the session." [1] This time the rule was not seriously debated in the House. As a matter of fact, it was not until March 16, 1910, that the rule was brought to test. On that Wednesday, Mr. Crumpacker of Indiana called up a census bill not under the rule. Immediately both Mr. Fitzgerald of New York and Mr. Mann of Illinois raised points of order, which Speaker Cannon overruled and said:

. . . Under the rules of the House it is perfectly clear that a question merely made privileged by the rules of the House would not be in order today; but this [census bill] is a higher question . . . presenting a privilege higher than any rule of the House would give. [2]

The ruling provoked a heated debate, the consequence of which proved to be very disastrous to the prerogatives of the Speaker. Mention has already been made of this great parliamentary battle which went on for three days in the House of Representatives. [3] But here only what has direct bearing upon the rule of Calendar Wednesday will be dwelt upon. First and perhaps the most convincing of all was the speech by Mr. Underwood of Alabama in opposition to the ruling of Speaker Cannon:

Mr. Speaker, I am very much opposed to the ruling of the Speaker in this case, and hope that the House will reverse the decision of the Chair, because I believe if the decision of the Chair is adopted as the ruling of the House in this case Calendar Wednesday will pass away and be of no more benefit to the House than is the original right to call the calendar. The reason you could not do business under the old rule on the call of the calendar was that the chairmen of committees, under the direc-

---

[1] *Cong. Record*, 61st Cong., 1st Sess., pp. 22, 23.

[2] *Cong. Record*, 61st Cong., 2nd Sess., pp. 3240, 3241.

[3] See *supra*, pp. 139 *et seq.*

tion of the Speaker or the Rules Committee, could inject between the House and the calendar other business that they demominated as privileged business, and your calendar was gone. Now, the House in its wisdom in adopting the rule for Calendar Wednesday, said that this Calendar Wednesday should not be interfered with except by a two-thirds vote of this House. That does not mean a ruling of the Speaker; that does not mean a decision of the Speaker as to whether the matter is privileged or is not privileged. It means a vote of two-thirds of the members of this House. . . . If it is in order because it is privileged . . . because it relates to the taking of census, it is equally in order to consider today a bill raising revenue. Does not the Constitution of the United States fix the duty on Congress and on this House to consider all revenue bills? Is a bill to take census of any more vital importance to the people of the United States than a bill to raise revenue to support the Government? Is it of any greater privilege or has it been considered of any greater privilege in the history of this House? Not at all. And therefore if this House today votes to sustain the Speaker and recognize the bill of the gentleman from Indiana as privileged, and thereby set aside the Calendar Wednesday, you open the door to inject between you and the call of the calendar an appropriation bill, a revenue bill, and other matters of privilege that will destroy the rule you adopted in the last session of Congress for the benefit of this House.[1]

The issue was very clear. As Mr. Mann has said:

Whatever the decision of the House may be, it will in my judgment, remain without question that this House has determined to give to Calendar Wednesday a fair and impartial trial and to preserve to the House Calendar Wednesday so long as, in its judgment, it can keep on transacting business of the country and maintain Calendar Wednesday, and I believe that will be forever.[2]

[1] *Cong. Record*, 61st Cong., 2nd Sess., pp. 3242, 3243.
[2] *Ibid.*, p. 3249.

As has been stated, Speaker Cannon overruled the point of order.[1] An appeal was taken, and by a vote of 112 against 163 the House reversed the Speaker's ruling. Thus the House, by its vote in this case, showed a decisive voice in preserving the Calendar Wednesday in defiance of the Speaker's ruling. It was from this never-to-be-forgotten struggle that the name " Holy Calendar Wednesday " was originated.

But it would be erroneous to assume that Calendar Wednesday is as sacrosanct as is commonly supposed. In the first session of the Sixty-first Congress, that is, from March 15, 1909, to August 5, 1909, not a single Calendar Wednesday was observed by the House. During the month of March the rule for the Calendar Wednesday was " automatically " dispensed with without a direct motion as was required by the rule, because there was no business on the calendar. The fact was that the House was during that time considering a tariff bill, and the House committees, except those on Ways and Means, on Rules, on Mileages and on Accounts, were not appointed until the last day of the session.[2] From April to August the House was never in

---

[1] In making the ruling Speaker Cannon said: "... If the rule were to be construed literally, without any exception whatever, whether it be statutory law or the fixed law of the land—the Constitution—that might stand in the way, then nothing else could be done on Calendar Wednesday except the call of the committees." Speaker Cannon seemed to have overlooked the fact that privileged matters could be in order on Wednesday if so decided by a two-thirds vote of the House. However, Speaker Cannon went on to say: "... If the Chair was four inches wide and a thousandth of an inch thick, the Chair would feel some gratification if the House should see proper to overrule the Chair upon the point of order that the action of the majority of the House under its rules, in reversing the present Speaker, would make it plain that he has no more and no less authority than any Speaker who has proceeded him, would set at rest the question whether the Speaker 'doth like Colossus, bestride the world.'" *Ibid.*, pp. 3250, 3251.

[2] *Cong. Record*, 61st Cong., 1st Sess., pp. 57, 5901, 5902.

session on Wednesdays, and was usually declared in adjournment either from Monday to Thursday or from Tuesday to Thursday, thus indirectly dispensing with Calendar Wednesdays. Whether the adjournment of the House on Wednesdays throughout the session was meant to evade the rule for Calendar Wednesday was immaterial. Probably not, as the House seemed to have been considering only the tariff bill, to the exclusion of nearly all other important business. Nevertheless, two important facts present themselves. In the first place, Speaker Cannon, by not appointing the committees, except a very few, until the closing day of the session, had prevented the House from legislating, and the consequence was that Calendar Wednesday, for want of business, was " automatically " dispensed with. Here, as elsewhere, the power of the Speaker in appointing committees was felt. In the second place, in declaring the House in adjournment either from Monday to Thursday or from Tuesday to Thursday, the majority leaders have an ingenious way of killing both the letter and spirit of the rule. To show how it was done in the first session of the Sixty-first Congress, the following table might be useful.

This device, let it be remembered, has been frequently resorted to in the later Congresses. During the first session of the Sixty-third Congress which convened on April 7, 1913, and expired on December 1, 1913, there were thirty-three Calendar Wednesdays without counting the last two weeks during which the rule for Calendar Wednesday is not applicable.[1] Of these thirty-three Calendar Wednesdays, thirty were dispensed with by the following methods: (1) sixteen Calendar Wednesdays found the House in adjournment either from Monday to Thursday or from Tuesday to

[1] See Rule xxiv, 7.

CALENDAR WEDNESDAY IN OPERATION DURING THE FIRST SESSION OF THE
SIXTY-FIRST CONGRESS

April 7, 1909 (Wednesday)	Tariff bill was considered.
April 12 to April 15 (Thursday)	House in adjournment.[1]
April 15 to April 19 (Monday)	" " "
April 19 to April 22 (Thursday)	" " "
April 22 to April 26 (Monday)	" " "
April 26 to April 29 (Thursday)	" " "
April 29 to May 3 (Monday)	" " "
May 3 to May 6 (Thursday)	" " "
May 6 to May 10 (Monday)	" " "
May 10 to May 13 (Thursday)	" " "
May 13 to May 17 (Monday)	" " "
May 17 to May 20 (Thursday)	" " "
May 20 to May 24 (Monday)	" " "
May 24 to May 27 (Thursday)	" " "
May 28 to June 1 (Tuesday)	" " "
June 1 to June 3 (Thursday)	" " "
June 3 to June 7 (Monday)	" " "
June 7 to June 10 (Thursday)	" " "
June 10 to June 14 (Monday)	" " "
June 14 to June 17 (Thursday)	" " "
June 17 to June 21 (Monday)	" " "
June 21 to June 24 (Thursday)	" " "
June 24 to June 28 (Monday)	" " "
June 28 to July 1 (Thursday)	" " "
July 1 to July 5 (Monday)	" " "
July 5 to July 8 (Thursday)	" " "
July 12 to July 15 (Thursday)	" " "
July 16 to July 19 (Monday)	" " "
July 20 (Tuesday) to July 23 (Friday)	" " "
July 23 to July 27 (Tuesday)	" " "
July 27 to July 29 (Thursday)	" " "
August 4 (Wednesday)	The last day of the session.

[1] In accordance with the standing order the House usually meets at
12 m. See Hinds, *op. cit.*, i, 104-109, 116, 117; iv, 4325.

During this session the House, upon a motion by a member on the
majority side, adjourned shortly after it convened. For instance, on
April 12, 1909, the House adjourned at 2:15 p. m. The procedure was thus:

"Mr. Dalzell. Mr. Speaker, I move that the House do now adjourn. The motion was agreed to; and accordingly (at 2 o'clock and
15 minutes p. m.) the House adjourned until Thursday next (April 15)."
See *Cong. Record*, 61st Cong., 1st Sess., p. 1344.

Friday; (2) on five Wednesdays the House adjourned shortly after it assembled, the time of adjournment varying from 12:15 p. m. to 12:40 p. m.; (3) one was taken for debating on the date of adjournment; (4) three were spent for the consideration of a tariff bill; (5) one, that is, July 2, 1913, was at first taken up by a question of personal privilege and then followed by a motion of adjournment; (6) on another Wednesday, July 9, the House considered as its special continuous order a resolution for the investigation of the influence of lobbyists over legislation; (7) another Wednesday, August 27, found the President of the United States addressing Congress at a joint session; (8) another day, September 10, was dispensed with by a unanimous consent request for the consideration of a currency bill; and (9) at last on September 17 the House, in accordance with the rule for Calendar Wednesday, dispensed with the regular business on that date by a two-thirds vote. In other words, during the entire first session of the Sixty-third Congress only three of the thirty-three Calendar Wednesdays were used for the purpose for which the rule was established.

The rule has shown imperfections in its operation and has thus furnished members of the House ample opportunities to violate its spirit, if not its letter. Even as early as the Sixty-first Congress the practice of calling up a lengthy bill was in evidence, a bill which would take several continuous Calendar Wednesdays for its consideration. Once in that Congress the House having devoted two continuous Wednesdays to a bill for the revision of the judiciary title of the Revised Statutes, Mr. Crumpacker of Indiana regretfully remarked: " It is an abuse at least of the spirit and purpose of Calendar Wednesday to take up a bill of this character, one that will take up all of the Calendar Wednesdays during the entire session of Congress." Mr. Crumpacker moved to dispense with Calendar Wednesday so as to enable the House to consider another bill. The motion was rejected by an overwhelming vote of 28 against 279.[1] And in the following Congress, August 10, 1911, Speaker Clark, apparently in keeping with the feeling of the House as shown in the Crumpacker motion, made a ruling that a bill undisposed of on Calendar Wednesday will be in order the following Calendar Wednesday as unfinished business.[2] The inevitable consequence of Speaker Clark's ruling was presaged by Mr. Hinds:

Now, I invite your attention, Mr. Speaker, to what will happen today if you rule that this bill must go over until next Wednesday. I infer from what happened yesterday that there was against this bill a large and a determined opposition. They have found, if you shall rule as many here urge you to rule, that by debating that bill until the time of adjournment yesterday they have thrown it over for a week; and next week, when you shall again call it up, they will find that by debating it through that day they can throw it over to another week.[3]

These tactics, the tactics of debating a bill called up on Calendar Wednesday from one Wednesday to another under the name of unfinished business, were effective in emasculating the rule, particularly during the second session of the Sixty-third Congress. During that session the Committee on Revision of Laws called up on April 15, 1914, Wednesday, a bill " to codify, revise and amend the laws relating to the judiciary." From April 15 to June 17, 1914, for a period of ten Wednesdays, the House had that single bill under consideration.[4] Then, on August 12, 1914, Wednes-

---

[1] *Cong. Record*, 61st Cong., 3rd Sess., pp. 1771, 1772.

[2] *Cong. Record*, 62nd Cong., 1st Sess., pp. 3814-3819; also see *ibid.*, 3rd Sess., p. 1929.

[3] *Ibid.*, 2nd Sess., p. 3816.

[4] *Cong. Record*, 63rd Cong., 2nd Sess., pp. 6764, 7087, 7429, 8177, 8523, 8903, 9319, 9747, 10193, 10691.

day, the Committee on Printing called up a bill for the revision of printing laws. This bill occupied nine Calendar Wednesdays, that is, from August 12 until October 15, 1914.[1] There was then no provision in the rule limiting the general debate on a bill when called up on Calendar Wednesday. And when a bill was thus called up, each member of the House, if recognized by the Speaker, was entitled to debate on it for an hour with the result that a bill could be held before the House from one Wednesday to another. " The Chair," as Speaker Clark commented on the rule for Calendar Wednesday, " is very frank to state publicly what he has stated privately, that he believes that rule ought to be changed and a limit fixed to the time that any gentleman can hold up the House upon that day." [2]

Determined efforts to reform the rule were made on the opening day of the Sixty-fourth Congress. Mr. Lenroot of Wisconsin spoke of the rule as " a farce." Mr. Mann of Illinois unsuccessfully attempted to move to recommit the customary resolution for the adoption of the rules to a committee of seven in the hope that the rule for Calendar Wednesday might be thereby amended.[3] Happily the defeat of the Mann amendment only temporarily arrested the movement to reform the rule. On January 18, 1916, the Committee on Rules reported a rule which provided that general debate on a bill called up on Calendar Wednesday shall be limited to two hours and shall also be confined to the subject, and that no committee shall occupy more than two Calendar Wednesdays unless the House by a two-thirds vote shall otherwise determine.[4]

[1] *Ibid.*, pp. 13655, 13988, 14279, 14614, 14869, 15224, 15595, 15963, 16677.
[2] *Cong. Record*, 62nd Cong., 2nd Sess., p. 7562.
[3] *Ibid.*, pp. 7-13.
[4] *Ibid.*, pp. 1209-1214.

The rule for Calendar Wednesday has since then remained unaltered. In its actual application there are, however, defects which work to the disadvantage of the individual members. In the first place, it was ruled that only the chairman of a committee can call up a bill on Calendar Wednesday.[1] The practical effect of this ruling amounts to this: the chairman of a committee, especially of an important committee, who is generally in accord with the party chieftains, including the Speaker, may not call up a bill on Calendar Wednesday which, for one reason or another, may have some objectionable features. This practice ultimately tends towards strengthening the party control in the House. The

[1] On December 15, 1920, Mr. Flood of Virginia called up a concurrent resolution from the Committee on Foreign Affairs during the absence of the chairman. Mr. Flood did so without the authorization of the committee. A point of order was made against Mr. Flood. Mr. Flood argued, however, that the rule for Calendar Wednesday provides that "... On a call of committees under this rule, bills may be called up from either the House or the Union Calendar ...," and that " it is not necessary for a member to have special authority to call it up, being favorably reported by the committee and being on the Calendar, it is presumed that it has been authorized ... If it should be held that only the chairman could call up bills, then the entire work of the committee would be placed at the mercy of the chairman of the committee." Speaker Gillett held, however, that Mr. Flood could not call up the resolution. *Cong. Record,* 66th Cong, 3rd Sess., pp. 395, 396. The concurrent resolution in question was for the purpose of expressing the sympathy of Congress with the Irish people for independence. Undoubtedly the nature of the resolution had something to do with Speaker Gillett's action.

Mr. Henderson of Iowa revealed the following fact regarding the practice of calling up bills: "... Some Committees have usually at the commencement of their work passed a resolution to the effect that any bill reported from that committee favorably should be subject to the control of the party reporting it, so that he could call it up by unanimous consent or on a call of committees, if on the House Calendar [before the inauguration of Calendar Wednesday], on committee or individual suspension day and all methods known under the rules." This was the practice of the Committee on Judiciary when Mr. Henderson was its chairman. *Cong. Record,* 56th Cong., 1st Sess., p. 5821.

other defect, arising out of a ruling of Speaker Gillett, is that a member in favor of the bill under consideration can move the previous question even after " one minute's debate." [1]   On the one hand, it may be argued that Speaker Gillett's decision is a wholesome one in curtailing some of the meticulous debates on Calendar Wednesdays.   But, on the other hand, it may also be argued on the same ground that the curtailment of debate in this wise is menacing the sound principle of government by discussion.

Calendar Wednesday might have served its purpose; but judging by its fruit, it is still far from being satisfactory. Echoes of complaints reverberate now and then.   And in the first session of the Sixty-ninth Congress, or to be more exact, on December 15, 1925, Mr. Luce of Massachusetts called the attention of the House to the following facts:

. . . Mr. Speaker.   I desire to use this opportunity to call the attention of the House [the] facts about the Calendar Wednesday; and I do this because in the last Congress I was the chairman of one of the committees that was not reached in the course of its deliberations.

The calendar shows 61 committees that might have been reached.   In the course of the two years 23 committees [out of the 61 committees in the House] were reached.   There were 35 days upon which committees might have an opportunity to be heard.   Of these only 21 were used, and they were used by only 15 committees of the House.   At the time of adjournment the call rested with the twenty-third committee.   Thus only about one committee out of three of the House was able to avail itself of the purpose of the rule about Calendar Wednesday.

It is true that in the first third of the list are many of the important committees, but farther down were these which are not altogether unimportant, that had no opportunity to be heard on Calendar Wednesday: Education, Labor, Patents, Immigration

[1] *Cong. Record*, 66th Cong., 2nd Sess., pp. 5310-5314.

and Naturalization, Census, Roads, World War Veteran's Legislation, and Flood Control.

My own committee [the Committee on Library] is a small committee, has but five members, and its business is not of vast importance. Yet its inability to take advantage of the opportunity presented by Calendar Wednesday caused, in my judgment, the loss to the city of Washington of a monument for which $100,000 had been offered, and of a memorial which by reason of the delay in action here now adorns the campus of an educational institution in West Virginia. These are but two instances of how our work was hampered in the Congress.

. . . The purpose of Calendar Wednesday is being rapidly thwarted, and should the present rate continue, Calendar Wednesday will almost wholly disappear.[1]

[1] *Cong. Record*, 69th Cong., 1st Sess., p. 879. As to the purpose of Calendar Wednesday Mr. Luce states that Calendar Wednesday " serves the purpose of the House in handling the bills of medium importance. As the procedure goes today, the bills that are reasonably certain of being considered here are the big bills or the very little ones; those on the one hand can get special rules, and on the other those arouse the opposition of not more than three Members of the House [that is the Consent Calendar]. There are not a few bills which, if they can have but a short hearing, would commend themselves to the judgment, I am sure, of a majority of the Members; but which might arouse the opposition of 5, 10, or 15 Members, but to which the majority would give a hearty approval.

"As it is today, the work of three-fourths of the committees on these bills goes for naught. They are too small for special rules ... And yet they are of grave importance to a large number of citizens and to the country at large to warrant the chance for consideration that was contemplated in drafting this rule about Calendar Wednesday." *Ibid.*, p. 879.

The following table shows the extent to which the House has made use of the rule for Calendar Wednesday since its inception on March 1, 1909. As the rule is not applicable during the last two weeks of a session, so the last two Calendar Wednesdays were not counted unless the House actually called up bills from this calendar.

CALENDAR WEDNESDAYS

Congresses	61			62			63			64		65			66			67				68		69	
Sessions	1	2	3	1	2	3	1	2	3	1	2	1	2	3	1	2	3	1	2	3	4	1	2	1	2
Total Calendar Wednesdays	19	26	9	20	37	9	33	42	11	37	10	26	46	9	25	24	11	29	35	··	11	24	10	27	10
Dispensed with by two-thirds vote	··	··	··	8	3	2	1	1	1	··	1	··	1	··	1	··	1	··	4	··	··	1	··	··	··
Not called due to adjournment or during adjournment or due to lack of business or other causes	··	··	··	··	··	··	··	··	··	··	··	··	··	··	··	··	··	··	··	··	··	··	··	··	··
Tariff bill considered	15	1	··	9	2	··	23	1	··	7	··	13	10	··	3	1	1	4	3	··	··	5	··	1	1
Questions of privilege considered or special rule as continuous order	4	··	··	··	··	··	3	··	2	1	··	··	··	··	··	··	··	2	··	··	··	··	··	··	··
Dispensed with by special rule from Committee on Rules	··	··	··	··	··	··	··	··	··	1	··	··	··	··	··	··	··	1	1	··	··	··	··	··	··
Dispensed with by unanimous consent	··	··	··	1	··	··	1	··	··	6	2	8	16	··	3	7	7	6	11	··	6	4	3	9	7
Calendar Wednesdays called	··	25	9	2	32	7	3	40	8	22	7	5	19	··	18	16	2	16	16	··	5	14	7	17	2

The rule as to Calendar Wednesday has not succeeded in preventing the leaders of the House from controlling its business. Take the Norris resolution, for instance. It was a joint resolution proposing an amendment to the Federal Constitution fixing the commencement of the terms of the President, Vice-President and members of Congress and the beginning of the Congressional session on the first day of January. It passed the Senate three times,[1] and each time when sent to the House, it was referred to the Committee on Election of President, Vice-President and Representatives in Congress, from which it was reported and placed on the House Calendar. However, with the exception of the fourth session of the Sixty-seventh Congress,[2] the resolution was prevented, by a few of the majority leaders in the House, the Speaker included, from coming before the House for consideration. The author was informed by a distinguished member of the House that if the resolution ever comes before the House for a vote, it would be passed by a majority of four to one. It could not come before the House through unanimous consent request, for a small minority of the members were opposed to it. It could not come before the House through a special order from the Committee on Rules, for the chairman of that committee was hostile to it. There then remained the call on Calendar Wednesday. The Committee on Election of President, Vice-President and Representatives occupies the thirty-fourth place among the House committees. During the Sixty-ninth Congress there were all together thirty-seven Calendar Wednesdays, sixteen of which were, however, dispensed with on motions by the majority

[1] See *Cong. Record*, 67th Cong., 4th Sess., p. 3540; *Cong. Record*, 68th Cong., 1st Sess., p. 4418; *Cong. Record*, 69th Cong., 1st Sess., p. 3971.

[2] See *Cong. Record*, 67th Cong., 4th Sess., p. 5204.

floor leader.[1]   On two Wednesdays[2] the calendar was not called.   In other words, the House used nineteen Calendar Wednesdays during the entire Sixty-ninth Congress, and did not reach the Committee on Election of President, Vice-President and Representatives in Congress.

It was believed that Mr. Tilson, the majority floor leader, was opposed to the resolution in question, and that his repeated request to dispense with Calendar Wednesday was to prevent the House from reaching the Committee on Election of President, Vice-President and Representatives in Congress, which might call up the Norris resolution for consideration.   Certain facts bear out this belief.   In the second session of the Sixty-ninth Congress the House used only two of the ten Calendar Wednesdays,[3] and these two days were used by the Committee on Territories, which occupies the nineteenth place among the House committees.[4]   On February 15, 1927, Mr. Tilson stated that he had reached the " limit " on Calendar Wednesday and " can go no further." [5] He then asked unanimous consent that if there was any time left after the Committees on Territories and on Insular Affairs had finished their business the following day, the 16th, the last Calendar Wednesday of the session, the House would proceed to take up the Private Calendar.[6]   No objection was heard.

---

[1] Practically in every case Calendar Wednesday was dispensed with during this Congress by unanimous consent request of the majority floor leader.   See *Cong. Record*, 69th Cong., 1st Sess., pp. 519, 879, 1505, 1934, 2328, 5713, 6173, 6585, 10426; *ibid.*, 2nd Sess., pp. 73, 289, 863, 1005, 1335, 1817, 2553.

[2] *Cong. Record*, 69th Cong., 1st Sess., p. 4087 and *cf.* pp. 4400 *et seq.*; *ibid.*, 2nd Sess., p. 863.

[3] *Cong. Record*, 69th Cong., 2nd Sess., pp. 2831, 3954.

[4] The order of the committees is arranged according to Rule xx.

[5] *Cong. Record*, 69th Cong., 2nd Sess., p. 3886.

[6] *Ibid.*, p. 3886.

Under the rule, the Speaker has no control over the business on Calendar Wednesday,[1] but it does not mean that he has no influence over it. In the case of the Norris resolution it was generally charged that the Speaker, the majority floor leader and the chairman of the Committee on Rules were responsible for having prevented the measure from being brought up for action. The letter of a rule, be it Calendar Wednesday or any other, can hardly be a sufficient check upon the influence of the Speaker in shaping the course of legislation, so long as he is one of the most important of the House leaders and the titular head of his party in the House as well as wielding the power of his great office.[2]

[1] The rule for Calendar Wednesday reads: " on Wednesdays of each week no business shall be in order except as provided by paragraph 4 of this rule unless the House by a two-thirds vote on motion to dispense therewith shall otherwise determine . . . " Rule xxiv, 7. Paragraph 4 of this rule is the morning hour call of committees. This part of the rule has been rarely used since the adoption of Calendar Wednesday. See Rule xxiv, 4.

[2] See *infra*, pp. 310 *et seq.* on leadership in the House.

CHAPTER VII

THE DISCHARGE CALENDAR

THE rules of the House provide that any proposal for legislation, be it a bill, a resolution or a memorial, shall be referred to a committee.[1] In Jefferson's *Manual* it is further provided that " the committees have full power over the bills or other papers committed to them, except that they cannot change the title or subject." [2] There was no rule requiring the committees to report to the House any bills.[3] During the Fifty-second and Fifty-third Congresses article 59 of House Rule XI stated that general appropriation bills should be reported within eighty days after the committees were announced in a long session, and within forty days after the announcement in a short session. And if any committee failed to so report, the reasons for such failure should be privileged for consideration when called for by any member of the House. This rule was, however, dropped by the Republican party when it gained control of the House in the Fifty-fourth Congress. Statistics have shown that literally thousands of bills and resolutions flood the House during each session of a Congress and are referred to appropriate committees, from which no more than a tenth are reported to the House for consideration.[4] As it is a general rule in

[1] Rule xi, 1; also *cf. supra*, pp. 109-111.

[2] Jefferson's *Manual*, xxvi.

[3] However, resolutions of inquiry not being reported back within one week a motion to discharge the committee from further consideration of it is in order. See Rule xxii, 4. For cases decided under this rule, see Hinds, *op. cit.*, iii, 1865-1870.

[4] See *supra*, p. 115 (footnote).

the House that all business should first go to committees before receiving consideration in the House itself, the nine-tenths of the bills and resolutions are consequently pigeon-holed in the committee rooms.

Prior to 1910 there was no provision in the rules of the House for a motion to discharge a committee from its further consideration of a bill which was not reported to the House. As early as 1792 a motion to instruct a committee to report a provision in a bill for a loan of the remaining debts of the individual States was made but was objected to as out of order.[1] Later, on December 17, 1867, Speaker Colfax ruled that a motion to discharge a committee was not a privileged one, because, in the regular order of business of the House, no provision was made which allowed time for the offering of a motion of this character,[2] and a demand for " regular order " would shut such a motion out. On January 30, 1882, Speaker Keifer stated that it was not in order to move to " instruct a committee on referring a bill on its introduction." [3] On February 15, 1887, Speaker Carlisle held: " It is not competent to move instructions upon the reference of a matter which has not been reported by a committee. Matters reported to the House by a committee can be recommitted with or without instructions under the rules of the House." [4]

However, these rulings by the Speakers had not all together prevented a member of the House from making a motion to discharge a committee which had pigeonholed or failed to report a legislative bill.[5] It could be done through

---

[1] Hinds, *op. cit.*, v, 5523.

[2] *Ibid.*, iv, 4693.

[3] *Ibid.*, v, 5524.

[4] *Ibid.*, v, 5522.

[5] It is, however, in order to move to discharge a committee from consideration of a resolution involving a question of privilege, such as related to a contested election case or a resolution of inquiry. See *ibid.*, i, 622; iii, 1865-1870, 2585, 2709; also see Rule xxii, 4.

unanimous consent. This procedure was resorted to on December 28, 1902, on which day Mr. Steel of Indiana requested unanimous consent, in the Committee of the Whole House on the state of the Union, to consider a pension bill. This bill which had been on the calendar of the Committee of the Whole House but had been recommitted to the Committee on Invalid Pensions, from which it was not reported. The chairman of the Committee held that the Committee of the Whole could not discharge the bill. Later, however, after the Committee of the Whole had risen, the House, by unanimous consent, discharged the Committee on Invalid Pensions from further consideration of the bill.[1] The difficulties in this procedure were that, in the first place, before the adoption of the Unanimous Consent Calendar,[2] a member who sought to make a request for unanimous consent had to obtain in advance the permission of the Speaker; in the second place, being a request for unanimous consent, any member of the House could raise objection to it, and particularly the majority members of the committee which pigeonholed it, or its chairman, would in most cases raise such objection.

Indirectly, there were three ways to discharge a committee. First, it could be done by a motion to suspend the rules and then discharge the committee, thereby bringing the bill before the House for action.[3] This method was very cumbersome, because motions to suspend the rules are in order only two days a month and must be accepted by a two-thirds vote. And, what is more, such motions are subject to the discretion of the Speaker in the exercise of his power of recognition.[4] There was also a second way to discharge

[1] *Cong. Record*, 57th Cong., 1st Sess., pp. 2256, 2259.

[2] See *supra*, pp. 179 *et seq.*

[3] See Hinds, *op. cit.*, v, 6850.

[4] *Cf. supra*, pp. 197 *et seq.*

a committee. Any committee of the House could move, and still can move, on any morning after the approval of the *Journal*, to change by unanimous consent the reference of a bill from another committee to itself, that is, to a friendly committee which will soon report it to the House for action.[1] This method, it should be noted, is not applied to private bills, resolutions and memorials. The third way was to refer a motion to discharge to the Committee on Rules, from which might come forth a special order to be agreed to by a majority vote of the House.[2] Here, again, prior to 1910, the power of the Speaker was felt, as he was Chairman of the Committee on Rules. Theoretically, should the Committee on Rules, or for that matter any other committee of the House, decline or neglect to report, any fifty members of the majority party could call a caucus meeting of the party and obtain a mandate therefrom to compel the committee to act.[3] But, in practice, with the Committee on Rules, no such action had ever been taken in the House.

No proposition, except by unanimous consent, can be considered by the House unless reported by a committee. And the committees of the House, prior to 1911, were appointed by the Speaker. Consequently the widely prevalent belief had been that the Speaker had control over the action—or non-action—of the committees. For instance, in 1908, *The Outlook* writes:

The Speaker of the House appoints all the committees; he determines to what committees each measure as it is introduced shall be referred; the committee may report or not as it pleases upon the matter thus referred to it. Thus it is possible for the Speaker, foreseeing the legislation likely to come before the House during an approaching season, to appoint a committee

[1] *Cf. supra*, pp. 109 *et seq.*
[2] *Cf. supra*, pp. 120 *et seq.*
[3] Hinds, *loc. cit.*, McClure, vol. xxxv, p. 198.

certain to be hostile to it, and to refer the proposed measure to that committee so that it may be smothered without public debate. By the power thus lodged in the Speaker's hands, it is possible for him not only to prevent the passage of any measure, but to stifle Congressional debate upon it, if he chooses so to do. . . .[1]

Even Mr. Hinds, a defender of the old centralized system which preceded 1910, admitted that the "grasp of the committees on the business of the House is the main citadel of the Speaker's power so far as it is dependent on the rules. The main element of it is the appointing power, since the discharging power is lodged in a committee." [2]

In the first session of the Sixtieth Congress a bill for the prevention of the shipment of intoxicating liquor to a dry territory was introduced in the House and was referred to the Committee on Judiciary. During this same session of Congress the Methodist Episcopal churches held a national convention in the city of Baltimore. This body of ministers, being interested in the passage of the bill, sent a delegation to Washington to interview the Speaker, who was then Mr. Cannon. Concerning the power of the Speaker as shown in connection with this bill, Mr. Norris writes:

It is important to note that it was conceded by all and taken for granted by everybody that the Speaker held the key to the situation.

The bill was pending before the Committee on Judiciary. The committee [of ministers] made no effort to have a hearing before this committee or to make any argument there in favor of its passage. It made no attempt to influence the different members of the House. It proceeded at once to interview the Speaker. It is worthy of note, too, that when they called on the Speaker he did not intimate to this committee of ministers that

[1] *The Outlook*, "Government by Oligarchy", vol. lxxxix, p. 12.
[2] *Cong. Record*, 61st Cong., 1st Sess. (appendix), p. 106.

they ought to go before the Committee on Judiciary, or that they ought to take it up with the different members of the House, but he practically told them in a very curt, if not disrespectful way, that the bill could not pass.

After their rebuke by the Speaker, the ministers began a campaign against what they termed " Cannonism ".[1]

As early as the Forty-sixth Congress an attempt was made to remove the difficulties in discharging the committees, thereby limiting the power of the Speaker over legislation through his influence over committees. In 1880, when the House was debating on a general revision of the rules, Joseph F. House of Tennessee offered an amendment [2] providing that when, for fifty days, a committee should fail to report a public bill or resolution, it should be in order, on any Monday, after the expiration of the morning hour, to move to discharge the committee and place the bill or resolution on the calendar. It is interesting to note, however, that the predominant note during the debate in support of the proposed amendment concerned the power of the majority of a committee as against the will of a majority of the House, and no reference was made to the Speaker. In the debate it was brought out that the Committee on Commerce had smothered an important interstate commerce bill. The

---

[1] *Cong. Record*, 61st Cong., 2nd Sess., p. 6277. For the report of the " interview" between the Speaker and the committee of ministers, see *Cong. Record*, 60th Cong., 1st Sess. (appendix), pp. 176-179.

[2] The proposed amendment read: " When a bill, resolution, or proposition of a public character has been referred to a standing committee or select committee of the House, and the committee shall fail for fifty days to make any report to the House thereon, it shall be in order on any Monday immediately after the expiration of the morning hour to move to discharge a committee from the further consideration of the same, which motion shall then be considered; and, if decided in the affirmative, the bill, resolution, or proposition shall be placed on the proper calendar unless the majority of the House shall determine then to consider the same." *Cong. Record*, 46th Cong., 2nd Sess., p. 1199.

chairman of the Committee declared himself in favor of this bill, but, owing to the opposition of a majority of the Committee, was unable to report it out to the House. As Mr. Townsend of Illinois argued:

What has been the result? Because that committee has a majority hostile to that measure we are deprived of the opportunity and the people are deprived of the opportunity of being heard upon it. What I want to do is to get some sort of rule adopted by which we can put aside the majority of that committee and allow the majority of this House to have something to do with regard to the legislation of the country. . . .[1]

The amendment was rejected by the House, by a vote of 94 against 65. Four years later, however, another attempt was made by Mr. Turner of Kentucky, but this too met with defeat. In 1884 he proposed an amendment [2] which provided that whenever a committee should have failed or refused for thirty days to report back a bill either favorably or adversely, it should be in order for the member who had introduced the bill to move on any Monday to discharge, with the object of having the bill considered by the House. Here, as in 1880, the attempt was to limit the power of the committee, and the Speaker was not once mentioned during the debate, although the Committee on Rules, of which the Speaker was chairman, was censored. To quote Mr. Turner:

[1] *Cong. Record*, 46th Cong., 2nd Sess., p. 1200.

[2] The amendment read: "When any bill or resolution shall have been referred to a committee and the committee shall fail or refuse to report said bill or resolution, back to the House of Representatives, either favorably or unfavorably, for thirty days, it shall be in order for the member who offered the bill or resolution, on any Monday, immediately after the morning hour, to move to discharge the committee from the consideration of the bill or resolution, and the House shall then dispose of the bill or resolution by recommittal or by final action, such as majority of the House may determine." *Cong. Record*, 48th Cong., 1st Sess., p. 964. Mr. Turner offered a similar amendment in 1880. See *Cong. Record*, 46th Cong., 2nd Sess., pp. 331, 1057, 1089.

No member would for a moment deny that the voice of a majority of this House ought to control in all matters of legislation. But, sir, let us look for a moment at the practical operation of the rules of this House. As soon as a bill or resolution is offered by a member it is immediately referred to a committee, and unless the committee reports it back to the House, the House is powerless to act upon it, although it may be a public bill affecting the interest of the whole American people, giving them some proper relief which is immediately demanded. But, sir, if a majority of the committee are opposed to the bill, they simply pocket it and refuse to report it back, and by their action prevent a majority of this House from voting for a public bill or resolution that a large majority may be in favor of.

One would hardly suppose that a committee would resort to this method to prevent action by this House; yet, sir, I state without fear of contradiction, that it has often been done and the fact is well known to every member who hears my voice. None will deny it. Why, sir, the pending amendment is an illustration of the evil sought to be remedied. I have offered this amendment at the beginning of four sessions of Congress, and it has been referred to the Committee on Rules [of which the Speaker was chairman], and, sir, up to this day the Committee has failed to make any report on this amendment. . . .[1]

It was not, however, until the Sixty-first Congress that a discharge rule was established. This change was brought about in the wake of the March revolution, 1910, but before the Speaker was deprived of the power of appointing committees. On June 17, 1910, Mr. Dalzell of Pennsylvania reported a rule from the Committee on Rules providing that any member of the House may file with the Clerk of the House a motion to discharge any of the committees of the House from further consideration of any public bill and joint resolution pending before a committee; that the motion should be recorded in the *Journal* as well as on the House

---

[1] *Cong. Record*, 48th Cong., 1st Sess., p. 964.

Calendar under an appropriate heading; that on each suspension day, after the call of the Unanimous Consent Calendar, motions on the Discharge Calendar which have been entered at least seven days prior thereto, will be in order to be called up; that a motion when called up should be seconded by a majority of the House by tellers; that if the motion be seconded, there should be twenty minutes of debate equally divided between the proponent and opponent of the motion; and that if the motion to discharge should prevail, the bill would be placed upon its appropriate calendar. It was further provided that the bill, thus discharged, should have precedence of all other bills reported by the committee subsequent to the time when it was discharged from the latter, and that recognition for such motions should be in the order in which they appear.[1]

Of all the speeches in support of the amendment, the most convincing was made by Mr. Sherley of Kentucky. Mr. Sherley's statement is so clear that it is worthy of note at considerable length:

. . . There have always been two schools of thought; there

[1] *Cong. Record*, 61st Cong., 2nd Sess., p. 8439. By way of comparison, it is interesting to note that about a year before, on March 1, 1909, Mr. Williams of Missouri, the Democratic minority leader, offered an amendment to the rules. It provided, among other things, for a discharge rule, which read: " Whenever a majority of the membership of the House shall, in writing, petition the Speaker that a day shall be given for the consideration of a public measure, when the said measure shall have been reported by a committee, or whenever a majority of the membership of the House shall, by petition in writing, request him to give a day for the consideration of the motion to discharge any standing committee from further consideration of a designated bill, and that the House shall proceed to the consideration of it, it shall be the duty of the Speaker, not later than the next legislative day, to designate a day and to announce to the House the day designated, which designated day shall be . . . no more than five days after the day of the Speaker's announcement." *Cong. Record*, 60th Cong., 2nd Sess., p. 3568.

will always be a difference of opinion along this line of cleavage. There are men who believe that the rules of the House should be used to prevent its Members from doing what they think necessary and proper, and leave it only to those elected to leadership to determine, and there are those who believe as I do, that the majority should really determine.

I do not believe that you can run a great body like this without any sort of rules, but I do believe that it ought to be within the power of a determined majority to legislate in the face of the Speaker or any particular committee or of the Committee on Rules. (Applause.)

This rule enables us to do that. I say to you that when you have taken a bill from a committee and placed it on the calendar it will require very daring leaders of any majority party to undertake to prevent the House legislating on that bill; and if that sort of situation arises in the future then I for one shall be willing to go forward and give to this rule such terms as will enable you not only to discharge the committee but to put the bill taken from that committee in any preferential position required.

. . . The adoption of this rule marks the greatest march forward that has been made during my service in the House. (Applause.) It is the greatest march forward because it is not depending for its success upon the personnel of any body. When you elected your Committee on Rules you did well, but you did not do half enough, because then, as when they were appointed, you were dependent upon whether those men were really of the right sort. Under this rule the rights of the membership of this House are not dependent upon personality.

It does not remain with the Speaker to determine whether he will recognize the mover of a motion to discharge a committee. That right is given to any Member here as a matter of right, and then it is safeguarded by requiring that after he moves to discharge the committee there must be a majority to second that motion, because you ought not to stop the ordinary procedure of the House with any proposition that a majority are not willing to second.

If a majority should second it, the proposition then comes whether you will discharge the committee, and here it is claimed that you have nullified the rule because you required the affirmative vote of a majority of those elected. I deny it. I would have been glad to see it a majority of the majority, but after all it is not to be doubted that matters of real merit that are to be taken away from a committee, and none other should be taken away, will have back of them a majority of those elected to the Congress of the United States. (Applause.)[1]

Speaking in favor of the pending amendment, Mr. Murdock of Kansas, a leading insurgent, said:

Two years ago a Member of this House had to go to the Speaker, hat in hand, to get recognition for unanimous consent. He does not have to go there [any] longer. That has been corrected. In the past there were entire sessions of Congress in which there were no calls of committees. There are calls of committees now—a call every week. That has been improved. Two years ago in this House the Speaker dominated the Committee on Rules. He does not today dominate it; he is no longer a member of it. These betterments in House procedure, in representation, with the change proposed today, are inevitably leading to a great change, the taking of the appointment of committees out of the Speaker's hands.[2]

Mr. Clark, of Missouri, the author of the rule, thought that " it is . . . a long step in the right direction, the same direction that we travelled on the 19th of March, 1910." [3] The father of the rule even predicted that " if this rule is adopted we will never have very much occasion to put it into operation, because it will be held in terrorism over the committees . . . and they will report out the bills desired by the membership of this House." [4]

[1] *Cong. Record*, 61st Cong., 2nd Sess., p. 8443.
[2] *Cong. Record*, 61st Cong., 2nd Sess., p. 8444.
[3] *Ibid.*, p. 8440.
[4] *Ibid.*, p. 8441.

Since the adoption of the rule, the House, indeed, has practically had no occasion to put the rule into operation, not because, as Mr. Clark predicted, the committees report out the bills desired by the membership of the House, but because it " was so defective in so many respects that a child could run through it, much less a man." [1]   From June 17 to December 19, 1910, there were forty motions to discharge committees.   And, then, to demonstrate the futility of the rule, Mr. Mann alone filed, on January 5, 1911, one hundred and seven motions to discharge various committees.[2]   As Congress was about to expire on March 4, the impossibility of considering even half of these motions filed by Mr. Mann was apparent.   On January 15, he called up eleven of those bills on the Discharge Calendar in succession, each time making dilatory motions of no quorum.   That Mr. Mann's motions to discharge committees were not made in good faith was evidenced by the fact that all of the eleven motions which he called failed of securing a second by a majority by tellers, as was required under the rule, and were consequently dropped from the Discharge Calendar.[3]   And in the extra session of the following Congress, the Sixty-second Congress, the Republican members, largely through the effort of the Republican floor leader, Mr. Mann, placed sixty-seven motions on the Discharge Calendar, forty-four of which were filed even a month before the convening of Congress.[4] What was all the more interesting was, however, that a large portion of these motions filed by the members on the Republican side was to discharge the Committee on Invalid Pensions.   The Democrats, who were in the majority, had

[1] *Cong. Record*, 61st Cong., 3rd Sess., p. 680.

[2] *Ibid.*, p. 690.

[3] See *Cong. Record*, 64th Cong., 1 Sess., p. 8.

[4] *Cong. Record*, 62nd Cong., 2nd Sess., p. 1689.

decided at a caucus meeting not to act on legislation pertaining to pensions during that session. Therefore Mr. Mann and his associates, by filing their motions to discharge committees, had virtually blocked the House from reaching other motions on the Discharge Calendar.[1]

Two attempts were made, in the Sixty-first Congress in which the discharge rule was established, to defeat the purpose for which it was set up. On December 19, 1910, a committee suspension day, the House having considered bills on the Unanimous Consent Calendar, Mr. Fuller of Illinois, by the direction of the Committee on Invalid Pensions, moved to suspend the rules and discharge the Committee of the Whole House on the state of the Union from further consideration of a pension bill. Immediately Mr. Sherley of Kentucky raised a point of order on the ground that under paragraph 4 of Rule XXVII it was the "duty" of the Speaker to call up motions on the Discharge Calendar before he recognized a member for the suspension of rules. In overruling the point of order, Speaker Cannon held that:

The motions to discharge the committee do not come up upon their own instance, but on the call of Members. They are merely privileged motions. Perchance no Member desires to call up such a motion. If called up, perchance the House might not desire to second such a motion. But no gentleman has arisen and addressed the Chair and designated any motion which he wishes to call up, and in the absence of such motion on the part of a Member the Chair recognized the gentleman from Illinois. The point is made by the gentleman from Kentucky that it is not in order to move to suspend the rules. The Chair thinks it is clearly in order. But whether or not the House shall proceed to consider that motion depends on whether or not a Member shall call up a motion having higher privilege.[2]

[1] *Cong. Record*, 62nd Cong., 2nd Sess., p. 1689.
[2] *Cong. Record*, 61st Cong., 1st Sess., p. 498.

Mr. Sherley contended that it was not that motions for the suspension of rules were not in order on a suspension day but rather that motions on the Discharge Calendar under the rule were of " higher order." Speaker Cannon, however, took exception to Mr. Sherley's contention and said :

. . . The calendar for motions to discharge is unlike the Unanimous Consent Calendar, because under the terms of the rule creating the latter calendar it is mandatory that it shall be called. There is nothing mandatory here. There are upon the calendar, as the Chair is informed, 20 or 29 motions to discharge the committees. Now, then, it may not suit the purpose of the individual Members of the House to consider any or all of the motions, so that the gentleman's point of order would, if sustained, make it practically impossible, if there were many bills on the calendar, to conclude consideration of it in time to enable a Member to move to suspend the rules. The gentleman has called up no motion to discharge the committee, but makes the point of order against this motion to suspend the rules, and the Chair thinks the point of order is not well taken.[1]

Then Mr. Fitzgerald and Mr. Mann rose to call up bills from the Discharge Calendar. Speaker Cannon conceded that " it seems to the Chair a motion to discharge the committee would take precedence under the terms of the Rule," [2] and recognized Mr. Mann who called up calendar number 1 to discharge the Committee on Post-Office and Post-Roads from the further consideration of a postal bill.

A little more than a month later, January 16, 1911, another test case occurred. After the House had considered some bills from the Unanimous Consent Calendar, Mr. Hull of Iowa moved that the House resolve itself into the Com-

[1] *Cong. Record*, 61st Cong., 1st Sess., p. 498.
[2] *Ibid.*, p. 499.

mittee of the Whole House on the state of the Union for the
further consideration of an Army appropriation bill.   Mr.
Fitzgerald of New York rose to call up a motion to discharge the Committee on Ways and Means from further
consideration of a revenue bill, and Mr. Mann of Illinois
called up another motion from the Discharge Calendar which
took precedence over that of Mr. Fitzgerald.   Speaker Cannon declined to recognize Mr. Fitzgerald for the purpose for
which he rose but would recognize him to make any point
of order against Mr. Hull's motion.   Fitzgerald argued that
under the rule motions to discharge committees were in
order " immediately " after the Unanimous Consent Calendar was called, and that it was not necessary to make a point
of order against the Hull motion.   He launched a vigorous
attack on the Speaker's ruling:

. . . It is a fact that it had been the practice in this House to
use the appropriation bills to shut out all other classes of
business and to put Members either in the position of voting to
consider an appropriation bill or of voting against the consideration of an appropriation bill.   Members did not desire to
be put in that position.
   They desire certain fixed times at which certain class of
business should come up in the House for consideration.   In
order that the Speaker should not have any control over these
motions—and I do not refer to the present occupant of the
Chair, but whoever may be the Speaker—it took from him, first,
any control over the question of recognition and permitted the
motion to be made by entering it in writing, regardless of the
will of the Speaker; and second, by taking from him all power
or control over the order of recognition, by providing that Members should be recognized to call these motions up in the order
in which the motions had been entered.[1]

And

[1] *Cong. Record*, 61st Cong., 1st Sess., p. 967.

If the construction given to the rule providing for the discharge of committees by the Speaker be followed, then those who have imagined that any opportunity would ever be given to consider such motions have indulged in a very idle dream, because there will always be some gentleman like the gentleman from Iowa (Mr. Hull) ready with an appropriation bill to shut out such motions, as there has always been in the past some gentleman ready to offer that privileged motion, so as to prevent the House ever coming to a call of the committees.[1]

Referring to the last case of December 19, 1910, Mr. Fitzgerald argued:

If the construction . . . urged by the Chair [on December 19. 1910] be adopted, this is what will happen: Suppose the gentleman from Iowa (Mr. Hull) rises for the purpose of being recognized to move that the House resolve itself into the Committee of the Whole House on the state of the Union to consider an Army appropriation bill, and the gentleman from Nebraska (Mr. Norris) rises and requests recognition to move to suspend the rules to pass some bill. The Speaker under the rules could recognize the gentleman from Nebraska to move to suspend the rules. The gentleman from Iowa would have no remedy. The Speaker would act within the rule, and no appeal could be taken from his decision on a question of recognition. Then it would be in order for myself or any other Member to insist upon a preferential recognition over the gentleman from Nebraska to call up one of the pending motions to discharge committees, and such a demand could not be ignored by the Speaker.

If, instead of recognizing the gentleman from Nebraska, as he had a perfect right to do under the rules, to move to suspend the rules, the Speaker declined to do so, but recognized gentleman from Iowa to proceed with the consideration of the Army appropriation bill, in order to test the sense of the House. then the motions to discharge committees could not be called

---

[1] *Cong. Record*, 61st Cong., 1st Sess., p. 967.

up at all, and the results would be to put in the control of the Speaker the power to prevent motions of this character ever being called up. The House having voted down the motion to consider the Army appropriation bill would have accomplished little, as the Speaker could recognize some other gentleman to move some other privileged motion under the rules.[1]

On the power of recognition by the Speaker on suspension days Mr. Fitzgerald said further:

On days except Wednesday and Monday, if the gentleman (Mr. Hull) demands recognition, after the reading of the *Journal*, to move that the House resolve itself into the Committee of the Whole House on the state of the Union to consider an appropriation bill, he is entitled to recognition, and the Speaker must submit that motion, but he can not compel the Speaker to submit such a motion on the first and third Mondays of the month if the Speaker prefers to entertain a motion to suspend the rules. And those motions having the higher privilege in the practice of the House, the design of the committee and of the House, as I understand, was to give these motions a privilege over business having the highest privileged status.[2]

By a vote of 126 against 146 the House overruled the decision of Speaker Cannon in holding that Mr. Hull's motion was in order. In doing so the House reversed a " uniform " practice since Speaker Randall that, although recognition for motions to suspend the rules was discretionary with the Speaker on suspension days, he could not, however, decline to entertain certain privileged motions, such as the consideration of appropriation or revenue bills.[3]

The defects of the discharge rule, as were shown in the Sixty-first Congress, made it necessary to bring about

[1] *Cong. Record*, 61st Cong., 1st Sess., p. 968.

[2] *Ibid.*, p. 971.

[3] *Ibid.*, p. 971.

changes in the rule itself. On April 15, 1911, Mr. Henry of Texas reported from the Committee on Rules an amendment which differed from the previous rule in two important respects: (1) Under this amendment a bill, prior to the filing of a motion to discharge, should have been in a committee for a period of fifteen days; and (2) no member should have upon the calendar more than two motions at the same time.[1] During the debate on the adoption of the amendment much light was thrown upon the ineffectiveness of the rule. To quote Mr. Mann:

What does the rule propose to do? When a motion is on the calendar to discharge a committee, and you call it up, if it is ever reached, which very likely it will never be, you first have to have it seconded by a majority of all the Members present before it can be put up to the House, and then when put up to the House it must receive a favorable vote from a majority of the entire elected membership of the House. Considering the fact that on the Mondays when this calendar will be called there is seldom much more than a quorum of the House present, it is not likely that a majority of the membership of the House will often be found to vote for the motion, if there be sufficient opposition to a bill to have a committee refuse to report it. But suppose you have a motion, and it is reached on the call of the calendar, and the majority of the Members present second the motion and the majority of the Members-elect of the House vote for your motion, then what happens? Does the bill come before the House for consideration? Why, not at all. The bill goes on the calendar. Any bill which has been previously reported from the same committee has priority over your bill when the calendar is called. It is not likely that a House in its early days will discharge a committee from the consideration of a bill, because that might be considered unjust to the committee, and even unfair to the House, which is usually to have the bene-

[1] *Cong. Record*, 62nd Cong., 1st Sess., pp. 58, 78.

fit of committee consideration first; and if the committee is not discharged until late in the Congress, the calendar will already be so full that there is scarcely any chance of the bill being reached for consideration in the House, even after the committee has been discharged.[1]

The imperfections of the rule necessitated a further change in the second session of the Sixty-second Congress. This time motions for the suspension of the rules were given precedence over the Calendar of Motions to Discharge Committee.[2] The order of business on these three calendars ran thus: (1) The Calendar for Unanimous Consent; (2) motions for the suspension of the rules; and (3) the Calendar of Motions to Discharge Committee. In its actual effect it was a change from bad to worse. As Mr. Dalzell of Pennsylvania pointed out:

. . . If you put the motion to suspend the rules in advance of the motion to discharge the committees, it is in the power of the Speaker to dictate what committee shall be discharged and what committee shall not be discharged, or whether any. . . . It will take away from the individual Members of this House the power of initiative and place that power in the hands of the Speaker. . . .[3]

The rule was also limited in its application. It did not apply to the Committee on Rules, which has jurisdiction over resolutions to make or to change the rules of the House and also over those to authorize investigation.[4] During the Sixty-third Congress there were referred to the Committee on Rules about seventy amendments to the rules of the House, only one of which was reported from it to the House

[1] *Cong. Record*, 62nd Cong., 1st Sess., p. 78.
[2] *Ibid.*, 2nd Sess., p. 1686.
[3] *Ibid.*, p. 1687.
[4] See Rule xi, 47.

for action,[1] and, in addition, nearly eighty resolutions for investigations. In the Sixty-seventh Congress the committee pigeonholed no less than thirty resolutions for investigation, the most important of which was the Woodruff resolution to investigate the Department of Justice.[2] The Progressive Republicans having attempted in vain during that Congress to have the resolution reported from the Committee on Rules, sought revenge in the following Congress.

The discharge rule, to quote Mr. Nelson of Wisconsin, became "the heart, the heart, the heart of the whole contest"[3] at the commencement of the Sixty-eighth Congress. As the Republican party had in this Congress no clear majority, the "Progressives" held the balance of power and succeeded in forcing the leaders of the Republican party to agree to a change of the rules.[4] Subsequently the Committee on Rules reported, on January 15, 1924, a number of amendments to the rules, the most important of which was naturally the discharge rule. For the Committee on Rules itself there was a special discharge rule which provided that it "shall present to the House reports concerning rules, joint rules, and order of business within three legislative days of the time when ordered reported by the committee."[5] If such reported rule or order is not considered immediately it will go to the calendar, and if not called up

---

[1] Hinds, *Your Congress* (Washington, 1915), p. 94.

[2] See *supra*, pp. 146-8. Another case may be cited to show the impotence of the discharge rule. Mr. Johnson of South Dakota filed, on February 1, 1922, a motion to discharge the Bursum bill for the retirement of the emergency officers. The bill was "peacefully slumbering" in the Committee on Military Affairs, although "two-thirds" of the membership of the House were in favor of having it considered. *Cong. Record*, 68th Cong., 1st Sess., pp. 894, 995, 1011.

[3] *Cong. Record*, 68th Cong., 1st Sess., p. 1049.

[4] See *supra*, pp. 32-4.

[5] Rule xi, 56.

by the member making the report within nine days, any member " designated " by the committee may call it up for consideration.   This particular rule received no serious consideration from the members of the House.   The reason was that the House was deeply aroused by another amendment to the general discharge rule which provided that " when Members to the total number of one hundred and fifty shall have signed the motion it shall be . . . referred to the Calendar of Motions to Discharge Committees." [1]   For five

[1] *Cong. Record*, 68th Cong., 1st Sess., p. 944; also see Rule xxvii, 4 in the Sixty-eighth Congress which read: "A Member may present to the Clerk a motion in writing to discharge a committee from the consideration of a public bill or resolution which have been referred to it thirty days prior thereto (but only one motion may be presented for each bill or resolution).   The motion shall be placed in the custody of the Clerk, who shall arrange some convenient place for the signature of Members.   A signature may be withdrawn by a Member in writing at any time before the motion is entered on the *Journal*.   When Members to the total number of one hundred and fifty shall have signed the motion it shall be entered on the *Journal*, printed with the signatures thereto in the *Congressional Record*, and referred to the Calendar of Motions to Discharge Committees.

" On the first and third Mondays of each month, except during the last six days of any session of Congress, immediately after the approval of the *Journal*, any Member who has signed a motion to discharge which has been on the Calendar at least seven days—prior thereto, and seek recognition, shall be recognized for the purpose of calling up the motion, and the House shall proceed to its consideration in the manner herein provided without intervening motion except one motion to adjourn.   Recognition for the motions shall be in the order in which they have been entered.

" When the motion shall be called up, the bill or resolution shall be read by title only.   After twenty minutes' debate, one-half in favor of the proposition and one-half in opposition thereto, the House shall proceed to vote on the motion to discharge.   If the motion prevails, it shall then be in order for any Member who signed the motion to move that the House proceed to the immediate consideration of such bill or resolution (such motion not being debatable), and such motion is hereby made of high privilege; and if it shall be decided in the affirmative, the bill shall be immediately considered under the general rules of the House.

days the House debated on this single provision in the absence of a " gag " rule.

Fundamentally there were two different points of view, diametrically opposed to each other. On the one hand, there were those who advocated that one hundred, instead of one hundred and fifty, members of the House should be sufficient to sign the motion to discharge, while, on the other, there were those who insisted that a majority of the members of the House should rule in this case as it was in other cases. To the former belonged a large section of the Democrats and the whole force of the Progressive Republicans, whose spokesman was Mr. Crisp of Georgia, an accomplished parliamentarian and a Democrat. Mr. Crisp commenced the debate with an amendment to the resolution that a motion to discharge, to be effective, should require only the signature of one hundred members of the House. In presenting the amendment Mr. Crisp indulged in a general stricture of the discharge rule since its beginning. He said in part:

After the revolution in the House along in 1910, when Mr. Cannon . . . was turned down and offered to resign, a discharge rule was provided. It was a delusion and a snare. It was a sugar-coated bill, and all the evils and bad taste of the original medicine were left. That rule was absolutely unworkable and never has worked up to this good hour. What is the old rule? It provided that a Member may file a motion for a discharge

Should the House by vote decide against the immediate consideration of such bill or resolution, it shall be referred to its proper calendar and be entitled to the same rights and privileges that it would have had had the committee to whom it was referred duly reported the same to the House for its consideration: *Provided*, That, when any motion to discharge a committee from the consideration of any public bill or resolution has once been acted upon by the House, it shall not be in order to entertain any other motion for the discharge from the committee of said measure."

and that on certain days—first and third Mondays—after the Unanimous Consent Calendar has been disposed of and after all motions to suspend the rules have been disposed of, that motion may be called up. If a majority of the House, by tellers, seconds the motion, then there could be 10 minutes of debate on a side and a vote would then come on the question of discharge, and if the House discharged, then the bill would go to the calendar, with no privilege and there abides its time and sleeps serenely.

Now, that was a long, circuitous, rocky road for the motion to travel. I have been here for 10 years and I do not remember one single instance where any legislative bill has been discharged from a committee. Therefore you will agree with me, I am sure; that to say the least it was a delusion if it was not a snare. Now, what was the evil? The evil is that when men are elected to this great body, entrusted with legislative responsibility, they are entitled to have a chance to express their views on momentous public questions. (Applause.). . .[1]

When Mr. Longworth of Ohio asked how Mr. Crisp arrived at the number one hundred as the basis for a motion to discharge, the latter replied:

. . . One hundred is your quorum in the Committee of the Whole House on the state of the Union. You will spend weeks and months, sometimes, in the Committee of the Whole House on the state of the Union, with 100 as a quorum, considering tax bills that tax the people billions of dollars. If it is competent for 100 Members of this House to take weeks of their time taxing and appropriating millions of dollars, is it not reasonable to say that 100 Members of this House on two days in each month are entitled to have 20 minutes—20 minutes of the time of the House—and one roll call to see whether or not they desire to proceed to consider a public bill of sufficient importance to secure 100 Members, representing 100 districts of these United States?[2]

[1] *Cong. Record*, 68th Cong., 1st Sess., p. 966.
[2] *Ibid.*, p. 967.

But by far the most important point was that made by Mr. Nelson of Wisconsin:

Now for the purpose of a party 150 is sufficient, because they can have a caucus and decide on a program, and of course, party members will march up and support it; but for the *individual* or *group* 150 might be prohibitive. . . .[1]

Objections to the Crisp amendment were, on the other hand, voiced with equal force. Mr. Graham of Illinois, who offered a substitute providing for a majority of the members of the House as the number to move to discharge, argued that the Crisp amendment, if adopted, would destroy the orderly conduct of the business of the committees of the House, and that a bill would be ill-considered if discharge is too easy to attain. Then, he went on to say:

. . . The effect [of the Crisp amendment] would be to take from the committee many times bills not considered, bring them on the floor of the House, moved by temporary expediency or political feeling, might make possible things to be done and legislation to be enacted which would not be the will of the majority of the deliberative body.[2]

Moreover, Mr. Graham contended that with the disappearance of the rule of majority would go what is called " responsibility." The inevitable result, so Mr. Tilson of Connecticut added, would be the government by " blocs " which " has so plagued continental Europe." [3]

As a matter of fact, the contentions of both Mr. Graham and Mr. Tilson were erroneously grounded. The Crisp amendment would not lead towards the destruction of the

[1] *Cong. Record*, 68th Cong., 1st Sess., p. 962.

[2] *Ibid.*, p. 997.

[3] *Ibid.*, pp. 1004, 1005. Fear was also expressed of the increasing influence of the lobbyist and propagandist under the Crisp amendment. See *ibid.*, p. 1099.

majority rule of the House. The one hundred members as provided therein could hardly do anything beyond presenting, or we would better say seconding a motion to discharge a committee so as to give a bill a chance of hearing. The motion, when called up on the first and third Mondays of each month, under the rule, would be of any effect only if it is passed by a majority of the House. In case the motion prevails, that is, by a majority vote of the House, the bill then, and not until then, is considered discharged and is in order for a motion for its immediate consideration. If the motion again prevails by a majority vote of the House, the bill or resolution so discharged would be " immediately considered under the general rules of the House." If, however, the motion is rejected by a majority vote, the bill or resolution so discharged would be referred to its proper calendar waiting for its turn under the general order of business in the House. At every step, after the bill or resolution is before the House upon the demand of one hundred members, the majority rule governs.

To say that the Crisp amendment was inimical to " government by Standing Committees" would be, however, nearer to the truth. It was after all the committee system of government that was really at stake. With the adoption of the Crisp amendment a bill, if pigeonholed at the will of a few members on the committee — and in some cases under the direction of the leader or leaders of the majority party— could be brought up on the demand of one hundred members of the House for a hearing. In a democracy such as the United States of America where popular government exists, if the judgment—or the wisdom—of one hundred members of the House, in filing a motion to discharge a committee, is less trusted than the judgment or wisdom of a handful of members on the committee or a few of the leaders of the majority party in pigeonholing it, it is time for thoughtful consideration.[1] "One hundred Members of this House," Mr. Nelson of Wisconsin reminds us, "represent 30,000,000 of American people . . . when 30,000,000 of people say they want a vote [on a bill] that is not something to be sneered at." [2]

Both the Crisp and Graham amendments were rejected. In their stead, the House adopted the resolution reported by Mr. Snell of the Committee on Rules. It was " a compromise rule," and " suits no one and never would have been adopted if either side had a clear majority." [3] During the entire Sixty-eighth Congress, so far as it can be ascertained, only one bill, the Howell-Barkly bill for labor arbitration, was discharged from the Committee on Interstate and Foreign Commerce, and was not passed owing to the objections of the leaders of the Republican party who, as it was charged, defeated its passage by resorting to filibustering tactics.[4] This case really threw light on the advantages as well as disadvantages of the discharge rule, and is therefore interesting to note in passing. Mr. Barkley of Kentucky is a Democrat. He introduced the bill on February 28, 1924, for labor arbitration, which was referred to the Committee on Interstate and Foreign Commerce, of which Mr. Barkley was the minority ranking member. Realizing that the bill would not receive favorable consideration from the members of the committee on the majority side and that it could not be reported by the committee,[5] Mr. Barkley, seconded by one

---

[1] *Cf.* Hasbrouck, *Party Government in the House of Representatives* (MacMillan, 1927), pp. 216, 217.

[2] *Ibid.*, p. 962.

[3] *Cong. Record*, 69th Cong., 1st Sess., p. 12.

[4] See *Cong. Record*, 69th Cong., 1st Sess., p. 14.

[5] See *Cong. Record*, 68th Cong., 1st Sess., pp. 6383, 6574, 6655, 7499, 7701, 7712, 7771, 7776, 7867 where charges were made and denied by those for and against the bill.

hundred and fifty members of the House, moved to discharge the Committee on Interstate and Foreign Commerce. On May 5, 1924, being Monday, Mr. Barkley called up the motion, which was passed by a vote of 194 to 181.[1] The bill was thus discharged. Then Mr. Barkley moved for its immediate consideration, which motion was again passed by a vote of 197 to 172. So far Mr. Barkley was successful. As the nature of the bill called for a sharp division of the House, Mr. Barkley could easily have the seconding of one hundred and fifty members. The Progressive Republicans seconded him, because the bill fell in with their economic point of view. His Democratic associates seconded him, partly because of the merit of the bill itself and partly, also, because of party politics. But, on the other hand, the action caused embarrassment of the majority leaders who apparently had little desire to see the bill before the House for consideration. Mr. Longworth, then the majority floor leader, led the filibustering in order to prevent the bill from being passed. On May 5, there were altogether sixteen roll-calls,[2] half of which were made either on motions for adjournment or on motions of no quorum—dilatory tactics frequently resorted to by members of the House. In this work Mr. Longworth had a lion's share. On May 19, when the bill was again under consideration, it met with the same obstruction. Mr. Longworth even moved to refer the bill back to the Committee on Interstate and Foreign Commerce,[3] but his motion was rejected by a vote of 181 against 201.[4] Finally Mr. Barkley, realizing the futility of his attempt, agreed to cease to press the bill for passage.

[1] *Cong. Record*, 68th Cong., 1st Sess., pp. 7874, 7875.

[2] See *ibid.*, pp. 7885 *et seq.*

[3] See *ibid.*, pp. 8894, 8939, 8943, 8945, 8947.

[4] See *ibid.*, p. 8940.

When the Sixty-ninth Congress convened on December 7, 1925, one of the important changes in the rules of the House was the change of the title of the rule from Calendar of Motions to Discharge Committees to Calendar of Motions to *Instruct* Committees.[1] The difference in the construction of this rule during the Sixty-ninth Congress and the preceding one is worth noticing. In the Sixty-eighth Congress a member might present to the Clerk a motion in writing, signed by one hundred and fifty members of the House, to *discharge* a committee from further consideration of a bill or resolution, which had been referred thirty days prior thereto (only one motion might be presented for each bill or resolution), and the motion was to be referred to the Calendar of Motions to Discharge Committees, whereas in the Sixty-ninth Congress any member may present to the Clerk a motion in writing, signed by a *majority* of the membership of the House, to " *instruct* a committee to report within 15 days a public bill or resolution which had been referred to it 30 days prior thereto."

In the Sixty-eighth Congress any member who had signed a motion to discharge could call up that motion immediately after the approval of the *Journal* on the first and third Monday of each month, except during the last six days of any session of Congress. When called up, the bill was read by title only. Twenty minutes of debate would be held without intervening motion except one motion to adjourn. After the twenty minutes' debate the House would then proceed to vote on the motion to discharge if the motion prevailed; any member who had signed the motion to discharge could move that the House proceed to immediate consideration of the bill thus discharged. And such immediate consideration would be in order should the House decide the motion in

---

[1] Rule xxvii, 4; also see *Cong. Record*, 69th Cong., 1st Sess., pp. 383, 384.

the affirmative; in case the House decided in the negative, the bill would be referred to its proper calendar. In the Sixty-ninth Congress it is provided in the rules that motions to *instruct* a committee are in order only on the third Monday of each month immediately after the approval of the *Journal*. When such motion is called up the bill will be read by title. After the reading the motion is, however, not as yet submitted to the House " unless seconded by a majority of the membership of the House to be determined by tellers, and clause 4 of Rule XV [1] shall not apply to such second." If the motion fails of seconding by a majority of the membership of the House, it will be stricken from the Calendar of Motions to Instruct Committees. But if the motion prevails, it will then be in order for debate under the forty-minute rule. And if again adopted by an affirmative vote of a majority of the membership of the House, then, and only then, the committee will report the bill or resolution within fifteen days thereafter, and such bill or resolution will be referred to its proper calendar. Now, under such circumstances, the difficulty of getting a bill out of a committee is well-nigh unsurmountable. In the first place, a majority of the membership of the House on each of the three occasions means 218 out of the 435 members if the House is full.[2] The trouble is that seldom, if ever, does the House have as many as two hundred members on the floor on Mondays.

[1] " Whenever a quorum fails to vote on any question, and a quorum is not present and objection is made for that cause, unless the House shall adjourn there shall be a call of the House, and the Sergeant-at-Arms shall forthwith proceed to bring in absent Members, and the yeas and nays on the pending question shall at the same time be considered as ordered ... "

[2] A majority of the membership means a majority of those Members chosen, sworn, and living whose membership has not been terminated by resignation or by the action of the House. Hinds, *op. cit.*, iv, 2889, 2890; also see *Cong. Record*, 63rd Cong., 1st Sess., p. 1457.

In the second place, as clause 4 of Rule XV does not apply to such second, it is impossible for a member to force a roll-call, a record vote, on a motion of no quorum or on a motion of the call of the House to compel the attendance of the members. And, furthermore, the rigidity of this rule seems beyond all range of reasonableness. For under the Constitution a majority of each House constitutes a quorum to do business,[1] that is, in a full House it means 218 members. Both in theory and in practice a majority of these 218 members can pass, as they have frequently passed, bills of grave importance, while under this rule no member can even move to instruct a committee to report a bill and to have it placed upon an appropriate calendar until 218 members of the House have signed a petition for his motion and the same number of members vote for that motion twice consecutively on the third Monday of a month.

Needless to say, during the first session of the Sixty-ninth Congress not a single motion to instruct a committee to report was filed by members of the House. In the second session, however, the Democrats made an unsuccessful attempt to instruct the Committee on Ways and Means to report a bill on corporation income tax.[2] With a few exceptions, the whole membership of the Democratic party[3] and a few Progressive Republicans—totaling one hundred and seventy strong—signed the petition, but fell far short of the number required under the rule. So the effort was of no avail. But the case is worth noticng. Suppose the rule provides that 150 members of the House are sufficient to file a motion to instruct a committee to report a bill, then in the case just referred to, the Democrats would have achieved

[1] Article I, 5.

[2] See *Cong. Record*, 69th Cong., 2nd Sess., pp. 2253-2255.

[3] The total Democratic membership in the House during the Sixty-ninth Congress was 181 as against the Republican membership of 246.

their purpose. The smaller the number of petitioners to instruct committees to report bills, the greater will be the danger of relaxing party control over legislation.

The present rule for Motions to Instruct Committees is unworkable, and, as a matter of fact, its framers intended to make it so. It has defeated the original purpose of the House in establishing a calendar whereby a bill suppressed by a committee might be brought before the House for action and a majority of the members of the House could legislate over the opposition of a handful of members of a committee or a few House leaders including the chairman of the committee, the majority floor leader and the Speaker. The rule in its present construction presents no occasion to call upon the Speaker to exercise his power of recognition.

CHAPTER VIII

The House Under Six Speakers

THE Fifty-fourth Congress convened on December 2, 1895. Thomas B. Reed of Maine was elected Speaker of the House by a vote of 240 against 95 for Mr. Crisp of Georgia, the Democratic nominee for the office. It was the second time, after four years of Democratic control, that Mr. Reed presided over the House of Representatives. The significance of his reelection to the Speakership was that it was a vindication by his party associates of his first administration. As a victor and not without an air of self-confidence, he said on being conducted to the Speaker's chair:

. . . Of the past, however, I shall not speak, for the past speaks for itself (Applause) in terms more fitting and appropriate than words which could come from my lips. Nor shall I speak of the future, for we are not now putting off the harness, but putting it on. Yet I think I may venture to say of the future in the light of the past, that if we do some things which for the moment seem inadequate it may be that time, which has justified itself of us on many occasions, may do so again. Those who have acted with wisdom heretofore may be fairly expected to act with wisdom hereafter.[1]

The Republicans had in the House a majority of more than one hundred and forty members over the Democrats, and this made things much easier for Speaker Reed. With such an overwhelming majority there could hardly be any need for the enforcement of the quorum rule.

[1] *Cong. Record*, 54th Cong., 1st Sess., p. 4.

Moreover, there was very little for Speaker Reed to do in the way of party legisation because of the political difference existing between the House and the Executive, who was then a Democrat.[1]   In domestic affairs there was during that Congress no legislation of great importance, while in the sphere of foreign affairs the boundary dispute between Great Britain and Venezuela was perhaps the only question of moment.   President Cleveland appointed a commission to investigate the dispute and asked Congress for appropriations, which the House granted.   It is hardly neccessary to narrate herein " the President's fearful blunder . . . in . . . his direct threat of war with his demand for a commission." [2]   The point of interest is, however, that in so far as Speaker Reed was concerned, the House sank into a sea of political tranquility.   The oratorical ripples, which occasionally rose in the House, could hardly be compared with the stormy sessions of the preceding Congresses.   Indeed, throughout this Congress Speaker Reed, as Mr. McCall writes, " took a placid enjoyment in presiding over the House, and his manner was much like that of a benevolent teacher." [3]   As Speaker, Mr. Reed was the leader of the House, and since the President was a Democrat, Mr. Reed was at the same time the titular head of his party in the country.   " It is doubtful," so continues Mr. McCall, " if he ever took more satisfaction in public life than during the first session of this Congress." [4]

On March 15, 1897, the Fifty-fifth Congress essembled in extraordinary session to revise the tariff.   Mr. Reed was for the third time elected Speaker of the House, having

[1] Grover Cleveland was President—in his second term—from March 4, 1893 to March 3, 1897.

[2] McCall, *Life of Thomas Brackett Reed* (Boston, 1914), p. 220.

[3] *Ibid.*, p. 217.

[4] *Ibid.*, p. 217.

received 200 votes against 144 for Mr. Bailey of Texas. It is, however, interesting to note that in his speech of acceptance he spoke very much after the fashion of a peace maker: he was conciliatory and apologetic. " I can not," he said, " having had experience, expect to please all of you always, but I do hope, with your kind assistance and your kind forbearance, to administer justice to each member and to both sides of the Chamber." [1] He did not look back upon the record of the past. Nor did he, as had done in the preceding Congress, venture to speak of the future " in the light of the past." Perhaps he might have sensed that the future would take care of itself. And in that Mr. Reed was unerringly right, as far as his leadership in the House was concerned.

Clearly the wounds which Mr. Reed received from the defeat of his presidential embition were not healed. In a moral sense, he was, to be sure, the victor,[2] but politically he was the vanquished. His leadership in the House was shortly challenged, as was shown in two instances in the Fifty-fifth Congress. In the first place, there was the Cuban question. The Island of Cuba was then in rebellion against the authority of Spain. The American Government dispatched the battleship Maine to Havana at the time when the rebellion seemed to be at the point of being crushed. On the night of February 15, 1898, while it lay at anchor in the harbor of Havana, the ship was blown up. The news set this country aflame. President McKinley at once ordered

[1] *Cong. Record*, 55th Cong., 1st Sess., p. 16.

[2] Mr. Reed believed that the use of money played an important part in securing the Southern delegates for Mr. McKinley. McCall, *op. cit.*, pp. 222, 223. The money raised and spent during the campaign in the interest of Mr. McKinley was estimated at $3,500,000, a much larger sum than any previous (but not any succeeding) presidential campaign. Croly, *Marcus Alonzo Hanna: His Life and Work* (New York, 1912), p. 220.

a board of inquiry by naval officers who reported that the destruction of the ship was due to external explosion.   This report made war with Spain inevitable.   In Congress a joint resolution for armed intervention was passed by the two Houses.   Mr. Reed who had little sympathy with the barbarism of war, was opposed to armed conflict with Spain. He at first exerted his influence in hope that an open break might be averted.[1]   And when the resolution for armed intervention went to the conference, he appointed conservative conferees on the part of the House but in vain.[2]   The conference report was passed, April 13, 1898, in the House, by a vote of 311 to 6.[3]   To one of these six who voted against the conference report Mr. Reed said: " I envy you the luxury of your vote.   I was where I could not do." [4]

About two months after the declaration of war upon Spain, the joint resolution " to provide for annexation of the Hawiian Islands to the United States " came before the House.   A foe of imperialism, Mr. Reed was again opposed to the annexation—so much so that he even went to the extent of holding the annexation resolution for some time from being reported from the Committee on Rules.[5] On June 15, 1898, just after the vote on the resolution was taken in the House, the Speaker *pro tempore,* Mr. Dalzell, said: " Before announcing the result of the vote, I desire to say that the Speaker of the House is absent on account of illness.   He authorized me to say that if present he would vote ' no ' " [6]   Such a procedure was unusual in the House. In this instance the Speaker's influence was of no avail.

[1] McCall, *op. cit.*, p. 233.

[2] *Ibid.*, p. 233; also see *Cong. Record*, 55th Cong., 2nd Sess., p. 4033.

[3] *Ibid.*, pp. 4062-4064.   Speaker Reed voted " yea."

[4] McCall, *op. cit.*, p. 234.

[5] Dingley, *op. cit.*, p. 467.

[6] *Cong. Record*, 55th Cong., 2nd Sess., p. 6019.

These two cases, occurring in rapid succession, had turned the House away from the leadership of Mr. Reed. In the first case, the popular impulse was for war. Members of the House—as well as Senators—were almost unanimously clamoring for war. The position of Mr. Reed under such circumstances was most embarrassing. Within the House he could not lead his party and be the party's mouthpiece on an issue of such momentous importance; without, he was out of sympathy with the nation at large. In the second case, that is, the annexation of the Hawaiian Islands, the House openly followed the leadership of President McKinley over the opposition of Mr. Reed. Mr. McKinley recommended annexation in his annual message of December, 1897, and on May 17, 1898, Mr. Hitt of Illinois, in carrying out Mr. McKinley's wishes, reported from the House Committee on Foreign Affairs the annexation resolution which, as has been shown, was passed by an overwhelming vote on June 15, 1898. These happenings were humiliating to Mr. Reed, because, on the one hand, he felt that his leadership was waning and, on the other, he saw not without fear the rise of American imperialism. " I have tried," he said to Mr. Hinds after the Philippine Islands were acquired by the United States from Spain, "perhaps not always successfully, to make acts of my public life accord with my conscience, and I can't do this thing." [1]

Mr. Reed was elected to the Fifty-sixth Congress, but resigned his seat before Congress met. This action was subject to varied interpretations, for he has never given out any reason for his resignation. The most common explanation, the one always attributed for the resignation of a public officer, was that the salary he received as Speaker was insufficient for his family, and that he had to enter the practice of law to recoup his finances. That might have been

---

[1] McCall, *op. cit.*, p. 238.

true, but still there were other reasons which might also have prompted his resignation. It was an open secret that Mr. Reed and Mr. McKinley were none too friendly to each other. After Mr. McKinley took the President's office, Mr. Reed never conferred with him and vice versa. If Mr. McKinley desired to obtain the views of the Speaker or the other House leaders, he conferred with Mr. Dingley.[1] The gulf of difference between the President and the Speaker deepened when the United States " purchased " the Philippines in the wake of the war with Spain. Mr. Reed did not believe in the existance of a colonial theory in the American constitution.[2] In the light of these facts, the action of Mr. Reed in resigning his seat in the House was both simple and understandable.

Mr. Reed best typifies the American type of Speakers, well grounded in law, profound as a parliamentarian, an avowed partisan and a ready debater. As a presiding officer, he was the *primus inter pares*. If he had an equal, it was Henry Clay. Like Clay, Mr. Reed was not the umpire but the leader of the House. As one of the Republican members has put it, he sat " in his chair with his feet on the neck of the Republican party." [3] And if need be, he, like Clay again, took the means which, in the words of Miss Follett, would most easily and quickly accomplish his end.[4] Both his quorum rule and his decision on dilatory motions were points in illustration. It was stated that on one occasion he overruled a point of order made by a Democrat. The latter discovered, however, that Mr. Reed, in his book on parliamentary procedure, " Reed's Rules," had entertained a different view, and hoping to embarrass the Speaker, he, with book in

[1] Dingley, *op. cit.*, p. 430.
[2] McCall, *op. cit.*, pp. 235 *et seq.*
[3] Follett, *op. cit.*, p. 117.
[4] See *ibid.*, p. 73.

hand, approached the Speaker, and pointing to the passage, asked him to explain it. After reading it over, the Speaker coolly replied: "Oh, the book is wrong." [1] Again, at another time when a matter to which he objected, came before the House, Mr. Reed anxiously inquired: " Is there objection? " No response. Then he rapped with his gavel and in a louder voice called out, pausing between the words: " Is—there— objection? " Still no response. At this point he pounded with the head of his gavel vehemently, shouting meanwhile: " Did—any—gentleman—object? " Finally one of his lieutenants found his wits and made an objection.[2]

During his first administration Mr. Reed established the right of the majority to rule. For fifty years, he writes, the " citadel of Do Nothing seemed unapproached from sea or shore. . . . Unless the House could be emancipated from the bad traditions of fifty years there was no hope of legislation." [3] And " emancipated " indeed was the House in the Fifty-first Congress. To quote Mr. Reed further:

. . . Fortunately for the country the House was strong enough to meet its duties, and, amid shouts and outcries, which already seemed strange and incomprehensible, broke down the barriers of custom and reestablished the right of the majority to rule. This was its greatest achievement, for which it will have a name in history.[4]

But, to enable the majority to rule, there must be something to keep that majority intact. And that something is discipline. Mr. Reed frankly regarded the Republican party in the House as an army, of which he was the Speaker-

[1] McCall, *op. cit.*, p. 247.

[2] Leupp, *loc. cit., Century*, vol. lxv, p. 764.

[3] Reed, " Two Congresses Contrasted," *North American Review*, vol. clv, p. 233.

[4] *Ibid.*, p. 233.

General. In criticising the Democratic party in the House during the Fifty-second Congress as a " mob," he says:

Whenever an army is like the famous army of Xerxes, essentially barbaric, it matters not how far the ranks stretch across the field of view, or how far off on the horizon's edge they pass glittering out of sight. They are useless alike for conquest or for slaughter. The numbers only emphasize the failure. They hasten its downfall, and serve only to astonish children in story books that so many could be conquered by so few. Whenever discipline or unity of purpose is lacking, numbers may be one of the elements of disaster. No army can fight the enemy if it must at the same time fight itself.[1]

Party discipline was best shown in the case of the Force bill. This bill was bitterly contested in the Republican caucus. Mr. Cannon of Illinois led the attack upon it. For three days the contest lasted, and finally it was adopted in the caucus but by a majority of only one. Mr. Cannon accepted the verdict and brought from the Committee on Rules a special order for its immediate consideration. What was all the more remarkable was that the bill over which the Republican members in the House had been evenly divided, received almost the unanimous support of the party when it was voted upon in the House.[2]

However, as party leader, Mr. Reed was not as successful as was Clay. When Clay wanted the United States to go into war with Great Britain in 1812, he succeeded in making it to do so. When Reed was opposed to the war with Spain in 1898, the annexation of Hawaii and the purchase of the Philippines, he met with defeat. When Clay and President Monroe contested for supremacy, Clay won. " In form," Miss Follett tells us, " the contest was between the President

---

[1] Reed, "Two Congresses Contrasted," *North American Review*, vol. clv, p. 227.

[2] McCall, *op. cit.*, pp. 175, 176.

and Congress; but Clay's practical success shows that when the legislative gains over the executive, it is the Speaker who gains the spoils of the battle." [1] When McKinley took the presidency, Reed's leadership in the House was defied. Clay had the vision of a constructive statesman: he favored internal improvements, a protective tariff, recognition of the South American governments. Reed, on the other hand, intiated no great measures to capture the popular imagination in the country. Tariff was one of the important issues in the presidential campaign of 1896 but it was personified with " McKinleyism." The other questions of the day, the money issue and the free silver question, were the battle cry of the Democrats, or a large portion of the Democrats.

Mr. Reed himself might well have suffered for his aphorisms and cynicism. His scorching wit,—his piercing satire—were like drops of poison that entered into the veins of a victim on the floor of the House. But the Speakership during his incumbency never suffered from them. On the contrary, he presided over the House with both honor and dignity. His vision of the office was unfolded in the resolution of thanks to Mr. Crisp in the Fifty-second Congress:

. . . The Speaker of the House holds an office of dignity and honor, of vast power and influence. The extent of that power and influence can not be described even by one who has been honored by its possession. All this dignity, honor, power and influence were created not to adorn or glorify any individual, but to uphold, support, and maintain the well-being of the people of the United States.

That that officer should be respected and esteemed concerns every Member of the House not only as a Member, but as a citizen of the United States.

No factional or party malice ought ever to strive to diminish its standing or lessen his esteem in the eyes of the Members or

[1] Follett, *op. cit.*, p. 78.

of the world. No disappointments or defeats ought ever to be permitted to show themselves to the injury of that high place. Whoever at any time, whether for purposes of censure or rebuke or any other motive, attempts to lower the prestige of that office, by just so much lowers the prestige of the House itself, whose servant and exponent the Speaker is. No attack, whether open or covert, can be made upon that office without leaving to the future a legacy of disorder and of bad government.

This is not because the Speaker is himself a sacred creation. It is because he is the embodiment of the House, its power and dignity.

If efforts of that kind have been made in the past, if at any time in the heat of passion or in the flush of resentment over unexpected defeat or overthrow, action has been taken which has been thus inimical to the public good and to the public order, let us leave to those who so acted the honor or shame, and in no way give their example the flattery of imitation.

While therefore, my associates and I have not forgotten the past, I am sure that I speak the sentiment of them all when I say that the Republican party, without regard what any other party may do, or what any other party has done, will buttress, by the respectful behavior of each and every one of its members, this high office. (Applause on the Republican side.)

Therefore, placing patriotism above partisanship, placing duty above even a just resentment, not withstanding we do not approve of the parliamentary law of the Speaker and his associates, and deem that the system reestablished is undemocratic and unwise, nevertheless, by offering the customary resolution, we tender to the Speaker of this House the expression of our belief that he, like all his predecessors, has performed the trying duties of his office with upright intention and honorable purpose. (Applause.)[1]

When Mr. Reed resigned his seat in 1898, David B. Henderson of Iowa was elected Speaker for the Fifty-sixth

[1] *Cong. Record*, 52nd Cong., 2nd Sess., p. 2614.

Congress. Mr. Henderson had been chairman of the Committee on Judiciary. The peculiar distinction which he could claim in his election was that he was the last of the Civil War Speakers and the first Speaker from a State beyond the Mississippi River. But the fact that he was elected over Mr. Cannon of Illinois, was a " mystery " which remains unsolved even to this day.[1]

Mr. Henderson presided over the House from the Fifty-sixth to Fifty-seventh Congress. During this time he practically made no advance in the importance of the Speakership. To do him justice, it must be stated, however, that he was at disadvantage in being the successor of Mr. Reed. Mr. Stealey, in his *Twenty Years in the Press Gallery*, sympathetically wrote that the House had grown restless under the iron hand of Mr. Reed, and was " ready to go to the other extreme and reduce the Speakership to a position of a mere presiding officer . . . and the power of the Committee on Rules was threatened and even its abolition was urged." [2] To appease this " reaction " with its attending uneasiness on the one hand and to avoid the appearance of desiring to play the role of " Czar " was the difficult task of Mr. Henderson.

How far Mr. Henderson was successful in applying his Doctrine of Mean, as the Chinese would say, is difficult to tell. Much of the happenings during his administration have remained obscure,[3] and it is hardly possible to form any

[1] Mr. Alexander of New York, a member of the House in the Fifty-sixth Congress, writes: " . . . To this day it remains an unsolved mystery why his [Mr. Cannon's] party preferred Henderson for Speaker in 1899." *Op. cit.*, p. 109. Mr. Henderson received assurance from President McKinley that he would not interfere with the contest for Speakership and that he would keep "hands off." Brown, *op. cit.*, p. 111.

[2] Pp. 304, 305.

[3] It was also stated that Mr. Henderson's obscurity was due to his unpopularity with the newspaper correspondents in Washington. While Speaker Mr. Henderson never cared to discuss pending legislation with the newspaper reporters for publication. *Ibid.*, p. 307.

intelligent judgment upon the extent of his success.   On the other hand, signs of dissatisfaction were in evidence among the members of the House, noticeably at the end of the Fifty-seventh Congress when Mr. Payne, the floor leader of the Republican majority, offered the customary resolution of thanks for the " able, impartial and dignified manner " in which Mr. Henderson presided over the deliberations of the House.   Usually such resolution is offered by the leader of the minority party.   Mr. Payne, fully conscious of what he was doing, said, apologetically, in addressing the House :

. . . It is not the first time, Mr. Speaker [Mr. Cannon in the Chair], that this resolution has been offered by a member of the majority party. . . . There are numerous cases, Mr. Speaker, in which the resolution was met with opposition, in which there have been votes in opposition, and in which a member in sympathy politically with the majority has offered this resolution.[1]

As soon as Mr. Payne concluded his speech, he demanded the previous question which cut off all debate and brought the House to a direct vote upon the pending resolution.[2]   Mr. Cockran of New York, however, demanded the yeas and nays, an action usually expressive of resentment or ill-will on the part of members towards the Speaker, although in this case he was not supported by enough members to secure a roll call.[3]

With the retirement of Mr. Henderson at the end of the Fifty-seventh Congress, the contest for the Speakership came to the front.   Among the prominent candidates were Mr. Cannon of Illinois and Mr. Hepburn of Iowa.   However, by the middle of October, 1902, Mr. Hepburn, having learned the futility of " butting his head against the stone

[1] *Cong. Record*, 57th Cong., 2nd Sess., p. 3071.
[2] See Rule xvii, 1.
[3] *Cong. Record*, 57th Cong., 2nd Sess., p. 3071.

wall," withdrew from the contest. In a letter to one of his friends in Washington he stated (1) that Iowa could not have two Speakers in succession; (2) that his stand on the rules reform made him unacceptable to the Old Guards; and (3) that Mr. Cannon had the support of the Western Congressmen which was essential to the success of Mr. Hepburn.[1] With the withdrawal of the latter, the Republican caucus unanimously elected Mr. Cannon to the Speakership. Commenting on his elevation to this high office, a close observer in the press gallery of the House noted that " Cannon did not come to this exalted political position by reason of the discovery of any great overwhelming genius. He came to it through long experience, close study and persistent effort "[2] in the House of Representatives.

In his first term as Speaker of the House in the Fifty-eighth Congress Mr. Cannon was unusually successful and extremely popular with members on both sides of the House. This fact can best be testified to by the overwhelming sentiment of the House as expressed on the closing day of the Congress, at which time the customary resolution of thanks is offered. A resolution of thanks, as we know, is a formal expression of sentiment on the part of the members of the House towards the Speaker; but, more frequently than not, it passes judgment upon the manner in which the latter performs his duties. Shortly before the House adjourned on March 4, 1905, a joint caucus of the two parties, Republican and Democratic, was held, over which Mr. Hay, of Virginia, chairman of the Democratic caucus, presided. Mr. Boutell of Illinois was recognized to make an address. The unanimity of approbation as exhibited on this occasion was very illuminating, in contrast with the loud denunciation of

[1] Briggs, *William Petters Hepburn* (Iowa, 1919), pp. 318, 319.
[2] Stealey, *op. cit.*, p. 230.

him during the later years of his administration. Mr. Boutell said:

This recess will afford us an opportunity for transacting some important business, which the Speaker . . . would have ruled out of order in the House. Fortunately, however, our control over the Speaker is now as complete as the control that we are accustomed to submit to with cheerfulness.

The Fifty-eighth Congress is rapidly approaching its close. During its three sessions the House has considered and passed, in addition to the great supply bills, an unusually large number of public measures of the first importance and of far reaching influence. . . . These measures have all been considered with exceptional candor and consideration, and the entire business of the House has been carried on without friction and in harmony. . . . This happy result, gratifying alike to the country and to ourselves, is mainly attributable to the unmatched qualities of leadership that have made the career of the present Speaker of the House unique in the history of this body. (Applause.)

. . . From the time that Muhlenberg's gavel called to order the House of Representatives of the first Congress down to this hour no Speaker ever had such a comprehensive and accurate knowledge of the working and needs of all the departments of Government as the present Speaker. (Loud Applause.) This profound knowledge enables him to determine with unerring precision the comparative merits of the vast number of measures clamoring as it were for recognition and preference and to exercise a power of elimination so judicious that its wisdom is never questioned by any Member. . . .

There are two kinds of leadership—one of the head and another of the heart. There are great leaders who sometimes have to drag their followers by the iron chains of conviction; the greatest leaders draw their followers with the golden cords of affection. (Applause.) Our Speaker has the chains, but he never needs to use them. (Loud Applause.)

This hour is wholly dedicated to his leadership . . . for we who know him best know that . . . his door has always been hospitably open to receive any Member of the House, his mind always impartially open to receive suggestions and advice, and, best of all, his heart has always been fraternally open to give out friendly counsel and encouragement. (Loud Applause.)

And

On behalf of all your colleagues in the House of Representatives of the Fifty-eighth Congress, I take great pleasure in presenting to you, Mr. Speaker, this loving cup. (Loud and continued applause.) Neither our words nor this mute token of our affection can adequately express our sentiments. But we want to give you a lasting memorial that could be transmitted from generation to generation. . . .

You will notice, Mr. Speaker, that the artist has engraved around the bowl and stem of this cup the leaves and flowers of the thistle. It is the favorite flower of those of Scotish lineage and is the emblem of the Ancient Order of the Thistle, whose motto is . . . no one assaults me with impunity, (Laughter) . . . and you can be assured, Mr. Speaker, that during the remainder of this session, and in the next Congress, and in whatever exalted office the people may summon you, no one within the hearing of any Members of this House can assault with impunity either you or one of your rulings. (Laughter and loud applause.)[1]

Mr. Williams of Mississippi, the minority leader, joined the chorus of exaltation and paid tribute to Mr. Cannon in " recognition of kindly services and kindly feeling already extended and already appreciated "[2] by both sides of the House. And Mr. Clark of Missouri added: " Historians of our times will record the fact that the Fifty-eighth Con-

---

[1] *Cong. Record*, 58th Cong., 3rd Sess., pp. 4038, 4039.

[2] *Ibid.*, p. 4039, 4040.

gress was celebrated above all its predessors for all its extra-ordinary kindness of feeling which prevailed among its Members." [1]

However, eight years later, March 4, 1911, the last day of the Sixty-first Congress, Mr. Clark of Missouri, under different circumstances and in a different spirit, presented the following resolution of thanks to Mr. Cannon:

Thanks are due to the Hon. Joseph G. Cannon . . . for the intelligent, constant, courteous manner in which he had presided over its important deliberations.[2]

The adjective " impartial " was absent in the resolution. And, what was more, the " extra-ordinary kindness of feeling " manifested in the Fifty-eighth Congress was no longer in evidence. In order to see the contrast, let us quote Mr. Clark further:

. . . The Sixty-first Congress . . . is . . . one of most important of all Congresses which we have had, and undoubtedly one of the stormiest . . . More bitter words have never been uttered or more riotous scenes enacted in any Congress of the United States than in this one. It began with a storm, and it came precious near ending with a storm just now. . . .

. . . I offer this resolution because the Hon. Joseph G. Cannon becomes this day a historic personage. It does not make a particle of difference whether we like him or we dislike him, whether we endorse what he has done in whole or in part, or not at all. . . .[3]

And pleading for the passage of the resolution, he went on to say:

[1] *Cong. Record*, 58th Cong., 3rd Sess., p. 4040.
[2] *Cong. Record*, 61st Cong., 3rd Sess., p. 4338.
[3] *Ibid.*, p. 4338.

. . . I offer this resolution without detracting in anything from the principles which we have advocated in this Congress or any other, without apologizing to any mortal man for any act of the minority in the House during this Congress, and according to others the same honesty and patriotism which we claim for ourselves, I believe this resolution is reasonably just and ought to be passed. (Applause.)[1]

Despite the open revolt of the insurgent Republicans in the Sixty-first Congress, Mr. Cannon was, on the whole, very successful in his control over legislation, even more so than Mr. Reed. It is indeed not too much to say that when Mr. Cannon was in the chair, the success or failure of a measure largely depended upon his pleasure. The Appalachian-White Mountain bill is a case in point. The bill provided for the preservation of certain forests in the East. It was repeatedly urged by President Roosevelt, passed without dissent by the Senate, and was unanimously recommended by the House Committee on Agriculture. It did not, however, meet with the approval of Mr. Cannon, and was therefore referred by him to the Committee on Judiciary which reported adversely on account of its unconstitutionality.[2] Another case shows the way in which Mr. Cannon dealt with President Roosevelt when they were at variance with each other. President Roosevelt sent, January 13, 1908, his annual message to Congress, but it was not considered in the Committee of the Whole House on the state of the Union until as late as April 2, 1908.[3] Moreover, many of the President's recommendations or measures remained unacted upon during that Congress. Influential as he was, Mr. Roosevelt even found it necessary to conclude a

---

[1] *Cong. Record,* 58th Cong., 3rd Sess., p. 4338.

[2] *Outlook,* lxxxvix, May 2, 1908, pp. 12-14. *Cf.* Busbey, *op. cit.,* p. 213 on Cannon's opposition to tariff revision.

[3] See *Cong. Record,* 60th Cong., 1st Sess., pp. 1381, 4325.

secret "pact" with Mr. Cannon and two other House leaders, Mr. Payne of New York and Mr. Dalzell of Pennsylvania.[1] It was agreed that Mr. Roosevelt would not insist upon an immediate revision of the tariff if certain specific legislation advocated by him was allowed to pass the House.

Two underlying forces were at work in favor of Mr. Cannon's control over the House. The first force is what one may call the conservatism of the American people in politics, a remarkable trait in a remarkably progressive people. " It may seem a paradox," writes Lord Bryce, the most sagacious critic of *Modern Democracies,* " that the Americans are a conservative people." [2] " They are conservative in their fundamental beliefs, in the structure of their governments." [3] Mr. Cannon was a conservative and had the support of the conservatives who at that time dom-

---

[1] *Cong. Record,* 68th Cong., 1st Sess., p. 562. It is interesting to compare with Mr. Roosevelt's own writings relating to his control over Congress. Mr. Roosevelt, like many other great men, was not without the fault of feeling his own greatness. On June 26, 1906, he wrote to Jacob Riis: "... For instance, I am criticized for interference with Congress. There really is not any answer I can make to this except to say that if I had not interfered we would not have had any rate bill, or any beef-packer's bill or any pure food bill, or any consular reform bill, or the Panama Canal, or the Employer's Liability Bill, or in short, any of the legislation which we have obtained during the last year." Bishop, *Roosevelt and His Time Shown in His Own Letters* (New York, 1920), vol. ii, p. 19.

On May 5, 1908, Mr. Roosevelt wrote to Whitelaw Reid in London: " Congress is ending, but by no means in a blaze of glory. The leaders in the House and Senate felt a relief that they did not try to conceal at the fact that I was not to remain as President, and need not be too implicitly followed; and they forget that the discipline that they have been able to keep for the last six years over their followers was primarily due to the fact that we had a compact and aggressive organization, kept together by my leadership, due to my hold..." *Ibid.,* vol. ii, p. 84. On January 31, 1909, he wrote to his son Theodore almost in a similar tune. See *ibid.,* p. 134.

[2] Bryce, *American Commonwealth* (New York, 1888), vol. ii, p. 253.

[3] *Ibid.,* p. 254.

inated the House of Representatives. These conservatives believed that the rules of the House upon which Cannonism was built, " are the best rules that could have been devised to conduct the business of the House." [1] " Why," declared Mr. Dalzell of Pennsylvania, a conservative leader, " the rules of the House, Mr. Speaker, are the evolution of one hundred and twenty years of parliamentary experience. They represent the wisdom of the best and most accomplished statesmanship, so far as our present rules are concerned, of the last two decades of our country." [2]

The second force was the strong personal regard, nay affection, that a majority of the members, especially the Old Guards, had for Mr. Cannon, or " Uncle Joe " as he was called. At the end of his fourth term as Speaker, Mr. Cannon had served in the House for thirty-four years, During this time he " had thumped and skinned and pummeled too many men. He had killed too many bills, both for Democrats and Republicans, . . . and yet the time has come when he is an exceedlingly popular man on both sides of this Chamber." [3] The sixth day of May, the birthday of Mr. Cannon, always afforded an occasion for eloquence, and for this purpose, a roll call was once interrupted [4] and at another time the House adjourned over the next day.[5] There was in him something typical of the Western frontiersman: he was courageous, crude, simple in manner and yet shrewd in politics. In debate " he reasoned and smiled, unbuttoned his vest, unloosened the band of his trousers, and then, with his left arm flying over his head," [6] tore down

[1] *Cong. Record*, 61st Cong., 1st Sess., p. 31.

[2] *Ibid.*, p. 31.

[3] *Cong. Record*, 59th Cong., 2nd Sess., p. 4670.

[4] *Cong. Record*, 60th Cong., 1st Sess., pp. 5901, 5902.

[5] *Cong. Record*, 67th Cong., 1st Sess., p. 1143.

[6] See Alexander, *op. cit.*, p. 132.

the arguments of his opponent. While in the Speaker's chair, he had his " feet in the soil ", considering all proposed legislation and examining all bills under requests for unanimous consent. He never dodged responsibility. He had a humane way of dealing with the discontented, too. To an insubordinate and turbulent member he would say, while laying his hand on the member's shoulder: " Now, my boy, let's us talk it over." [1]   And yet he was a " Czar; " He admitted it but not, however, without foundation. Thus he said:

yes, I know I am a Czar in Democratic platforms and in some of the moral-uplift magazines, but only just so long as I have a majority behind me who like a Czar. There has been much said about Tom. Reed and his rules, and he was the first Czar. Tom Reed led, but he would have stood naked before the minority if he hadn't been clothed with a majority. That is what makes a Czar in this House, a majority, and it makes no difference whether it is on the Republican or Democratic side.[2]

During the election of 1910 the Democratic party made the reform of the rules of the House one of the campaign issues, and upon that issue, though not upon that alone, it was returned with a majority of 228 to 162 Republican members in the House. When the Sixty-second Congress assembled on April 4, 1911, Mr. Clark of Missouri was elected Speaker of the House. As floor leader of his party in the preceding Congress, Mr. Clark had taken a conspicous part in the March revolution, 1910, in overthrowing Can-

---

[1] *Cong. Record*, 64th Cong., 4th Sess., p. 5500.

[2] McClellan, "Leadership in the House Representatives," *Scribners*, vol. xlvix, p. 595. It was stated that once a constituent of a Representative asked for a copy of the rules of the House and received a copy of a picture of Mr. Cannon instead. This was indicative of the popular conception of the power of Mr. Cannon wielded in the House. See *Outlook*, vol. xciv, April 9, 1910, pp. 789-792.

nonism, and had been one of the ardent advocates for the liberalization of the rules of the House. "Although I am going to be Speaker next time," he once declared in the Sixty-first Congress, " I am going to sacrifice the Speaker's power to change the rules." [1]

Mr. Clark presided over the House under a new system of rules, and for this reason to his administration attaches a peculiar importance. Under this system he was denied the power as well as the privilege of appointing the standing committees in the House. Nor was he the chairman of the powerful Committee on Rules. The power of recognition also was reduced considerably under the rules for Calendar Wednesday and the Calendar for Unanimous Consent. Out of these new conditions whether a new character of Speakership was to come depended wholly upon the conduct of Mr. Clark.

Almost on the first day on which Mr. Clark ascended the Speaker's chair it was very clear that the new Speaker would not be content with being a mere presiding officer. In his inauguration speech he enunciated a legislative program,— six " promises " on which he expected the endorsement of the people, namely, (1) a revision of tariff downward; (2) the passage of a constitutional amendment for the election of Senators by the people; (3) a change in the House rules; (4) economy in public expense; (5) publicity of campaign contributions; and (6) the admission of Arizona and New Mexico as one State.[2]

Mr. Clark's active participation both in debate and in voting while in the Speaker's chair has already been shown in a preceding chapter,[3] and it is only necessary to reiterate

---

[1] See *Cong. Record*, 68th Cong., 1st Sess., p. 960.

[2] *Cong. Record*, 62th Cong., 1st Sess., p. 7.

[3] See *supra*, pp. 46-48, 56-58.

here that in frequency of debate Mr. Clark has not as yet been equaled by any of the Speakers of the House either before or after him and in frequency of voting he was seconded only to Speaker Cannon. As Speaker, Mr. Clark made both his power and influence felt in the House. He preserved and continued the duality characteristic of the American Speaker-ship. On one occasion he regarded himself as " the Dean of the Faculty," [1] and on another he vigorously declared that he " refused absolutely to be either a ' rubber stamp Repre-sentative ' or a ' rubber stamp Speaker.' " [2]

Frederick H. Gillett of Massachusetts succeeded Mr. Clark in the Sixty-sixth Congress as Speaker of the House upon the return to power of the Republican party. As elsewhere stated, Mr. Gillett was elected over Mr. Mann of Illinois by the Republican caucus through the assistance of Senator Lodge, Senator Penrose of Pennsylvania and Chairman Hays of the National Committee of the Republican party.[3] But in addition to the political reinforcement from the Re-publican chieftains, we may also add that Mr. Gillett had practically no personal enemy in the House through his political activities, or perhaps we had better say his political inactivities. Mr. Mann, on the other hand, was probably the most active of all members in his time. As Mr. Clark has said, Mr. Mann was " the most industrious, indefatigable human being that I [Mr. Clark] ever clapped my eyes on. How he learns all he knowns about these bills is an im-penetrable mystery to me, and I do not believe that any being in the universe, except Brother Mann, his secretary, and God Almighty Himself, know." [4] He read and ex-

[1] *Cong. Record*, 62nd Cong., 2nd Sess., p. 11840.

[2] *Cong. Record*, 63rd Cong., 2nd Sess., p. 6057.

[3] See *supra*, pp. 25-7.

[4] *Cong. Record*, 62nd Cong., 3rd Sess., p. 4807.

amined all pending measures in advance and was always in
his seat, watchfully waiting for a chance to criticize them.
And, indeed, happy would be the member whose bill was
passed under unanimous consent without being killed by the
torrent of questions asked by Mr. Mann. The true character of his activities was succinctly described by Mr. Longworth, the present Speaker:

. . . The gentleman from Illinois (Mr. Mann) undertakes
to play the role of Hamlet in this House, and does with it with
skill, grace and tact, and I think no one will begrudge him that
role, but when . . . he undertakes not only to play Hamlet, but
the fair Ophelia and the King and the Queen and the first
grave digger and sometimes, as now, carries a spear, he might
be criticized for carrying the thing too far.[1]

The election of Mr. Gillett united for the first time the
Fatherhood and the Speakership of the House in one man.[2]
But what was of far more interest was that his election gave
one more evidence to the saying of Mr. Reed that " parties
seldom follow their best man. They follow their average
sense." [3] Time proved the shrewdness of this " sense."
For Mr. Gillett was genial and of judicial temperament and
made no attempt towards autocracy. During his three terms
as Speaker, he voted and debated much less than any of his
immediate predecessors, and did much towards the restora-
tion of the judicial character of the Speakership. His
first term was " unusually free from party rancor and bitterness." [4] For two Congresses, the Sixty-sixth and the Sixty-

---

[1] See *Cong. Record*, 67th Cong., 4th Sess., p. 1717.

[2] Mr. Gillett had continuously served in the House for twenty-six years
at the time when he was elected Speaker. Also see *Cong. Record*,
66th Cong., 1st Sess., p. 8.

[3] McCall, *op. cit.*, p. 228.

[4] *Cong. Record*, 66th Cong., 3rd Sess., p. 4546.

seventh, Mr. Mondell of Wyoming and Mr. Campbell of Kansas, chairman of the Committee on Rules, were the powers in the House.   The Mann influence was particularly strong in the Sixty-sixth Congress, as was shown in the Committee of Committees.[1]   All this while Mr. Gillett showed no signs of asserting his leadership.   At the end of the Sixty-eighth Congress and before he took his seat in the Senate he said:

You may remember that when first elected Speaker I said that I had attained the goal of my desires and my ambition was completely satisfied.   I feel exactly now as I did then.   Thanks to you, my friends, my enjoyment of it has been equal to my anticipation.   I would rather be Speaker of this House than holding any other position in the world, and it was no ambition or initiative of my own that let me to relinquish it.[2]

With the election of Mr. Gillett to the Senate the mantle of Speakership fell upon Mr. Longworth of Ohio, who was the majority floor leader in the Sixty-eighth Congress.   The election was made in a secret caucus held in February of 1925 by the Republican members to the exclusion of the Republican Progressives.[3]   When the Sixty-ninth Congress convened on December 7, 1925, more than half a year after the caucus action, the House formally ratified the election of Mr. Longworth as its Speaker.   The importance attached to his election derives from his vigorous stand on party regulartiy.   During the Sixty-eighth Congress he spoke, before the Ohio Society in New York, January 10, 1925, and more than once on the floor of the House, of " the baneful effect of bloc government." [4]   In his inauguration speech as

[1] See *supra*, p. 80.
[2] *Cong. Record*, 68th Cong., 2nd Sess., p. 5623.
[3] *Cong. Record*, 69th Cong., 1st Sess., p. 6.
[4] *Cong. Record*, 68th Cong., 2nd Sess., pp. 2712-2715.

Speaker, on the opening day of the Sixty-ninth Congress, he reiterated, with additional emphasis, what he had uttered on previous occasions. Referring to the political duties of the Speaker, he said:

The political side, to my mind, involves a question of party service. I believe it to be the duty of the Speaker, standing squarely on the platform of his party, to assist in so far as he properly can the enactment of legislation in accordance with the declared principles, policies of his party and by the same token to resist the enactment of legislation in violation thereof.[1]

During the first session of the Sixty-ninth Congress Mr. Longworth presided over the House with unusual dignity and justice. He did not answer a single roll-call. He appeared once on the floor of the House to announce the birthday of Mr. Tilson, the majority floor leader.[2] As a Democratic member from Nebraska testified, it was unusual " to find a Speaker who can rise to the occasion under every condition and give fair treatment to minority members of this House, be he a Democratic or Republican Speaker, as [can] the present Speaker." [3] In the second session of the same Congress he spoke three times.[4] " I know," he said, as he arose from the floor of the House to debate on the Navy bill, " that it is a rather unusual thing for a Speaker to take part in debate. I am glad that it appears that you do not seem to mind very much." [5] Applause greeted his words.

Only once did Mr. Longworth arbitrarily exercise the power of recognition during his first Speakership in the Sixty-ninth Congress. It was upon the occasion when the

[1] *Cong. Record*, 69th Cong., 1st Sess., p. 382.

[2] *Cong. Record*, 69th Cong., 1st Sess., p. 6692.

[3] *Ibid.*, p. 11030.

[4] *Cong. Record*, 69th Cong., 2nd Sess., pp. 1244, 2672-2673, 4703-4704.

[5] *Ibid.*, p. 4703.

House debated February 24, 1927, on the Senate cruiser amendment to the Naval appropriation bill. Mr. French of Idaho moved to disagree to the Senate amendment and and asked for a conference. Thereupon Mr. Butler of Pennsylvania moved that the House recede and concur with the Tilson amendment providing for $14,200,000, of which $450,000 " shall be immediately available toward the construction of the last three of the eight scout cruisers authorized by section 2 of the act of December 18, 1924." After several members had spoken, Mr. Vestal of Indiana rose to offer an amendment to which the Speaker was opposed. Thus the *Congressional Record* reads:

> Mr. Vestal rose.
>
> The Speaker. For what purpose does the gentleman rise?
>
> Mr. Vestal. I rise to offer an amendment to the motion of the gentleman from Pennsylvania.

The Speaker then turned his head to the Democratic side of the House. The *Record* continued:

> Mr. Vinson of Georgia. Mr. Speaker, I move the previous question on the motion of the gentleman from Pennsylvania.
>
> The Speaker. The question is on ordering the previous question.
>
> Mr. French. But, Mr. Speaker, the gentleman from Indiana (Mr. Vestal) as I understand it, has offered a substitute, although I have not seen it.
>
> The Speaker. The Chair has not recognized the gentleman from Indiana for that purpose. . . . The gentleman from Georgia has moved the previous question on the motion of the gentleman from Pennsylvania.[1]

A vote was then taken on the previous question, thereby depriving Mr. Vestal of the opportunity of offering his sub-

---

[1] *Cong. Record*, 69th Cong., 2nd Sess., p. 4705.

stitute to the Butler amendment. Speaker Longworth was criticized for his " unfairness " in refusing to recognize Mr. Vestal. In the days of Speaker Reed and Speaker Cannon such action, on the part of the occupant of the Speaker's chair, was rather to be taken for granted by the members of the House. But time changes, particularly since the European War. Party discipline—party regularity—has been little by little waning. Members of both parties are less willing to subject themselves to the lashes of the party leaders who in turn become more conscious of the sentiments of the membership of their own party. As a member, Mr. Longworth may be a " militant Republican," [1] but, as Speaker of the House, he can not go very far at the expense of the rights of the members of the House. For " in the House of Representatives," as Mr. Longworth himself has well said on the closing day of the Sixty-ninth Congress, " a majority can at all times carry out the will of the people of the United States and . . . a minority [of party leaders] can at no time thwart it." [2] And that majority, which he referred to, is not a party majority but a temporary majority made up of members of both parties. During the last few years that majority has at times asserted itself to defeat the stand of the party leaders on measures of importance.

[1] Speaking before the Women's Republican Club of Boston, Mr. Longworth declared that he went there as a " militant Republican." See the New York *Times*, March 16, 1927, p. 2.

[2] *Cong. Record*, 69th Cong. 2nd Sess., p. 5707.

CHAPTER IX

The Speaker and Leadership in the House

LEADERSHIP in the House of Representatives is a much-mooted question. On the one hand, Mr. Wilson in his well-known book on *Congressional Government* writes that there is " in this country . . . no real leadership; because no man is allowed to direct the course of Congress." [1] He then goes on to explain:

> The leaders of the House are chairmen of the principal Standing Committees. Indeed, to be exactly accurate, the House has as many leaders as there are subjects of legislation; for there are as many Standing Committees as there are leading classes of legislation, and in the consideration of every topic of business the House is guided by a special leader in the person of the chairman of the Standing Committee, charged with superintendence of measures of the particular class to which that topic belongs. [2]

And further:

> . . . This scheme of distributed power and disintegrated rules seems a very excellent device whereby we are enabled to escape a dangerous " one-man power " and an untoward concentration of function. [3]

Six years later, however, Professor A. B. Hart gives us a different version of the very same subject. Mr. Hart writes

[1] Wilson, p. 205.

[2] *Ibid.*, pp. 60, 61.

[3] *Ibid.*, p. 92.

of the Speaker as Premier whose power and leadership in the House of Representatives then, and for some years to come, were comparable to those of the English Premier:

The powers now exercised by the Speaker will probably be exercised by each succeeding Speaker and will somewhat increase. Since the legislative department in every Republic constantly tends to gain ground at the expense of the executive, the Speaker is likely to become, and perhaps is already, more powerful, both for good and for evil, than the President of the United States. He is Premier in legislation; it is the business of his party that he be also Premier in character, in ability, in leadership, and in statesmanship.[1]

These views, from the pens of two competent students of American Government, bear evidence of the possibility of arriving at most divergent conclusions upon the question of leadership in the House of Representatives. Broadly speaking, " the leaders of the House are chairmen of the principal Standing Committees," but it is, however, not accurate to say that " the House has as many leaders as there are subjects." " The leading classes of legislation " are only confined to a few of the more than sixty House Standing Committees. Mr. Hinds thought that sixteen of these committees handle nearly all the legislation of the House.[2] Mr. McCall reduced the number to less than a dozen, although at times a half-dozen more may be prominent.[3] Speaker Clark set the number as still smaller, saying that six committees " are always the greatest of our legislative committees." [4]

[1] Hart, *Practical Essays in American Government* (New York, 1893), p. 19. In fact, "The Speaker as Premier" was an article which Professor Hart wrote in 1891 for the *Atlantic Monthly* magazine.

[2] Hinds, *loc. cit.*, *McClure*, vol. xxxv, p. 200.

[3] McCall, *The Business of Congress* (New York, 1911), p. 47.

[4] *Cong. Record*, 65th Cong., 2nd Sess., p. 318.

The chairman of a committee has power to control legislation. The Rules of the House provide that " all proposed legislation shall be referred to the committees," [1] and according to a general rule, all business must first go to committees before receiving consideration in the House. [2] Certain committees are accorded the privilege " to report at any time on matters " [3] over which they have jurisdiction, and such matters must receive immediate consideration in the House. The chairmen of these committees are generally influential leaders of the House and are able to exercise a considerable amount of power over the business of the House. With their privileged status, they may bring forth a report at any time, thereby preventing the House from considering measures to which they are opposed.

Referring to the power of the chairmen of the House committees, Mr. Anderson of Minnesota said:

Of course the chairman of a committee can not report a bill without the consent of a majority of the committee, but the unwritten, and, I believe, the unbroken, rule [is that] no majority has ever reported a bill without the consent of the chairman. On the floor the bill is absolutely in his hands.

It is obvious that the power to say that legislation shall not be considered is the power to legislate. It is the negative power which lends real significance to these chairmanships. This negative or obstructive power rests in the hands of a few men and may be exerted at any of the various stages of the bill's progress toward final passage. It is greatly enhanced by the restrictive character of the rules and the inefficiency of the legislative system in general. [4]

[1] Rule x.
[2] See *House Manual*, section 439, Sixty-ninth Congress.
[3] Rule xi, 56.
[4] *Cong. Record*, 63rd Cong., 1st Sess., p. 4761.

Here is a case which shows the power of the chairman of a committee over a bill. In the third session of the Sixty-second Congress the Senate passed a bill, S. 7723, " to regulate the hours of employment and safeguard the health of females employed in the District of Columbia." The bill went to the House and was referred to the Committee on the District of Columbia. The chairman of the committee, Mr. Johnson of Kentucky, was opposed to the measure. " The chairman of that committee," Mr. Lafferty of Oregon stated, March 4, 1913, " after a written request submitted yesterday by myself and the gentleman from Wisconsin (Mr. Cooper), the gentleman from Minnesota (Mr. Davis), and the gentleman from California (Mr. Kent), refused in writing to send that bill over here to the Speaker's table, so that the engrossed copy might be present when the motion to discharge the committee and pass the bill could be presented." [1] Mr. Lafferty moved to suspend the rules and discharge the Committee on the District of Columbia from further consideration of the bill. But under the precedents the House cannot suspend the rules and pass a bill unless the engrossed copy is on the Speaker's table. So Mr. Johnson moved to discharge the Committee on the District of Columbia so as to bring the bill before the House. No sooner had Mr. Lafferty entered his motion, than Mr. Underwood, the majority floor leader, moved the House to take a recess, thereby preventing the House from considering Mr. Lafferty's motion. Mr. Underwood's motion was agreed to. [2]

The Speaker has never been, and under the Constitution will never be, " Premier in legislation." Such a position he cannot attain under the peculiar organization of the House, regardless of how powerful and influential he may

[1] *Cong. Record*, 62nd Cong., 3rd Sess., p. 4845.
[2] *Ibid.*, p. 4845.

be. Elsewhere attempts have been made to show the checks and balances over the power of the Speaker, even at the time when that power was at its greatest height. For instance, in the appointment of committees, he was bound by certain established usages and practices. Speaker Cannon was sharply criticized for the removal of certain members from their former committee places in the Sixty-first Congress.[1] In recognition also there are restrictions to which the Speaker has to conform. The only power which seems to have no bounds is the personal influence of the Speaker. But that is a factor upon which he cannot ultimately rely for leadership. Every Speaker is possessed of a certain degree of personal influence, and likewise also of a coterie of loyal friends who are forever with him, right or wrong, in success or in defeat. Speaker Reed had it, but it did not help him to successfully oppose the passage of the Spanish war resolution and the bill for the annexation of Hawaii. Speaker Cannon had it, but it did not help him to subdue the onslaught of the insurgents in the Sixty-first Congress. Speaker Clark had it too, but it yielded before the invasion of the superior force of President Wilson. By and large, the House is a club of shrewd politicians. Sectional interests, local claims and personal advancements—all these things are dearer to the hearts of the members of the House than the party emblems which are now mere labels on empty bottles.[2] Few, if any, would follow the leadership of a member, be he Speaker or not, just because of his personality or even his influence. The chain of union is founded upon the plain of reciprocity.[3]

[1] See *supra*, pp. 66-7.

[2] See Professor Holcombe's *Political Parties of Today* (New York, 1924) in which he realistically painted the economic and sectional basis of the national politics. It is a book worthy of serious consideration.

[3] Mr. Lynn Haines gives us one instance: "Once from the House

Leadership in the House is in commission.[1] It is not in the Speaker's chair alone, although the Speaker, particularly an ambitious and aggressive one, is an important member of the commission. Nor is it to be found wholly on the floor, although the floor leader is one of the most powerful leaders in the House. Before 1910 the commission consisted of the Speaker, the two majority members on the Committee on Rules, the majority floor leader, the chairman of the Committee on Ways and Means, the chairman of the Committee on Appropriations, and one or two members who were either chairmen of important committees or merely members who had the confidence of the Speaker. As to the last case, we may cite Mr. Mann of Illinois, in eulogy of whom Speaker Gillett said: " Under Mr. Cannon's Speakership he had so won his way, and the House so recognized his ability that although he was not the nominal leader, yet he was the real representative of the Speaker and the dominating force upon the floor." [2] It must be pointed out that Mr. Mann was not appointed by Speaker Cannon to the important chairmanship of the Committee on Interstate and Foreign Commerce until the Sixty-first Congress.

Since 1911 when, owing to the change of the House organization under the Democratic control, the commission in-

gallery I saw a group of congressional 'leaders'— political leaders— gathered about a young Congressman who had just voted for a measure of rules reform which would have worked to curtail the undemocratic power of these same 'leaders.' They tried to persuade him to change his vote. Afterwards I learned that they had promised him an easy, assured political fortune, through an abundance of pork, if he would stand with them . . ." *Searchlight*, vol. iv, no. 5, p. 3.

[1] While these pages were being written, Mr. Luce's *Congress: An Explanation* (Harvard University, Cambridge, 1926) appeared, in which Mr. Luce writes: " . . . Nowadays the leadership of the House is in commission, with the membership of the commission more or less fluctuating and shadowy," p. 117.

[2] *Cong. Record*, 67th Cong., 4th Sess., p. 1713.

creased in size, it has been composed generally of the
Speaker, the floor leader (who, under the Democratic practice, is chairman of the Committee on Ways and Means and
chairman of the Committee on Committees, and who, under
the Republican practice, is ex-officio chairman of the Committee on Committees as well as that of the Steering Committee), chairman of the Committee on Rules and chairman
of the Committee on Appropriations. Under the present,
Republican, system we should also add the chairman of the
Committee on Ways and Means and the eight members of
the Steering Committee.

Of this small number of directors the Speaker is merely
one of the most important. These directors decide upon the
legislative program, usually but not always direct the course
of its progress, and finally get laws enacted. Curiously
enough, they do not meet, and in fact have probably never
met as a body, except the members and the ex-officio members of the Steering Committee. But during the second
session of the Sixty-ninth Congress the Steering Committee
seldom met and was superseded by an inner conclave, with
which we shall deal presently. However, in one way or
another the members of the commission confer with each
other and push things forward. Never was there a time
when the Speaker, or the floor leader, or any other person,
no matter how influential and powerful he was, has single-
handedly pushed a measure of importance through the wheels
of the legislative mills in the House of Representatives. We
can point out with approximate accuracy the names of those
members who formed the component part of the commission
during the administration of the several Speakers. Suppose
we take the Cannon régime, during which time the power of
the Speaker had reached its apex. Speaker Cannon did not
rule alone: he ruled with Payne of New York and Dalzell

of Pennsylvania. In other words, he ruled in commission. When President Roosevelt made an " alliance " with the House for the enactment of certain legislation which he recommended, he dealt with the three of them, Speaker Cannon, Mr. Payne and Mr. Dalzell.[1] It was a quadruple alliance. The truth of this political observation can also be shown in the following incident. Once when the House was in the Committee of the Whole House on the state of the Union for the consideration of the resolution to distribute President Roosevelt's message, Mr. Hughes of New Jersey rose from his seat and said:

Mr. Hughes of New Jersy. I desire to offer the following amendment.

The Clerk read as follows:

. . . " So much as relates to new legislation be referred to the ' Big Five ' of the House."

(Laughter.)

Mr. Payne. Mr. Chairman, I am afraid I shall have to raise point of order on that.

Mr. Williams. Upon what ground does the gentleman from New York raise the point of order—that is new legislation or new rules?

Mr. Payne. Because there is no such committee in the House except in the exuberant imagination of the gentleman from Missouri. (Laughter.)[2]

The floor leader has been one of the mainstays of the commission form of leadership in the House. Since the division of the Committee on Ways and Means in 1865 the floor leader was often the chairman of the Committee on Appropriations.[3] But from 1896 to 1910 the floor leadership

---

[1] See *supra*, pp. 299-300.

[2] *Cong. Record*, 60th Cong., 1st Sess., p. 2105.

[3] Alexander, *op. cit.*, p. 107.

was for the most part of the time in the hands of the chairman of the Committee on Ways and Means. Mr. Cannon, as chairman of the Committee on Appropriations, held the office of floor leader during the Fifty-fourth and Fifty-fifth Congresses when Mr. Reed was in the chair. But when Mr. Henderson was elected Speaker in the Fifty-sixth Congress, he selected Mr. Payne of New York as floor leader, who became at the same time chairman of the Committee on Ways and Means in that Congress. Throughout the Speakership of Mr. Cannon, Mr. Payne remained as the floor leader. In the Sixty-second Congress the Democratic party continued the practice by electing as its floor leader Mr. Underwood of Alabama, who was chairman of the Committee on Ways and Means and in addition was chairman of the Committee on Committees, whose sole function it was to organize the Democratic House. Then the Republican party came into power in the House in the Sixty-sixth Congress, and a somewhat different system was inaugurated. Under this system the floor leader was chairman ex-officio of the Committee on Committees as well as of the Steering Committee, but was no longer a member of any of the legislative committees of the House.

Before 1911 the Speaker wielded the power of appointing the floor leader, but since then that power has been taken away from him. Before 1911, the Sixty-second Congress, the Speaker in selecting a floor leader either named his opponent in the Speakership contest or appointed the ranking member of the Committee on Ways and Means or of the Committee on Appropriations or rewarded a faithful lieutenant.[1] From the Sixty-second to the Sixty-fifth Congress, during which the Democrats were in control, the practice still held for the floor leader to be the chairman of the Committee on Ways and Means, although by " election " at the

[1] *Cf. ibid.*, pp. 110, 111.

party caucus. Thus Mr. Underwood of Alabama was so chosen during the Sixty-second and the Sixty-third Congresses, and Mr. Kitchin of North Carolina during the two succeeding Congresses. But since the Sixty-sixth Congress there has been no sure criterion in determining the floor leadership. Mr. Mondell of Wyoming, the Republican floor leader in the Sixty-sixth and Sixty-seventh Congresses, was ranked third on the Committee on Appropriations and second on the Committee on Woman Suffrage in the Sixty-fifth Congress on the Republican side. It was stated that he owed his position as floor leader to the Steering Committee and not to the Committee on Ways and Means,[1] to which, indeed, he never belonged. When Mr. Mondell " retired " from the House in the Sixty-eighth Congress, Mr. Longworth of Ohio was elected by the party caucus to succeed him. Mr. Longworth had been a member of the Committee on Committees and of the Steering Committee, in addition to being third placeman on the Committee on Ways and Means in the Sixty-seventh Congress. With the election of Mr. Longworth to the Speakership in the Sixty-ninth Congress, the Republican caucus chose as Mr. Longworth's successor Mr. Tilson of Connecticut who, in the preceding Congress, ranked fifth on the Committee on Ways and Means and was also a member of the Committee on Committees, but was not a member of the Steering Committee. It is indeed interesting to note that of the three Republican floor leaders since the Sixty-sixth Congress two stood high in the Committee on Ways and Means and one in the Committee on Appropriations. Since tariff is the most important of all party issues, it is important that the party leader on the floor should be thoroughly acquainted with its problems.

The House organization initiated by the Democratic party in 1911 and complicated by the Republican party in 1919 has

[1] See Brown, *op. cit.*, p. 201.

enhanced the power of the floor leader. Prior to 1911 the floor leader owed his position to the grace of the Speaker, but since 1911 he has been elected by the party caucus in the same manner as is the Speaker. Prior to 1911 it was the Speaker who organized the House, but since then the Committee on Committees, of which the floor leader is chairman, has been entrusted with this duty. As was pointed out, during the Democratic control from 1911 to 1919 the Committee on Committees was composed of the Democratic members of the Committee on Ways and Means, with the majority floor leader as chairman. Generally, members of the Committee on Ways and Means are the regular of the " regulars," and are more apt to " follow the leader " than the rank and file of the House. In the organization of the House the floor leader, who was chairman of the Committee on Ways and Means, was apt to possess a power greater than any other member of the committee. In this regard—the organization of the House—the floor leader under the Democratic system exercised more power than his Republican successors since 1919. Under the Republican system the Committee on Committees, consisting of one member from each State having Republican representation, was established upon the principle of states rights. The size of the committee has been large—usually more than thirty in number—and each member of the committee has as many votes as there are Republicans in the House from his State. The floor leader is chairman ex-officio, but he has no vote unless he is a member of the committee from his State. Even so, he is probably no more powerful than any other member of the Committee on Committees. The strength of a member under this system depends upon the number of votes he casts.

However, under Speaker Gillett the power of the floor leader made visible gains. Although able and accomplished, Mr. Gillett was the least assertive of all the Speakers since

1896, and this fact was accountable for the extension of the activities of the floor leader in the person of Frank W. Mondell of Wyoming. Mr. Mondell was first elected to the Fifty-fourth Congress, and, with the exception of the Fifty-fifth Congress, had continuously served in the House through the Sixty-seventh Congress — an aggregate of twenty-six years. He was trained in the political school of Mr. Cannon, and consistently voted to support the latter during the March revolution, 1910.[1] An exponent of the old centralized system, he undertook the floor leadership with force and firmness, and greatly augmented the power of the office of the floor leader at the expense of the Speaker. In the Sixty-seventh Congress it was charged that Mr. Mondell and Mr. Campbell of Kansas, chairman of the Committee on Rules, virtually ruled the House.[2] Of the control of Mr. Mondell over the House, Mr. Blanton of Texas said:

I appreciate the splendid control which the gentleman from Wyoming has over the House; that he has everything oiled up; that things have to go just like he wants them to go or they are not going at all. That is an awfully good condition for things to be in. It is well for the country that what you think about legislation or what you other Republican colleagues might think is immaterial unless you go to the gentleman from Wyoming first and have an understanding with him, for he is not going to let any of you take things in hand. The quicker you realize that the better off you are going to be. Our young friends who lately came here through the great upheaval of affairs last November, the quicker you realize the fact that you can not

---

[1] Mr. Mondell did not make any speech in defence of the old rules, but he voted consistently to sustain Speaker Cannon and against proposed changes in the rules. See *Cong. Record*, 61st Cong., 2nd Sess., pp. 3247, 3251, 3288, 3290, 3308, 3312, 3323, 3324, 3389, 3415, 3417, 3426, 3427, 3428, 3435, 3436, 3437, 3439.

[2] See *supra*, p. 146.

do anything unless the gentleman from Wyoming is willing the better off you will be. (Laughter.)[1]

In the first session of the Sixty-sixth Congress Mr. Aswell of Louisiana asked unanimous consent to address the House for thirty minutes, for which purpose recognition was denied by Speaker Gillett. Immediately Mr. Aswell went to the Speaker's desk and inquired as to the difficulties. The Speaker replied that he had not informed the Chair in advance, and then asked on what subject Mr. Aswell intended to speak. The latter answered that it was " on war expenditure and this Congress." Upon hearing the answer the Speaker " smiled pleasantly " and told him that he had " best see Mondell." Mr. Aswell went to Mr. Mondell, repeating his " request very humbly as Members have to," and asked if he " might " not speak. Mr. Mondell retorted " no." As Mr. Aswell tells it:

A week ago I went to the gentleman from Wyoming (Mr. Mondell) and asked his permission, bowing as I did to the autocratic rule established by him that each ordinary Member must go and get on his knees and beg his permission—I went and asked to speak for 35 minutes. . . . He refused to let me speak. . . .

In reply Mr. Mondell said:

I followed the rule that I followed heretofore, to which no exception has been made, except in the case of the gentleman from Ohio (Mr. Sherwood) who, by reason of his age and his long and honorable Army service and his long distinguished service in this House, I believe was entitled to that distinction. . . .[2]

Thoughtful students of American Government have asked

[1] *Cong. Record*, 67th Cong., 1st Sess., pp. 2168-9.
[2] *Cong. Record*, 66th Cong., 1st Sess., pp. 7907-7910.

the question whether the floor leader, when he loses control of the House, would resign his office. One writer thought that he would. " If he had lost control of the House," the writer says of Mr. Underwood, the floor leader of the Democratic party, " he would have resigned and the caucus would have been confronted by the necessity of electing a new Floor Leader, and this would have carried with it the necessity of electing a new Committee on Ways and Means.' " It so happened," the same writer continues, " that Mr. Underwood never lost control of the House during the period . . . . as the actual leader of the House." [1] If, by the loss of the control of the House, the writer meant that on an important question the Democratic majority took a different position from and voted in opposition to him, then Mr. Underwood had at least once lost control of the House. This was on the bill to repeal the provision of the Panama Canal Act of August 12, 1912, which exempted vessels engaged in the coastwise trade of the United States from payment of tolls on the Panama Canal. Mr. Underwood— Speaker Clark, too—was opposed to the passage of the bill, on the ground that it was in violation of the Democratic party pledge.[2] On March 31, 1914, when the roll-call was made on the passage of the bill in the House, the vote stood 247 against 162. Mr. Underwood voted in the negative with the minority. The bill passed the House in spite of the opposition of Mr. Underwood who, on March 27, 1914, had

[1] Brown, *op. cit.*, p. 177.

[2] Mr. Underwood said: " I have served from one Democratic administration to another. I have never scratched a party ticket ; I have always endeavoured to live up to and sustain my party's platform. (Applause.) The Democratic Party, not I, wrote this provision as to free tolls in its platform. I believe this plank of the platform is right. (Applause.) Believing it is right, there is but one position that I can take, and this is to sustain the position of my party as expressed in its convention and in its platform." *Cong. Record*, 63rd Cong., 2nd Sess., p. 5616.

openly declared on the floor that " I regret that the bill should be before the House.   I hope it will be defeated." [1] But it was not defeated.   Yet Mr. Underwood remained as the floor leader of his party.

A more recent case was the passage by the House of the McNary-Haugen bill in the second session of the Sixty-ninth Congress.   Mr. Tilson, the majority floor leader, was opposed to the bill, which he termed as " vicious legislation." But he did not have his way.   On the contrary, he lost control of the House.   On February 17, 1927, after the House debated on the bill for the entire day and when twilight was ushering in, Mr. Tilson rose to offer a motion of adjournment, which was defeated by a vote of 198 to 170. [2]   On the passage of the bill the vote was 214 to 178.   Mr. Tilson was among the minority, [3] but, like Mr. Underwood, he remains as the floor leader of his party.

[1] See *ibid.*, pp. 5616, 5617.   The following table shows the party division on the passage of the bill in question.   There were 290 Democrats in the House during this Congress.   And, to repeat, Mr. Underwood answered " nay " on the passage of this bill.

	Yeas	Nays
Democrats	220	51
Republicans	24	95
Independent	1	
Progressives	1	11
Progressive Republicans	1	5
Total	247	162

As the table shows, only 50 Democrats followed the leadership of Mr. Underwood, while 220 Democrats did not.   It is also interesting to point out that two other Democratic leaders, Speaker Clark and Mr. Fitzgerald of New York, chairman of the Committee on Appropriations, also voted in the minority with Mr. Underwood.   See *ibid.*, pp. 6088, 6089.

[2] See *Cong. Record*, 69th Cong., 2nd Sess., p. 4051.

[3] The following table shows the party division on the passage of the McNary-Haugen bill.   There were in the House 246 Republicans, 181 Democrats and 5 Third party men:

The prevailing American theory, says Mr. Luce, is that "leaders are not discredited if occasionally disobeyed." [1] He thinks that this " political independence was the fruit of the widespread personal independence " " in a land of pioneers," such as is the United States of America. Besides this, there is, however, another practical and important reason for the independence of the party members. On great national and international issues, like the prohibition and the World Court issues, the two majority political parties maintain an attitude of golden silence, having no declared policies, either in one way or another, in their platforms. In such cases, party lines are obliterated; members vote either in accordance with the dictates of their own conscience, or in obedience to the wishes of the party leaders, or in deference to the prevailing opinion of their respective districts. And, in such cases, too, the party leaders, in the absence of express mandates from the people, can have no authority over the members of their respective parties. Party leaders have at times been placed in the hopeless minority on certain issues, but such occurrences have never been interpreted as signs of lack of confidence which would call for their resignation. Plainly the doctrine of political responsibility as it is understood in England is incapable of application in the House of Representatives, as elsewhere stated.

	Yeas	Nays
Republicans	113	108
Democrats	97	70
Independents	1	
Farmer Labor	2	
Socialist	1	
Total	214	178

Luce, *op. cit.*, p. 474.

Here, however, we have one of the most important developments in the evolution of party politics in the House (as well as in the Senate). Particularly after the close of the European War there has been a steady decrease of partisan controversy along party lines. Time and again a majority of Democrats and Republicans line up on one side in opposition to a minority of Democrats and Republicans on the other, or vice versa, on measures of major importance. The effect of this development is therefore the weakening of party leadership.

Caucus played an important part in the machinery of party government in the House of Representatives. It is a secret meeting of the members of a party for the purpose of deciding in advance upon party programs or political measures before the House. The decisions, in the form of resolutions, arrived at in the caucus have a binding force upon those members who attend the meeting. A meeting of caucus is also held for the election of officers of the party or for nomination of candidates for the offices in the House. The Speaker is first elected—or " nominated "—in the party caucus before he is elected in the House. Usually the chairman of the Congressional Committee, before the beginning of a new Congress, calls a meeting of the members-elect of the party, at which a chairman for the party caucus is elected. Usually, too, a secretary to the caucus is elected, but sometimes, as in the Sixty-ninth Congress, the Republican reading clerk acts as clerk of the Republican caucus.[1] The caucus has no official status in the House. It has " no established rules as to quorum, procedure, or methods of voting." [2] But, custom has it that general parliamentary law, with such

[1] From a letter of Mr. Tilson, the majority floor leader, to the author under the date of June 4, 1926.

[2] Mr. Tilson's letter just cited.

special rules as may be adopted, governs the meetings of the caucus. Generally a majority of the members of the party elected to the House constitutes a quorum of the meeting, and questions therein are decided by a majority of those present. In the Sixty-second Congress it was provided in the rules of the Democratic caucus in the House that meetings of the Democratic caucus were either called by the chairman upon his own motion or upon the request in writing by twenty-five members of the caucus. In the election of officers and in the nomination of candidates for offices in the House a majority of those present and voting was of binding force upon the members of the caucus, but questions involving party policy or principle should be decided by a two-thirds vote of those present and voting.[1] It was further provided that resolutions adopted in the caucus should be entered in the *Journal*, which was kept open not only to members of the caucus but also to the press and persons interested in the proceedings.[2] Roll-calls in the caucus were to be published upon the demand of one-fifth of the mmbers present.[3]

Caucus was the "drilling ground"[4] where leadership in the House was crystallized,[5] and where discipline was strengthened. It must be remembered that Speaker Cannon demoted the insurgent Republicans in the Sixty-first Congress largely because they "refused to respect the will of

[1] Haines, *Law Making in America* (Maryland, 1912), p. 10; also see *Cong. Record*, 63rd Cong., 1st Sess., p. 4903.

[2] *Cong. Record*, 63rd Cong., 1st Sess., p. 224.

[3] Luce, *op. cit.*, p. 513.

[4] See Wilson, *op. cit.*, pp. 327, 328 where he also said: "The silvern speech spent in caucus secures the golden silence maintained on the floor of Congress, making each party rich in concord and happy in cooperation."

[5] See Luce, *op. cit.*, p. 513.

the Republican caucus." [1]   "This being a government
through parties," said Speaker Cannon, ". . . . the Speaker
of the House, responsible to the House and to the country,
made the [committee] appointments with respect to these
gentlemen[2] as he conceived it to be his duty in the execution
of the trust reposed in him." [3]   When the Democratic party
gained control of the House in the Sixty-second Congress,
the party caucus practically became "the second House" [4]
of Representatives.   Mr. Underwood took almost everything
to the Democratic caucus before it was presented before the
House.[5]   In the first session of the Sixty-third Congress the
Democratic caucus even passed a resolution forbidding the
House Standing Committees to report bills before the House
without the express permission from the caucus.[6]   And
when bills were discussed in the caucus, some such resolution
as the following would be presented and adopted upon the
motion of Mr. Underwood as in the case of the chemical
schedule of the tariff bill:

[1] *Cong. Record*, 61st Cong., 2nd Sess., p. 3321.

[2] They were Mr. Fowler of New Jersey, Mr. Cooper of Wisconsin,
Mr. Murdock of Kansas and Mr. Norris of Nebraska.

Mr. Cooper stated that he refused to stand by the Republican caucus
in the appointment of a committee to investigate the Department of
Interior and the Bureau of Forestry. The Republican caucus decided
to select the Democratic members of the committee and have the Democratic party confirm the selection. Mr. Cooper insisted that the Democratic caucus should have the right to choose the two Democratic members on the committee, *ibid.*, pp. 3323, 3323. Also see *supra*, p. 101,
regarding Mr. Fowler.

[3] *Ibid.*, p. 3322.

[4] *Cong. Record*, 63rd Cong., 1st Sess., p. 5157.

[5] Brown, *op. cit.*, p. 185. On important matters the average attendance
of the Democrats in the Sixty-third Congress at caucus meetings was
about sixty-five per cent of the 291 Democratic members. See Luce,
op. cit., p. 513.

[6] Haines, *Your Congress* (Washington, 1915), p. 78.

Resolved, That the bill adopted by the caucus revising schedule [the chemical schedule] is hereby declared to be a party measure and the members of the caucus bind themselves to vote for the bill without amendment, or motion to recommit.[1]

However, since the Sixty-sixth Congress in which the Republicans regained the control of the House, the influence of the caucus has waned. Rarely have either the Republicans or the Democrats been called together to meet in caucus.[2] The principal reason was that on the Republican side there came into existence, almost simultaneously with that of the Committee on Committees, a small but extremely important organization called the Steering Committee. The germs of this committee came into being in the Sixty-fifth Congress, in which it was called the Advisory Committee of five members with Mr. Mann, then the minority floor leader, as its chairman.[3] In the following Congress it was changed into what is now the Steering Committee.

The Steering Committee, like both the Committee on Committees and the caucus, is a party organization having no official status as a legislative committee in the House of Representatives. In the beginning even its existence was denied. The names of the members seldom, if ever, appear in any public print, and much less have the activities and proceedings of the committee been discussed in the press. Only the privileged few are acquainted with its inside stories, and these few have been in the habit of maintaining a golden silence as to the doings of the committee.

The majority floor leader is chairman ex-officio of the Steering Committee. In the Sixty-sixth Congress the committee consisted of five members,[4] " five millionaire mem-

---

[1] Haines, *Law Making in America* (Maryland, 1912), p. 13.

[2] Luce, *op. cit.*, p. 513.

[3] *Cf.* Brown, *op. cit.*, p. 202.

[4] The members of the Steering Committee since the Sixty-sixth Congress are listed on the following page.

bers," not one of them represented an " agricultural district " or was " in sympathy with the laboring class of the American people." [1]   An agitation was thus started for the increase of its membership.   Mr. Longworth of Ohio, himself one of the " millionaire " members of the committee, played a leading role in this movement.   He believed that the committee should consist of nine rather than five members, so that it " might be more representative, geographically, and in cleavage of thought, of the body of majority." [2]   So in the Sixty-seventh Congress the membership of the committee was increased to seven, and ever since then the number has remained unchanged.   In theory, the Steering Committee is a creature of the Committee on Committees which presents the names of its members to the caucus for ratification. In practice, the selection is made in secret by the leaders of the party " not only outside the House but even outside the caucus." [3]

Members of the Steering Committee of the House of Representatives are as follows:

66th Congress;

    Mondell, Frank W., Wyoming, chairman ex-officio
    Dunn, Thomas B., New York
    Longworth, Nicholas, Ohio
    Madden, Martin B., Illinois
    Winslow, Samuel E., Massachusetts

67th Congress;

    Mondell, Frank W., Wyoming, chairman ex-officio
    Anderson, Sydney, Minnesota
    Darrow, George P., Pennsylvania
    Dunn, Thomas B., New York

[1] *Cong. Record*, 66th Cong., 2nd Sess. (Appendix), p. 9333.
[2] *Ibid.*, p. 6177.
[3] See Brown, *op. cit.*, p. 204.

Greene, Frank L., Vermont
Longworth, Nicholas, Ohio
Nolan, John I., California
Sanders, Everett, Indiana

68th Congress;

Longworth, Nicholas, Ohio, chairman ex-officio
Anderson, Sydney, Minnesota
Darrow, George P., Pennsylvania
Graham, William J., Illinois
Magree, Walter W., New York
Sanders, Everett, Indiana
Sinnott, Nicholas J., Oregon
Tincher, J. N., Kansas

69th Congress;

Tilson, John Q., Connecticut, chairman ex-officio
Darrow, George P., Pennsylvania
Denison, Edward E., Illinois
Magee, Walter W., New York
Newton, Walter H., Minnesota
Sinnott, Nicholas J., Oregon
Tincher, J. N., Kansas
Treadway, Allen T., Massachusetts

The function of the Steering Committee was plainly stated
by Mr. Mondell of Wyoming in reply to Mr. Kitchin of
North Carolina who criticized this committee as the "over-
lord of all the standing committees." Mr. Mondell said:

We have a steering committee. The Republicans of the
various committees of the House, after giving careful consideration to the matters that come before their committees, very
frequently say to the Speaker, or to the chairman of the Steering Committee, or some members of it, " we have some matters
with regard to which there is some difference of opinion as to
the proper policy to follow. We are trying to carry a policy
of economy. We want to provide properly for the public ser-

vice, but we want to cut out all unnecessary appropriations and the members of our committee would like to take up with the Steering Committee and with the Speaker, and with such other members as you see fit to invite in, the general policy before our committee." We frequently have conferences thus suggested. We have done that with regard to every appropriation bill that has been presented to the House thus far. . . . The conference not only takes in the Republican members of the committee having the matter in charge, the members of the Steering Committee, and the Speaker, but generally the chairman or members of other committees interested in the carrying out of the general policy and having to do with legislative and appropriation matters. . . . After full consideration we have always reached an unanimous consent. . . .

And he went on to conclude:

. . . I have a notion it is the best way to legislate and appropriate —that is, to bring the membership of the House together frequently in groups, first one and then another; bring those who desire to be heard, those who are particularly interested in the matter before us, those who have a special responsibility with regard to the general policy of the party, and finally coming to an agreement as to what we shall do . . . .[1]

Actually, however, the Steering Committee exercised a power much more absolute than Mr. Mondell just stated. Despite the veil of secrecy surrounding the proceedings of the committee, there had at least one case come above the surface which argues well for the arraignment of Mr. Kitchin. That was the case of the bill to amend the act " for the retirement of employees in the classified civil service, and for other purposes," as approved May 22, 1920. The bill was introduced in the first session of the Sixty-eighth Congress both in the Senate and the House. In the same session

[1] *Cong. Record*, 66th Cong., 2nd Sess., p. 1999.

a joint hearing was held by both the Senate and the House Committees on Civil Service. On March 24, 1924, the House Committee on Civil Service unanimously reported the bill to the House and at the same time requested the Committee on Rules to bring in a special order for its immediate consideration. For ten months the Committee on Civil Service stood on the door-step of the Committee on Rules for the desired special order, but with no success. Meanwhile, however, the Administration made itself clear in favor of the bill. In the second session of the Sixty-eighth Congress, on January 26, 1925, the Secretary of the Interior wrote the chairman of the Senate Committee on Civil Service:

I am authorized to state that the members of the President's Cabinet favor an increase in annuities for the Government employees and hope that Congress at the present session will come to an early decision on the retired Federal salaries by increasing their annuities under the present law.[1]

On February 24, 1925, the bill passed the Senate.[2] In the House no action was taken towards its enactment. Mr. Woodrum of Virginia, a member of the Committee on Civil Service, canvassed among the members of the House in both parties and found no opposition to the bill. The chairman of the Committee on Rules (Mr. Snell of New York) even " promised " the chairman of the Committee on Civil Service that the bill would be reported for consideration early in the session of the Sixty-eighth Congress, but the Steering Committee did not allow it to come before the House. The bill was doomed. Thus Mr. Woodrum said on the floor:

. . . I here now say and charge that its demise will be upon the heads of the steering committee of the Republican Party

[1] *Cong. Record*, 68th Cong., 2nd. Sess., p. 2737.
[2] *Ibid.*, p. 4518.

in this House.   Indeed, I now lay at the door of this committee, individually and collectively, an indictment charging them with the murder of the Federal retirement legislation that they are pledged to enact into law at this session of Congress.[1]

The Speaker of the House, the chairman of the Committee on Rules and the Republican whip are not members of the committee.   In fact, both the Speaker and the chairman of the Committee on Rules were deliberately excluded from the membership of the committee in accordance with the plan adopted by the Republican caucus at the beginning of the Sixty-sixth Congress, but later, however, they gained access on invitation of Mr. Mondell.   The whip was also admitted, when Mr. Longworth was the floor leader.   And now all three of them " are always present at the meetings and take part in the proceedings of the committee." [2]   In its actual existence the committee has really eleven members.

The presence of the Speaker at the meetings of the Steering Committee was regarded as of importance.   In the first place, his presence would lend weight to the policy or policies decided by the committee.   In the second place, a strong, ambitious, able and tactful Speaker could under this system accomplish a great deal in the way of attaining his personal end in legislation.

However, during the last session of the Sixty-ninth Congress the Republican party organization in the House assumed an interesting aspect of development.   In place of the powerful Steering Committee, of which the Speaker was originally not a member and then was invited to be present at its meetings, there came into being a sort of inner conclave, the " Big Four," with Speaker Longworth as head. " The party Steering Committee," writes a New York *Times*

[1] *Cong. Record*, 68th Cong., 2nd Sess., p. 5170.
[2] From a letter of Mr. Tilson to the author under the date June 4, 1926.

correspondent, " no longer framed legislative programs, and
. . . . this authority had been usurped by the ' Big Four,'
composed of Chairman Snell of the Rules Committee, Representative Tilson, the party floor leader, Representative
Begg of Ohio and the Speaker." [1] The relation of Mr. Begg
to Speaker Longworth is analogous to that of Mr. Mann to
Speaker Cannon. Mr. Mann came from the State of Mr.
Cannon. So does Mr. Begg from the State of Mr. Longworth. Mr. Mann was in the confidence of Mr. Cannon and
became influential during the Speakership of Mr. Cannon
not by virtue of his official position but as the personal representative of the Speaker. [2] The same is true of Mr. Begg.
Mr. Begg was Mr. Longworth's right-hand man during the
latter's campaign for the office of Speakership and has remained so since the election of Mr. Longworth. From the
point of view of material advantage, Begg receives one of
the choicest of offices, on the front of the ground floor of
the House wing, a fact which, to quote the opinion of a
leading member of the House, " strengthened our surmise
that the Speaker wanted him close at hand." His unofficial
place in the House was best described by Mr. Blanton of
Texas: " The gentleman from Ohio occupies a unique position here in the House. If there is an assistant Speaker here
in the House, it is the gentleman from Ohio. If there is an
assistant floor leader, it is the gentleman from Ohio." [3]

This development in the House organization was both
natural and inevitable. The Steering Committee, large in
size and organized on a geographical basis with members of

---

[1] The New York *Times*, February 22, 1927, p. 21.

[2] See *supra*, p. 315.

[3] *Cong. Record*, 69th Cong., 2nd Sess., p. 1800. Mr. Begg occupied
only a third place on the House Committee on Foreign Affairs in the
Sixty-ninth Congress, and had no other position which might give him
a claim to leadership.

different economic interests, if not of economic creed, lacks unity of purpose and unity of legislative policy. Take the much-talked-about McNary-Haugen bill, for example. Two of the members of the committee from the agricultural West voted for it, while six—if including Mr. Tilson, ex-officio chairman of the committee—voted against it.[1] During the last session of the Sixty-ninth Congress the committee never met except the last few days of the session, and even when it met, no legislation of importance was discussed.

Some members of the House have frankly expressed their belief that the Steering Committee has not come to stay in the organization of the Republican party. It is not decentralized enough to allow the Republican membership to have " a say " in legislative policy. Nor is it centralized enough to permit a few of the majority leaders of like mind to direct the course of business in the House. The exclusion of the Speaker from the membership of the committee necessarily leads him to seek means to assert his leadership by virtue of his position as the presiding officer as well as the titular leader of his party of the House. No strong Speaker would be content with an ambiguous status on a committee, like the Steering Committee, which was intended to be in fact the central executive committee of the House. The growth of the power of this committee since the Sixty-sixth Congress was in the main due to the non-assertiveness of Speaker Gillett. Under the leadership of the present Speaker, Mr. Longworth, there is, however, little likelihood that the committee will regain its former position of strength, although it still possesses all the formal attributes of power.

[1] Those who voted for the bill were Denison of Illinois and Sinnott of Oregon. Those who voted against the bill were Tilson of Connecticut; Darrow of Pennsylvania; Magee of New York, Newton of Minnesota; Tincher of Kansas; and Treadway of Massachusetts. See *Cong. Record*, 69th Cong., 2nd Sess., pp. 4064, 4065.

The relation of the Speaker to the President since 1896 has for the most part of the time been none too friendly. Speaker Reed and President McKinley never conferred with each other on any legislative question. Such, also, was the relation between Speaker Clark and President Wilson. When Mr. Mondell was the Republican floor leader during the last part of President Wilson's second term, he asked Mr. Clark how to get advice from the Administration in legislation, apart from the official recommendations and suggestions. Mr. Clark told him to go somewhere else for information, and said " they never confer with me." [1] The fact that both McKinley and Wilson succeeded in enacting some of their measures over the opposition of Reed and Clark in the House was largely due to the influence of patronage wielded by the chief executive.[2] Speaker Cannon and President Roosevelt acted in consonance during the latter's first years of administration, but they finally found themselves at variance. Mr. Roosevelt, however, appealed " over the heads of the Senate and House leaders " [3] to the people for the support of the measures he advocated and won his way in consequence thereof. To be sure, such differences are by no means worse than those which existed prior to 1896; [4] they are only consequences of the system of separation of powers. Under this system of separation of powers the difference of points of view of the President and the Speaker on political and economic measures is indeed to be expected. But the bitterness of personal enmity, arising

---

[1] *Cong. Record*, 68th Cong., 1st Sess., p. 564.

[2] See Alexander, *op. cit.*, p. 380 where Mr. Alexander says that President McKinley appointed members of Congress to " distinguished and lucrative places on various commissions, to negotiate treaties, to locate boundaries, and to confer with foreign representatives respecting other matters ... "

[3] Roosevelt, *An Autobiography* (New York, 1913), p. 383.

[4] See Follett, *op. cit.*, pp. 319-330.

from personal ambitions, which rends further apart the
" latent " unity between the legislative and executive bodies,
must be deplored. It is therefore useful to remember what
Speaker Reed said of the Speakership (although he failed to
live up to the ideal himself) : " No disappointments or defeats ought ever to be permitted to show themselves to the
injury of that high office." [1]

In summarizing the place of the Speaker in the House of
Representatives as it was occupied up to 1910 and the ulti-
mate aim of the March revolution, 1910, in relation to the
Speakership, we can do no better than to quote Mr. Underwood of Alabama. On that eventful day, March 19, 1910,
Mr. Underwood, then a leader of the Democratic minority,
rose amid great applause from the floor of the House, and
said:

> Mr. Speaker, if this resolution [the Norris resolution][2] is
> adopted by the House, we have reached the end of an era in the
> parliamentary history of this body. More than a decade ago,
> when Mr. Reed was elected Speaker of this House, the House
> on account of the large number of members here, found it im-
> possible under the rules then existing to do business. Speaker
> Reed adopted a system of rules that would allow the majority

---

[1] See *supra*, p. 292.

Mr. Longworth, the present Speaker, publicly stated that " there must
be teamwork, too, between Congress and the Executive, certainly if the
Executive be a member of the majority party in Congress." He then
went on to say: " I am by no means advocating that Congress should be
a rubber stamp for the execution of the Executive will. I am utterly
opposed to Executive domination of the legislative branch of the Government, just as I would be opposed to the legislative domination of the
Executive, but that does not mean that a just balance between these two
great constitutional branches can not be preserved with both functioning
in friendly cooperation.

" I am confident that this situation will exist in the next (the Sixty-
ninth) Congress..." *Cong. Record*, 68th Cong., 2nd Sess., p. 2712.

[2] See *supra*, pp. 141, 143.

of this House to do business at any time, but in doing so he lodged the power of the House in the Speaker, and there has remainded since that time. Now, we have no fight to make on the personality of Joseph G. Cannon, of Illinois. We are fighting a system, and that system is the system that enables the Speaker, by the power invested in him, to thwart and overthrow the will of the majority membership of this House. We recognize today that there has to be leadership, that some one must be the leader of the majority and some man must be the leader of the minority, but we say the place for that leadership is not in the Chair. (Applause on the Democratic side.)

If this resolution goes through—ultimately, if not today—the Speaker of the House of Representatives will cease to be its leader and the Chairman of the Committee on Rules elected by this House will become the leader of the majority party in the House. It does not deprive the House of one scintilla of its power to control its business. It does not deprive it of the right leadership, but it divorces from the Speaker the leadership of the House. . . . I say that, no matter how high or of what pure character a man may be who occupies the Speaker's chair of this House, that leader can not divorce the leadership and the partisanship of the leader from the Speaker when he is presiding over the deliberations of this House. This great parliamentary body is entitled to a presiding officer who wields the scales of justice between man and man, between the two contending political parties, and that is what we are standing for today. (Applause on the Democratic side.)[1]

Has the Speaker since 1910 ceased to be the leader of the House? Hardly so. Has the chairman of the Committee on Rules, " elected " by the House, become the leader of the majority party in the House? No. When the Democratic party was returned with a majority in the House in 1911, and before the convening of the Sixty-second Congress, President Taft, in his first act in relation with the forth-

---

[1] *Cong. Record*, 61st Cong., 2nd Sess., p. 3433.

coming House, " sent for " both Mr. Clark, who was to be the Speaker of the next House, and Mr. Underwood, who was to be the Democratic majority floor leader, to discuss the date for the calling of an extra session of Congress,[1] the first session of the Sixty-second Congress. President Taft did not send for the chairman of the Committee on Rules. Elsewhere in this treatise, attempts have been made to show that since the March revolution, 1910, the leadership of the House has not been divorced from the Speaker; it has only been weakened. In 1910 the Speaker was removed from the Committee on Rules. In 1911, while he was deprived of the power of appointing the standing committees, he was, however, not deprived of the power of appointing conference managers on the part of the House, select committees and the chairman of the Committee of the Whole House on the state of the Union. This power of recogniton has only been reduced but was not completely taken away from him. On suspension days (on which both the business on the Consent Calendar and on the Calendar for Motions to Instruct Committees [2] are in order) the Speaker has a discretionary power of recognition over motions to suspend the rules.[3] On days other than the consent calendar days [4] the Speaker also exercises a discretionary power in according recognition to the members who claim the floor.

Here is a concrete case. On February 15, 1923, Mr. Cramton of Michigan moved to discharge the Committee on Judiciary, a resolution of inquiry calling upon the Depart-

---

[1] Clark, *op. cit.*, vol. ii, pp. 7, 8.

[2] According to House Rule xxvii of the Sixty-ninth Congress, motions to instruct committees are in order only on the third Monday of each month immediately after the reading of the *Journal*.

[3] See *supra*, chap. v.

[4] For the limitations upon the Speaker's power of recognition, see *supra*, pp. 191 *et seq.*; chapter on Calendar Wednesday.

ment of the Treasury for "certain facts." Mr. Campbell of Kansas made the point of order that the motion made by Mr. Cramton was not privileged. A debate followed. Speaker Gillett "thinks that unquestionably it is privileged,[1] but the Chair also understands that the gentleman from Kansas (Mr. Campbell) claims the floor with a report from the Committee on Rules." In response to the suggestion of the Speaker, Mr. Campbell rose to offer a resolution from the Committee on Rules which "is of higher privilege." During the debate Mr. Cramton argued:

. . . My resolution was presented to the House and the resolution of the gentleman from Kansas was not yet offered; and in case they were of equal privilege, then mine, of course, would have priority, having been first offered.

But in any event I further urge that mine is of higher privilege for the reason that we are approaching the end of a session, and if the Committee on Rules, which will govern the business of the House very largely in the next two weeks—very little will get up for consideration except through a rule from that committee—if the gentleman from Kansas can now set my resolution aside by offering a resolution to make in order this Navy bill, that may provide for one day's debate or five day's debate—the question of privilege would be the same—then they can follow that with another rule that will make some other bill in order and follow that with another, and in that way they can absolutely delay, under that situation, the right that a Member of the House has for the consideration of inquiry. I urge, therefore, that for the protection of the rights of the Members of the House the resolution that I have offered is of higher privilege than the other.[2]

---

[1] Rule xxii, 5. "All resolutions of inquiry addressed to the heads of executive departments shall be reported to the House within one week after presentation."

[2] *Cong. Record*, 67th Cong., 4th Sess., pp. 3701, 3702.

However, Speaker Gillett gave Mr. Campbell prior recognition. Mr. Cramton appealed from the decision of the Speaker. The House sustained the Speaker's decision. What was the most important was the statement made by Speaker Gillett after the announcement of the vote. The Speaker held that the Cramton and Campbell resolutions " are questions of privilege," and " stand on the same basis," and that " it is entirely a matter of recognition by the Chair." [1]

There will probably never come the time when the Speaker is "Czar," but it seems inevitable that the leadership of the Speaker, under the "American system," will pass from its present position to a much stronger one. That there has been a tendency toward the augmentation of the power of the Speaker was visibly marked by the existence of an inner conclave, like the " Big Four," to supersede the party Steering Committee in the last session of the Sixty-ninth Congress. How far this tendency will go depends upon two conditions: (1) the character of the person in the Speaker's chair, and (2) the extent of interest the American people show in the work of the House of Representatives. " Government," according to William Penn's *dictum,* " like clocks, go from motion men give them; and as governments are made and moved by men, so by men they are ruined, too. Wherefor governments rather depend upon men than men upon governments." In a representative form of government the qualities of the governors are determined by the intelligence of the governed. So are the qualities of the members of the House of Representatives, and the Speaker is only one of them. In the last analysis, conditions (2) governs condition (1).

Under the present commission form of leadership in the House, which is invisible to the eyes of the nation at large,

[1] *Cong. Record,* 67th Cong., 4th Sess., p. 3702.

there has been an increasing difficulty in fixing responsibility for either the success or the failure of a measure. Prior to 1910 the eyes of the nation turned to the Speaker who, justly or unjustly, was held responsible for the legislation of the House. Since 1910 that responsibility has been divided. Between the Speaker and the majority floor leader there existed a dual leadership.[1] No one knows how much the Speaker is responsible for the success or the failure of this or that measure. With the curtailment of the power of the Speaker, one may well ask, has the House become its own master? How much has the House gained under the guidance of a secret unofficial Steering Committee or an inner conclave as compared with the time when it was dominated by the Committee on Rules, of which the Speaker was chairman? Assuming that the Steering Committee will continue to exist and restore its former position, what then should be the status of the Speaker? If, however, the committee is to be abolished, what then will be in its place so as to bring about direct and efficient responsible leadership in the House? These are the questions which the author, being a foreigner, leaves with the American people and with the American students of government to ponder and to answer.

[1] Mr. Luce observes: "The division of responsibility between a two-party Rules Committee and a one-party Steering Committee is reasonably sure to make trouble sooner or later. And the same is true of the like division of it between the Speaker and the floor leader. So far things have gone along with tolerable smoothness by reason of the happy chance that has filled these positions with men tactful and conciliatory, capable of working in harmony; but experience does not encourage the hope that such conditions will always prevail. The masterful, dominant leadership of some one man may yet be required." *Congress: An Explanation*, p. 118.

BIBLIOGRAPHY

Books

Alexander, De Alva Stanwood, *History and Procedure of the House of Representatives*, Houghton Mifflin Co., New York, 1916.

Atkinson, Charles R., *The Committee on Rules and the Overthrow of Speaker Cannon*, New York, 1911.

Bishop, Joseph Bucklin, *Theodore Roosevelt and His Time Shown in His Own Letters*, Charles Scribner's Sons, New York, 1920, 2 vols.

Briggs, John Ely, *William Petters Hepburn*, The State Historical Society of Iowa, Iowa City, Iowa, 1919.

Brown, George Rothwell, *The Leadership of Congress*, The Bobbs-Merrill Company, 1922.

Bryce, James, *American Commonwealth*, MacMillan, New York, 1923 abridged ed.

——, *Modern Democracies*, MacMillan, New York, 1921, 2 vols.

Busbey, L. White, *Uncle Joe Cannon: The Reminiscences of A Pioneer American*, Holt, New York, 1927.

Clark, Champ, *My Quarter Century of American Politics*, Harpers, New York, vol. i, 1919, vol. ii, 1920.

Congressional Record from the Fifty-fourth Congress to the Sixty-ninth Congress, 1896-1927.

Croly, Herbert, *Marcus Alonzo Hanna: His Life and Work*, MacMillan, New York, 1912.

Dickson, Harris, *An Old Fashion Senator: A Story—Biography of John Sharp Williams*, Frederick A. Stokes Co., New York, 1925.

Dingley, Nelson, Jr., *Life and Times of Nelson Dingley*, Ihling Bros. and Evereard, Kalamazoo, Michigan, 1902.

Follett, M. P., *The Speaker of the House of Representatives*, Longmans, Green and Co., New York, 1909 ed.

Fuller, Herbert Bruce, *The Speaker of the House*, Little, Brown and Co., Boston, 1909.

Haines, Lynn, *Your Congress*, The National Voter's League, 931-33, Woodward Building, Washington, D. C., 1915.

Hasbrouck, Paul DeWitt, *Party Government in the House of Representatives*, MacMillan, New York, 1927.

Hinds, Asher C., *Precedents of the House of Representatives*, Government Printing Office, Washington, D. C., 1907, 8 vols.

344

Luce, Robert, *Congress: An Explanation*, Harvard University Press, Cambridge, 1926.

——, *Legislative Procedure*, Houghton Mifflin, Boston, 1922.

May, Sir Thomas Erskine, *A Treatise on Laws, Privileges, Proceedings and Usages*, 12 ed., Butterworth and Co., Bell Yard, Temple Bar, London, 1917.

McBain, Howard Lee and Lindsay Rogers, *The New Constitutions in Europe*, Doubleday, Page, New York, 1922.

McCall, Samuel W., *The Business of Congress*, Columbia University Press, New York, 1911.

——, *The Life of Thomas Brackett Reed*, Houghton Mifflin Co., Boston, 1914.

MacDonagh, Michael, *The Pageant of Parliament*, T. Fisher Unwin Ltd., London, 1921, 2 vols.

——, *The Speaker of the House* (of Commons), London, 1914.

McConachie, Lauros Grant, *Congressional Committees*, Thomas Y. Crowell Co., New York, 1898.

McCowin, Ada C., *The Congressional Conference Committee*, New York, 1927.

Olcott, Charles S., *The Life of William McKinley*, Houghton Mifflin Co., Boston, 1916, 2 vols.

Page, William Tyler, *Congressional Hand-Book*, Washington, 1913.

Redlich, Josef, *The Procedure of the House of Commons*, Archibald Constable and Co., Ltd., 1908, 3 vols.

Rogers, Lindsay, *The American Senate*, Knopf, New York, 1926.

Roosevelt, Theodore, *An Autobiography*, Macmillan, 1913.

Stealey, O. O., *Twenty Years in the Press Gallery*, Publishers Printing Co., New York, 1906.

Wilson, Woodrow, *Congressional Government*, Houghton Mifflin Co., Boston, 1885.

House Manual, edited by Lehr Fess, Sixty-ninth Congress, Government Printing Office, 1925.

ARTICLES

Alexander, DeAlva S., "Speaker, Committees and the House," *Outlook*, lxxxi (1908), pp. 129-130.

Atkinson, C. R. and C. A. Beard, "Syndication of the Speakership," *Political Science Quarterly*, xxvi (1911), pp. 381-414.

Barrows, I. C., "Personal Side of the Fifty-sixth Congress," *Outlook*, lxiv (1900), pp. 21-31.

"Big Four of the House of Representatives," *Independent*, lxiv (1908), pp. 1185-1190.

Brooks, S., "Congress and Parliament," *North American Review*, clxx (1900), pp. 78-86.

Cannon, J. G., " Powers of the Speaker," *Century*, lxxviii (1909), pp. 306-312.

Cockrell, E., "Congress or Parliament?" *Arena*, xxiii (1900), pp. 593-605.

Dalzell, John, " Rules of the House of Representatives," *Independent*, lxiv (1908), pp. 577-582.

" Committee on Committees," *Outlook*, lxxxxvi (1910), pp. 987-988.

Davenport, F. M., "Aftermath of the Congressional Insurrection," *Outlook*, cxii (1916), pp. 667-671.

" Degradation of the House of Representatives," *Arena*, xxxix (1908), pp. 615-618.

Todd, C. T., " Congress and Anarchy. A Suggestion," *North American Review*, clxxiii (1901), pp. 433-436.

Gardner, A. P., " Rules of the House of Representatives," *North American Review*, clxxxix (1909), pp. 233-241.

Hall, W. B., " The Speaker and the People," *The World's Work*, xix (1910), pp. 12805-12812.

" Has the Speaker too Much Power?: A Symposium," *The World Today*, x (1906), pp. 507-509.

Hinds, Asher C., " The Speaker and the House," *McClure*, xxxv (1910), pp. 195-202.

" Insurgent and Speaker Cannon," *Current Literature*, xxxxviii (1910), pp. 127-131.

Leupp, F. E., " Humors of Congress," *Century*, lxv (1903), pp. 760-768, 938-945.

Lowry, E. G., " The Downfall of Cannon," *Harpers Weekly*, liv (1910), p. 8.

——, " In the Insurgent Camp," *Harpers Weekly*, liv (1910), p. 8.

McCall, S. W., " The Fifty-ninth Congress," *Atlantic Monthly*, lxxxxviii (1906), pp. 577-586.

McLellan, G. B., "Leadership in the House of Representatives," *Scribners' Monthly*, xxxxix (1911), pp. 594-599.

Maxey, E., " Powers of the Speaker," *Forum*, xxxxi (1909), pp. 344-350.

Mondell, Frank W., " What is the Matter with Congress? " *Review of Reviews*, lxviii (1923), pp. 61-72.

Murdock, Victor, " Congressman's First Bill," *American Magazine*, lxvi (1908), 545-550.

——, "After Cannonism—What?" *Independent*, lxix (1910), pp. 622-625.

——, " Insurgent Movement in Congress," *North American Review*, clxxxxi (1910), pp. 510-516.

Nelson, H. L., " Making Laws at Washington," *Century*, lxiv (1902), pp. 169-187.

——, " New Congress and the Old," *Harpers Weekly*, xxxxiii (1899), pp. 1203-1204.

Richards, J. W., "The Passing of Speaker Henderson," *Independent*, lv (1903), pp. 651-655.

Rogers, Lindsay, "Conference Committee Legislation," *North American Review*, ccxiv, pp. 300-307.

Smith, H. H., "Parliamentary Reform in the National House of Representatives," *Chautauquan*, xxx (1899), pp. 239-245.

"Speaker's Influence on Legislation," *Review of Reviews*, xxi (1900), pp. 85-86.

"Speaker Cannon and the Complete Destruction of the Popular Rule in the House," *Arena*, xxxx (1908), pp. 89-91.

Stevens, F. C., "Rules of the House of Representatives: A Defense," *Review of Reviews*, xxxix (1909), pp. 470-474.

Swanson, C. A., " Rules of the House of Representatives: A Criticism," *Review of Reviews*, xxxix (1909), pp. 465-470.

Taylor, H., "Speaker and the Powers," *North American Review*, clxxxviii (1908), pp. 495-503.

"The Final Outcome of the Steering Committee," *Congressional Directory*, ii (1923), pp. 163-165.

Thurston, J. M., "Rules of Congress," *Independent*, liv (1902), pp. 961-964.